Beyond tribalism
Managing identities in a diverse world

IE Business Publishing

IE Business Publishing and Palgrave Macmillan have launched a collection of high-quality books in the areas of Business and Management, Economics and Finance. This important series is characterized by innovative ideas and theories, entrepreneurial perspectives, academic rigor and practical approaches which will make these books invaluable to the business professional, scholar and student alike.

IE Business School is one of the world's leading institutions dedicated to educating business leaders. Palgrave Macmillan, part of Macmillan Group, has been serving the learning and professional sector for more than 160 years.

The series, put together by these eminent international partners, will enable executives, students, management scholars and professionals worldwide to have access to the most valuable information and critical new arguments and theories in the fields of Business and Management, Economics and Finance from the leading experts at IE Business School.

Beyond tribalism

Managing identities in a diverse world

Celia de Anca

First published 2012 by
PALGRAVE MACMILLAN

Palgrave Macmillan in the UK is an imprint of Macmillan Publishers Limited,
registered in England, company number 785998, of Houndmills, Basingstoke,
Hampshire RG21 6XS.

Palgrave Macmillan in the US is a division of St Martin's Press LLC,
175 Fifth Avenue, New York, NY 10010.

Palgrave Macmillan is the global academic imprint of the above companies
and has companies and representatives throughout the world.

Palgrave® and Macmillan® are registered trademarks in the United States,
the United Kingdom, Europe and other countries.

ISBN-13: 978–0–230–27694–9

This book is printed on paper suitable for recycling and made from fully
managed and sustained forest sources. Logging, pulping and manufacturing
processes are expected to conform to the environmental regulations of the
country of origin.

A catalogue record for this book is available from the British Library.

A catalog record for this book is available from the Library of Congress.

10 9 8 7 6 5 4 3 2 1
21 20 19 18 17 16 15 14 13 12

Printed and bound in Great Britain by
CPI Antony Rowe, Chippenham and Eastbourne

Para Nachito y Almudenita
Y sus hermanos Álvaro y Alicia
Y para Tobias y Violeta

CONTENTS

Contents

Part III Civilization and identity

LIST OF TABLES

LIST OF FIGURES

LIST OF MAPS

Author's Note

Neotribalism, and ways that new forms of communities are influencing the business world, have been of great interest to me for many years. In my experience working with organizations to manage diversity, it has become clear that communities are beginning to take on different shapes, superseding the traditional diversity groups. New community-based business networks seem to be leading the way to the future, and thus it seems worthwhile to explore them in some depth. With the encouragement of my editor, I decided to write about my experiences with neotribalism and its effects on business behavior. However, for some time it was difficult to get beyond the working title of "Beyond Tribalism." I was not clear about which approach would be best. I felt that things were changing very rapidly around the world, and a new model for "being together" was the key to understand some of these new dynamics. But I never had enough time away from my daily activities to provide the peace and quiet that reflection requires.

Arpad, my mentor, kept on telling me that I needed to take some time-off to explore, think and write, otherwise I would exhaust myself with the everyday routine. As I have always done in the last 25 years, I obeyed him.

So I took some time off, and used it to travel around the world to organize my ideas and see whether reality proved them right. Time was the key; not just to write, but also time to think and to explore the work of those who came before, those who had the clarity of mind to explain some of the fundamental characteristics of human behavior, since, as Aristotle said, to truly understand things it is necessary to see them develop, to take them at their beginning.[1] It is often said that there is nothing new, all ideas come from some old tradition, and this book is by no means an exception to this maxim. Everything has already been said, or is about to be said, or should have been said before; but we keep on thinking and writing, since we all see the same thing with different perspectives. Our only contribution is to add our different perceptions to the world and together create our human legacy.

On January 10, 2011, I managed to get things in order at the office so that I could leave. I only knew one thing: I needed to spend time in Cairo.

Everything seemed to be in the right place over there: friends, interesting companies to explore, good local universities whose representatives I knew well, as well as a colleague from our own office. My plan was to go to Cairo on January 10 and stay there for three months, then making visits to other Arab countries such as the United Arab Emirates, Bahrain, and Saudi Arabia. After all, I am also a philologist of Arabic, and this trip could also help me to refresh my language skills. Eventually, from the Middle East I had plans to spend three months in other countries, including Brazil, the USA, and Turkey.

But things never work out as planned. Shortly after my arrival in Cairo, the revolution started, and then the whole of the Middle East rose up in turmoil. My colleagues felt sorry for me, since it was the first time in my life that I had taken time off just to travel and think, and my plans had collapsed in the turmoil. But in fact, I really thought that I was lucky. I was never in danger during the revolution because I took refuge with some great people who were kind and well-informed. Everyone who helped me was enormously pleasant and considerate. And above all, I had an incredibly well-placed platform from which to witness what I believe to be the biggest change in the Arab world in the last 50 years.

After Cairo, I went to the Emirates, and spent quite a lot of time talking with Arabs from many different nationalities, all united in their Arab identity, very concerned, and experiencing first-hand everything that was going on…

When I began to analyze what was going on in the Middle East, I saw clearly how the book had to be organized…

The Egyptian revolution gave me the key to understand what I was trying to visualize with the book: the interplay of the different identities in movement.

Identities

Diversity is still a valid word to describe the society we live in with all of our differences in identity. However, when we talk of managing diversity, what we really manage is the myriad of conflicting identities we all carry inside. These can be roughly organized in the following categories:

1. **Personal identity and the right of self-development.** The Egyptian revolution was full of middle-class individuals who wanted a better future for themselves. Food and security were no longer enough to keep them quiet, because they wanted more: the right to self-development, to have options in life.

2. **Communal identities.** If there was one thing that impressed me more than anything else, it was how the organization of the Egyptian revolution interconnected communities. It was the kids on Facebook who orchestrated a change in their destinies: Facebook groups such as the "We Are All Khaled Said" or the "6th of April," that, despite not having a clear leader, managed to get all their members actively distributing information, recording what was happening, and even organizing the logistics for the people in Tahrir Square. But the Facebook kids were just one example of communal life during the revolution. In the neighborhoods far away from the square we can find a lesson in planning. After the police left the streets, the neighborhood committees wasted no time in organizing themselves to protect their neighborhoods from looters, controlling traffic, setting up a night-watch and other crucial aspects of neighborhood life.

3. **Civilizational identity.** Egyptians knew that the Arab world would be looking at them, that Tunisia could be just an anecdote or the small beginning of a dramatic change in the region. Everything depended on how the Egyptian situation would resolve itself. Following Cairo I went to other Arab countries, where I found that all Arabs were united through watching Aljazeera. They all felt connected with the soul of the Egyptians. In short, I felt that the Arab identity was back. For the last decades Arab identity faded away in the tension between each country's nationalism and Pan-Islamism – but now it was back! People all over the Arab world felt identified and stepped out into the streets to demand changes ... Arab identity was on the move.

We all have different basic identities inside our societies. In the case of the Egyptian revolution these aligned to reach a common goal. In other words, the individual person and the community were working in tune within the framework of a civilization that aspired to a better future.

Identities are multiple and in constant movement. They change because of the need for self-development, the desire to act in the multiple communities we all belong to, or aspire to be a part of. It is through this movement, from the self to the community and back, that we grow as humans. As we grow we can contribute to our community, and in turn we are influenced by this community, and back and forth in a permanent movement – from the solitude of the self to the company of the community and back. This movement has always been there but now, more than ever, we are becoming conscious of it.

What I observed, not only in Egypt but everywhere else I went during my research trip, is that there really is a major change happening: people are becoming increasingly conscious of who they are and the control they can have over their multiple identities and destinies. People are beginning to understand that they can control these processes; they are aware of their capabilities, but also of the necessity of working together in various groups.

Understanding identities and their movements is, then, crucial to understanding today's world, with its myriad of internet-based microgroups living in a global world with multiple cultures. But it also becomes essential in the business world, since individuals are much more aware of their choices, choices that they identify with: choosing a job, creating a new project or in buying a product or service.

Whatever happens afterwards, and with all the hardships they are likely to face in reorganizing their country, the Egyptians have taught us a lesson: that this world in transition must understand that identity matters, that to be conscious of one's own self is far better than unconscious identification. And on top of all this, they taught us how to keep a smile and the joy to live even in the hardest moments.

Difficult times are ahead, all over the world: the financial crisis, the spike in oil prices, the energy crisis, the economic system, the unemployment rate, the dismantling of the social welfare state, the increasing poverty gap, environmental deterioration, the scarcity of resources, and the other difficulties we all have to survive. This is a world in transition, but examples such as the ones described in this book illustrate the myriads of people working with enthusiasm in different economic initiatives, contributing their best efforts to the improvement of their societies, and helping us think that there is hope ahead.

"Consciousness is a very recent acquisition of nature and it is still in an 'experimental' state. It is fragile, menaced by specific dangers and easily injured," said one of the greatest psychologists, Carl Jung (1978, p. 7).

I believe the sign of our times is consciousness, in the individual's self-development as well as in the need to act to achieve the aspirations of our communities. We need the consciousness to identify with the community we want to work in and with the products and services we want to consume. Unlike the social engineering of earlier times, nowadays our communities tend to emerge naturally, and only by accepting them can organizations use them to their advantage.

At the beginning of this quest, Edgard Gouveia from Brazil told me that he, too, was on sabbatical leave, travelling around the world, and his main realization was that there is much more positive in the world than negative. And I have to admit a few months later, that yes, there are quite a lot of problems ahead and negativity is everywhere; but, honestly, I believe there are many, many young professionals working to find solutions.

A new generation of young people, is working enthusiastically on their internet-based business initiatives, and I believe they have the intelligence to improve their societies. This is a generation that has two key differences from mine:

- They are not ideological, they come together not to argue options but to take the best of each one. They are aware of their individuality and at the same time they are aware of the need to work as a community. Therefore, they share ideas, processes and even adjust their consumption so there is more for all.
- And they are practical; they can connect and integrate all options, resources and people in order to find ways to get ahead.

These young professionals do not represent the majority of new generations in the world, I am aware of that, not in the west nor in developing countries, but it does exist and in large numbers. I do think that they have a fair chance to create new organizations that will fit within the conditions of new markets and a world that is in a process of constant movement. Any new situation in human evolution needs new organizations, and the organizations and institutions we have right now are becoming too old to support these changes. "You should not put new wine in old bottles," Arnold Toynbee said. I am not sure what the new organizations that will support our world will look like, but I do believe there are good new ideas that, with time, will consolidate into new organizations. For the moment this generation is building new patterns that are leading to new way of organizing businesses; but this is only the beginning. I hope the world will give them a chance because this new generation deserves it, and it is working hard for a better world that has place for everyone.

Thus, the only intention of this book is to give a framework for some of the processes that are developing right in front of our eyes. They have many positive aspects, and with some synergies and some good luck, they can result in new and profitable ways of working and consuming together, and can open doors to many new great things in the future.

Acknowledgments

Co-creation is one of the words that describes the new tendencies I depict in this work, and the book itself illustrates what co-creation is all about; the generous participation of many to build something greater than the sum of the individual contributions. This section thus attempts to acknowledge the real authors of the book. I apologize to the ones I have forgotten, whose absence here is not due to the relevance of their contributions in the book but rather to my bad memory.

First I would like to acknowledge all the companies that have illustrated the different sections of the book by their daily work. The Journey began a year ago with a visit to JAK Medlemsbank in Skövde, Sweden, where Miguel Ganzo and his colleagues shared their enthusiasm for their project. My next visit was to SEKEM in Cairo, where Bianca Fliss and Philip Maximiliam Boes taught me a lesson on how to keep focus and concentrate even in the middle of a revolution. ADIB in Abu Dhabi was the next step, there, thanks to Fatima Iliasu, in addition to Islamic banking, I learned how enjoyable and fruitful it can be to jointly write a case, with different perspectives adding to a common purpose. Adriana Barboso in São Paulo taught me a lesson on how resilience and purpose can help overcome any difficulty, as her work at Instituto Feira Preta shows, and nearby, in Rio de Janeiro, Leila Velez showed me how it is possible to fly with the force of the conviction. The final step was at HUB, where some of its wizards, Pablo Handl in São Paulo, Indi Johar in London, Tatiana Glad in Amsterdam, and Max Oliva in Madrid, opened new doors for me to explore how things are really moving. Finally, I would like to thank Edgard Barki, Cristina Trullols, and Newton Campos, for their work in the development of some of these cases.

Max also lead me to Edgard Gouvia, and his contagious optimism gave me the idea to ask more entrepreneurs like him for their testimonies. So Edgard introduced me to Jay Standish in Seattle and to Sheri Herndon who, through our Skype conversations, helped me to understand the new energy that penetrates the world. Sheri in turn introduced me to her entrepreneurial friend in Istanbul, Filiz Telez, then in turn led me to Ayşegül Güzel, whose testimony in Chapter 5, together with those of Nisrine Abasher and

Lotfi El-Ghandouri, give me hope and the conviction that the coming generation is ready to improve the world.

Salvador Aragon deserves special mention: he always had, at the right moment, the perfect book, writer, expert, or idea, as well as the understanding I needed in each and every angle of this book, and his encyclopedic knowledge of everything is explicitly manifest in the outstanding fiction-history letters he and Franco Llobera produced for the chapter on the Mediterranean, letters beautifully illustrated by the geographic expertise of D. Juan Antonio Martinez Romera. Franco has special relevance in this book: someone with whom I have experienced the deep joy of co-thinking, in this work since its earliest beginnings, and in many works before this one. My thanks need to go also to Rodrigo Reyes, who helped me with my English expression, and to Daniel Conde, whose beautiful picture on the back-cover managed to show the happiness I felt during the journey

I also would like to thank all those who accompanied me through the journey in different places: Margarita, Omeima, Conchita, Rima, Khawla and her beautiful family, Nadia and her courageous family, who sheltered us and help us to understand the new emerging Egypt; and Najwa, Rahma, Rayana and Sandy, with whom I shared the intense and unique moments of the Egyptian uprising. And of course I need to recognize the influence of Arpad Von Lazar in this book, the best of mentors who always knows better than I what I am able to do.

I also feel I must acknowledge all those whose words keep me the greatest of companies all these months, some long gone, others still with us, thanking them for their thinking that pushes the human legacy further and allows us to build whatever contribution we can on really solid ground. In particular, I would like to thank Hannah Arendt, Arnold Toynbee, Carl Jung, Ibn Sina, Henri Corbin, Pierre Hadot, and Fernand Braudel, whose works constitute the theoretical ground behind the book

Finally I would like to thank IE, which, without hesitation, gave me the flexibility, time, trust, and support that I needed to carry out this venture.

And now, a word from the mentor ...

This work of Celia's started out with a conversation between us about the nature of business organizations, how women fit in modern and complex structures and why some countries prosper and others don't. The whole thing happened in my office in Madrid between inane bureaucratic faculty meetings and flavored by the imminent prospect of my having to leave for the airport for a flight to Boston. Celia was explaining things by doodling circles, arrows and connecting lines for me on a soiled coffee napkin, not losing my attention but testing my patience, since I was not about to miss my flight. So I did what seemed to be the simple, fastest and cheapest way out of such a conundrum, and said to her: "Why don't you write a book about this?" So, here it is.

I don't want to talk about the content of this excellent volume. You must read it for yourself. But I want to make a brief comment what it means for we readers and how we should approach its message and meaning. So let me regress for a minute. Almost thirty years ago my late dear friend and colleague Sam Huntington, a political scientist at Harvard, started talking to, actually more like pestering, a few of us about his idea of the role of religious fanaticism in the coming clash of civilizations. We listened but I just did not get the point. Sadly, it was only years later that I did begin to get the point, the relevance and the conceptual meaning of his ideas and that of the subsequent product of his vision, Huntington's by now world-famous book.

I think it is a bit like that with Celia's current work. This is an important book about a circumstance, a condition and a behavioral and structural given with which we are already living, but the full implications of which we do not understand. Celia explains, as always at some length; but more than anything else she forces us to think and reconsider many of our pre-conceived notions of how and why society, individuals and business work and coexist.

Celia is a hard taskmaster. She is, as an author and a thinker, a relent-less aggressor on our mind and attention. This work simply forces us to be more innovative and speculative – certainly in the case studies, a totally fresh departure from anything that I have encountered before in documenting an intellectual argument. This is not an easy or conventional book, but it provides us with a fresh and innovative look into the future we are already living with.

Professor Emeritus Arpad von Lazar
The Fletcher School of Law and Diplomacy
Tufts University, Medford, MA, USA

Neotribalism

At the end of the 1980s, sociologist Michel Maffesoli (1988) coined a new meaning of the term "tribalism" to explain an increasingly prevalent issue in western society. His use of the word "tribe" illustrated a significant shift in society since the "European Enlightenment," from a society built around the individual to a world populated by "affective communities." Driven by the emotional bonds of the community, individuals seek to belong to a proximity environment, and, occasionally, to dissolve their "own" identity to bring about complete identification with the group.

Against the backdrop of the excessive "rationality" of the last century, "emotionality" seems to be taking its revenge by means of a search for emotional bonds as the pillar of identity. The main change of paradigm we are witnessing constitutes *a shift from a longing for independence from a society made up of communities, to a longing for belonging from a society made up of individuals.*

The need to belong and feel useful to "my kind" went beyond urban tribes when it began to penetrate the business world toward the end of the twentieth century. Corporations, having understood the challenges posed by community bonds and the potential opportunities in them, have developed a series of policies and instruments now known as diversity policies, designed to tap into the forces resulting from the diversity among company employees, in order to help reach diverse clients in a diverse world.

The challenge is, however, fraught with complexity. Although diversity management has penetrated our corporations with varying degrees of success, new tribalism continues to grow in increasingly different forms that do not always work to the advantage of large corporations. The issue of tribalization goes beyond the recognition of a series of identities of origin (cultural, gender or sexual). Some individuals feel only weak bonds to their identities of origin, but close proximity with their identities of destiny (neo-oriental spirituality, ecological activism, etc.), identities they aspire to belong to. It is, therefore, difficult to plan policies aimed at capturing communal energies when it is not clear to which communities each individual belongs. Furthermore, the identity of individuals tends to be multiple and flexible, and thus subject to change in different phases of their lives.

In recent years, innovative businesses in different cultures and different locations have shown that the best guarantee for corporate success is to unite suppliers, workers and clients using the same "identity bond," which in turn generates a strong emotional affiliation. Hence "identity" corporations are flourishing, not only in terms of good results but also in the sense that they are sustainable corporations which can cope with the turbulent times we live in thanks to the strength of their identity bonds. Meanwhile, some large corporations are struggling to harness the energies of their human resources, as employees focus their attention on external social networks where they feel they can contribute more than they can inside the organizations they are working in.

The question at this stage is not about judging the good or bad of traditional or new ethnicities. New tribes are real and now play a pivotal role in society. The only way forward is to try to understand how tribalism works and how to manage it to move our organizations forward.

Traditional tribalism, history shows, constitutes a considerable danger, namely the total annihilation of the individual for the *good* of the community; *good* being defined by whoever is considered to be the leader or guru. This form of tribalism tends toward exclusion and toward a one-dimensional identity. The key to resolving the paradox of individual independence and belonging lies in the consciousness of individuals who can voluntarily and temporarily suppress their individuality for the good of the community without losing said individuality.

The individual capacity for independent thinking and the need to belong to a group do not need to be incompatible. The conscious, voluntary, and temporary annihilation of the ego for the common good is a key feature of some of the most successful companies in the twenty-first century, and this conscious contribution is what organizations need to capture from their human resources if they want to compete. If tribalism represents the annihilation of human individuality, beyond tribalism one can find new forms of ethnicity that illustrate the paradox of conscious annihilation – the sense of totally belonging to a community without losing individual consciousness. This is the phenomenon that can drive organizations to success and humanity to survival.

Individuals will have to learn to manage their different identities, which will shape their personality as well as serving as a base for personal growth and external contribution. Leaders in governments and organizations will have to accept and understand the ethnicities (setting basic common rules for all), and will have to help train individuals in all their capacities to enable them to choose and belong to their different identities, and thus contribute from within their own individuality.

The challenge ahead is to embrace community without renouncing universality. Multinationals have played the role of universality throughout the twentieth century, with the idea of equal employees in different cultures and settings, selling universal products to universal clients. Local businesses, on the other hand, represented the idea of local communities bound together in the same value system. Could we, in the twenty-first century, find a way to integrate both? A global organization made up of individuals freely linked to a variety of economic units with which they identify? Companies today competing against each other using human and capital resources could serve as the ideal platform to try out new systems of human and economic understanding.

This new tribalism is the direct result of movement, movement from a period of excessive individualism and movement away from old forms of tribalism.

Understanding movement

Popular sayings teach us that a pendulum-like movement is a matter of fact. A liberal period ends with the beginning of a traditional one, from a revolutionary father comes a traditional son. So we are not surprised when our children like to wear the fashion styles of our grandparents.

A swing backward and forward is not only what we hear in the streets but also what sociologists and historians tell us is happening.

Maffesoli talks about the decline of individualism in postmodern societies, which brought neotribalism as a consequence of an excessive individualism and the rationality that started during the Enlightenment.

Zygmunt Bauman clarifies the drama of community vs. individualism in terms of the paradox of security and freedom: "Promoting security always calls for sacrifice of freedom, while freedom can only be expanded at the expense of security" (Bauman, 2008, p. 20). Following this idea, societies struggle to find a model of freedom to turn it back into a model that sacrifices freedom and individuality in favor of security and community wellbeing.

Historians and politicians also stress a pendulum-like movement in our times, from globalization where all peoples are reunited thanks to technology and open markets, to an era that goes back to the local. National feelings can be seen everywhere in the world, from geographic nationalism to cultural or religious nationalism.

Each movement has in itself the seed of the next movement. Individualism becomes latent in periods of communitarianism, and then begins to reshape itself and move back to the surface. On the other hand, after each period of nationalism, latent universalism and globalization emerge with renewed force. In a period of excessive community, a longing exists for independence, equal to the desire to belong found in individualistic periods, as shown in Figure I.1.

No-one is surprised by movements, even cyclical ones, because movement is at the heart of our human condition, as the old principle of the Kybalion states: "Nothing rests; everything moves; everything vibrates."[1]

Eastern and western philosophers since the beginning of recorded times have tried to convince us to accept movement in our lives, from Lao Tse to the modern Gestalt psychologists, all attempting to make us at ease with the fact that nothing stays the same and that the best we can do is to accept it and go with the flow. Not only philosophers but also poets, singers, and even TV commercials recommend us to "enjoy the ride" and not to think too much on what is behind and what is ahead.

However, we still search for stability and refuse to accept the constant changes in our lives. We try to fight against movement the same way that we try to fight against time. Perhaps if all the effort we make to try to control movement was instead spent on trying to understand it and accept it, we would have a somewhat easier road. It seems that this is probably one of the most difficult things to do, as illustrated by the way our society works.

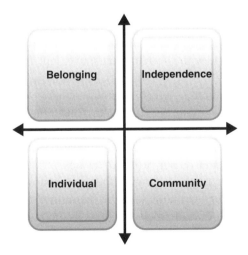

Figure I.1 Belonging, Independence, Individual, Community

This book is not attempting to manage movement but rather to understand it, and especially the way the movement of our identities affects the market. The question we want to explore is not so much whether this movement exists but whether there is any purpose in it. Is there anything to learn in the ebb and flow? Are we growing in the process?

I believe movement (particularly the movement from the self to the community and back, as individuals, and in societies from individualistic periods to communitarian ones and back), is one of the keys of growth as individuals and as societies. This new swinging back to community that we are witnessing in western societies is, in many of its manifestations, of a different nature than the one found in the old tribal period, if only because we have come from a long individualistic period that began with the Enlightenment, which focused on the capacities of the human mind, and both components, the individual self and the focus of the mind, have had a great effect in the making of a new communitarian way of being together.

Many new forms of tribalism, specifically the ones integrated with the myriad of internet-based networks, are not sect-based where individuals are emotionally glued regardless of their personal interest. New forms of tribalism are open-ended communities, with weaker emotional attachments than in previous tribal modes. Now, individuals want to keep their individuality and yet contribute to a common good by putting their thinking together with the thinking of others. Thus an emotional attachment exists; yet, this need to combine their thinking is, in my belief, stronger than emotional attachment. This is illustrated by the number of words for this new tribe: "thinking together," co-thinking, co-creation, co-design, co-invent, design thinking...

All through history, different thinkers of humanity have talked about the rhythm of things, with the idea that movement is not in vain. Every year we see spring followed by summer, which is followed by fall and in turn by winter; and thanks to that constant movement we can all advance and change, and so every spring find us as a different person in a different shape.

Ibn Khaldun, during the fourteenth century, explained the rhythm of history and the rise and fall of ruling dynasties as the product of internal forces and external actions.[2] Likewise, the great historian Arnold Toynbee in his *Study of History* explained, at the beginning of the twentieth century, the rise and fall of human civilizations as a constant advancement in human consciousness.

Toynbee saw history as a constant movement of challenges and responses, where individuals first, and then societies, rise above themselves in a constant spiritual growth that helps make mankind more complete with each step forward.

> The action of the creative individual may be described as a twofold motion of withdrawal and return: withdrawal for the purpose of his personal enlightenment, return for the task of enlightening his fellow men. This can be illustrated with Plato's parable of the cave, with Saint Paul's analogy of the seed, the story of the Gospel, as well as in the lives of the greatest individuals such as Buddha or Muhammad. (Toynbee 1957, p. 365)

Toynbee was accused of "idealism," a pejorative label in the twentieth century, a world of excessive focus on science, in which intuition and reflection had little value in academia. His understanding of history as constant growth movement had very much to do with spiritual growth and conscious development, words unacceptable in a world in which rationalism and positivism were the only possibilities allowed for human understanding.

Harmonizing actions with emotions and the mind

If one of the fundamental human questions is how to harmonize the conflicting but necessary tendencies towards independence and belonging, another is how human individuals can harmonize their actions with their feelings and thoughts.

Philosophers as well as psychologists have long tried to understand the basic components of human behavior. And following the correspondence of the nano- to the macro-, social scientists and development scholars follow some of the basic patterns of human behavior to explain the behavior of societies and cultures.

In a very interesting work, Don Beck and Clare Graves (Beck and Cowan, 2006) integrate horizontal and vertical movement into a map for understanding human evolution as well as individual evolution. *Spiral Dynamics* draws a map of the different levels in evolution of man's consciousness that in turn are illustrated in different stages in the history of mankind. These authors, and others with similar ideas, such as Ken Wilber, William Torbert, Susanne Cook-Greuter, and Robert Kegan, are well-known consultants who work in many programs helping political as well as economic organizations in the world today.

If we integrated together the individualism and collectivism movements with the vertical harmonization of physical, emotional and intellectual spheres, we can see a picture that can help us to understand the movements in identity, as shown in Figure I.2

Homo sapiens, many paleontologists affirm, represented probably the first big success for community organization, since these new patterns of community organization made community members fit to survive external factors as well as internal weaknesses, while giving them the strength that Neanderthals lacked. *Homo neanderthalensis* tended to live in small groups, and in such structures could not face the enormous challenges of survival, unlike the sophisticated organization of *Homo sapiens* (Carbonell and Sala, 2000).

At the opposite end of history, the European Enlightenment is probably the most successful achievement of individuality. Both individuality and community are necessary but at different periods, and so as individuals we could try to harmonize our bodies, our hearts, and our minds. In parallel, societies need also to harmonize their communities, in terms of the physical security of their members, emotional comfort of their members, and the pursuit of inventions to help in the development of their members.

Humanity has grown from following its instincts to being motivated by the heart and then by the mind. Mind, heart, and body often interact in disharmony, since each one tries to run the decision-making. The question we may bring forward is not what part of us is making the decision, but are we conscious of what our actions are? It is thus a growth in consciousness that helps increasingly identify what motivates us. In parallel, the trend keeps on moving from the need for independence to the quest for belonging.

Trends, however are not fit for everyone, because the rhythm in each one of us is different. In addition to belonging to humanity, each one of us belongs to a civilization, and to a number of communities, each with a different movement. To make things more complex, we are all at different stages in our self-motivation. These facts result in making the shift towards communitarianism appear as a growth movement for one community and as a regression movement for another community that is coming from

Figure I.2 Individuality vs. Community

the opposite end, for whom a movement towards individuality is what is needed. On the other hand the possibility of growth represented by a movement does not mean that everything will grow and that it will do so in the same way. For many, this pendulum-like movement represents a regression towards former stages. What is important is that a critical mass should be able to advance and in this way help the advancement of society.

I believe that these two movements, harmonizing instincts with heart and mind, and harmonizing independence and belonging, are the reason behind our actions in society and in the market. Therefore, the thesis of this book is to understand our identities in order to be conscious of their movement. The book is thus organized in three parts:

- The first part will be dedicated to understanding the meaning of identity, in its personal and social forms, with a particular reference to gender identity.
- The next part will take a look at how identities in action affect the marketplace, as well as our market behavior as producers and consumers.
- And finally, we will look at how these identities behave in the context of civilization.

These three areas will help us to move into business organization and see how a model can be applied in which we can move from managing diversity to managing flexible and multiple identities.

PART I

Understanding identity

CHAPTER 1

Identity and the self

Who am I?
First movement: Identity and the self, a continuous process of development from the ego to the self

1 Who am I?

I really need to go on vacation … and leave myself at home!

My friend Jamal used to tell me this expression and I loved it, since I really did identify with it. Sometimes one really feels like taking a break and leaving the self aside for a while, just to rest from one's worries, fears of the future, decisions that need to be made, etc. … But the self will just not leave us! No matter where we go and no matter what we do, the self is with us, regardless of whether we think it's good company or not. And if fact, any other option would be worse, since it would mean that either we are dead or that we have lost our personal identity and thus our sense of reality.

But what is the self? Is there such a thing as personal identity? Is the self my consciousness? Is it a real substance? Is it only my mind inventing my personality? Does my mind define my personal identity or am I defined by birth?

With the explosion of the European Enlightenment in the seventeenth century came the idea of fully understanding human nature scientifically. Pioneering philosophers such as Locke attempted to understand the scientific basis of personal identity.

Locke, in an essay concerning human understanding published in 1694, composed a chapter entitled "Identity and Diversity" where he gives the first scientific definition of personal identity.

> To find wherein what personal identity consists we must consider first what person stands for; which I think, is a thinking intelligent being, that has reason and reflection, and can consider itself as itself, the same thinking thing, in different times and places; which it does only by that consciousness which is inseparable from thinking, and as it

seems to me, essential to it.... Since consciousness always accompanies thinking; it is that which makes every-one to be what it calls self, and thereby distinguish himself from all other thinking things. In this alone consists personal identity, i.e. the sameness of rational being and as far as his consciousness can be extended backwards to any past action or thought so far reaches the identity of that person. (Locke 1694, 2008, pp. 33–53)

Bishop Butler in 1736 criticized Locke, since for him the self was more than memory, as Locke's article could be thought to imply. In his view, each individual person had an essence, a mental property which all his states of consciousness exemplified, even if he did not remember them (Butler 1736, 2008, pp. 99–107).

The controversy of self and whether it was related to memory, or whether it was a real substance, has continued up to our times in the work of philosophers such as H.P. Grice, Antony Quinton, Bernard Williams, Sydney Shoemaker, and John Perry among many others.

Other philosophers, such as David Hume, even questioned that such a thing as personal identity existed. In his *Treatise of Human Nature*, first published in 1739, he affirmed that identity was only a fictitious positioning between unity and diversity:

I may venture to affirm of the rest of mankind, that they are nothing but a bundle or collection of different perceptions, which succeed each other with an inconceivable rapidity and are in a perpetual flux of movement. ... Since, we can find impressions corresponding to unity and impressions corresponding to number or diversity but not impressions corresponding to identity, which is somehow between these two ideas. (Hume 1739, 2008, p. 170)

Putting aside the controversy of finding what scientifically constitutes the self, whether a substance or a memory impression, or an invention of our mind, philosophers throughout time have sought not particularly what self-identity is but, rather, its function. In other words, how to understand our self; what makes an individual strong and another weak; what are the attributes of the self; how can we develop our self to the best of our capabilities; and most of all, *how to make our self happy.*

2   The quest for human happiness: Getting to know yourself, *mode d'emploi*[1]

We all want to be happy! Or from another perspective, we all want to be away from suffering and sorrow. Our ancestors were not very different from us because they too, at least for the last 3000 years, have searched for ways to overcome fear and anguish so that they could enjoy fulfilling and happy lives.

The first schools of thought that we have record of were led by exceptional individuals, who, once they found their inner happiness, began to dedicate their lives to help others overcome their daily sorrows. For the majority of the traditional systems of thought, true happiness was not related to external circumstances; rather, it was found with a personal effort, with the process of detachment from the ego and its demands and connecting with the self to find inner peace. In other words, happiness was found by establishing a connection with the true essence of each individual.

The early thinkers of many different cultures and historical eras focused their thoughts in trying to understand human nature; and thus they offered their recommendations for the management of the *self* so that human beings could make the most of their lives in earth. In other words, thinking was necessary not so much to create a theoretical framework to explain things, but to guide human actions. *The quest of self-identity is in fact the quest for happiness.*

Human happiness in ancient thinking

Three of the most important thought movements in human history arose in different geographical areas, yet inside a relatively small time-frame of the seventh and sixth centuries BC. And although all three have significant differences, they also share remarkable coincidences, particularly in what they have to say about the human quest for happiness and their practical recommendations for human self-development.

The oldest human teachers include: Confucius in the sixth century BC, in Lu, China (currently Shandong); the Indian writers of the first *Upanishads*, in northern India around the eighth century BC; and the first Greek thinkers, (also known as the Seven Wise Men), around the seventh and sixth centuries BC, first in the periphery of the Greek zone of influence in the colonies of Asia Minor, and then followed by the Athenian philosophers led by Socrates.

Confucius (551–479 BC)

Also known as the Teacher, Confucius left his legacy in the so called *Lun-Yu* (*Analects*), short sayings compiled by his disciples after his death, where some of the most influential ideas that shaped Chinese civilization can be found.

His main idea for self-development is to pursue the Way of the Sage. In his thinking, material well-being does not depend upon us but on destiny, and for that reason it is worthless to try to pursue material happiness; instead, we should follow the path to morality described in the Tao (The Way of the Sage) as far as our capabilities allow us. (Stevenson and Haberman 2004, p. 10).

Confucius believed in human talents and in their potential, and his philosophy tries to help people to become wiser. He analyzed the sad situation of humanity during his time and defined some of its main problems:[2]

- **Human egoism**. Humans are attached to material benefits; a noble man sees the good of an action, while a regular man only sees how the action will benefit him. "To be thinking only of salary is shameful." (*Analects* XIV.1)
- **Lack of filial piety**. Egoistic conduct reflects a total lack of respect for others in any given society, which in turn reveals inappropriate relations within the family and shows a lack of discipline, since the family is the Pillar of Society.
- **Lack of sincerity.** The differences between what is said and what is done, and thus people are unfaithful to their promises.
- **There is a general ignorance of the past.** People are not longer familiar with the Way of the Sage.
- **Benevolence is lacking in human affairs**. Benevolence (*rén*) is the highest quality any human being can have, and the best way to approach it is to put the self in the position of the other and then treating the other accordingly. "Do not do to others what you would not like done to yourself." (*Analects* XII.2) The written character for benevolence represents two people living together in harmony, since benevolence has a lot to do with human relations. The state of benevolence is based on internal serenity and equanimity, both of which result from the detachment from things we have no control over, such as fortune or disgrace. The prescription to help cure humanity's illness is self-discipline. When asked about the characteristics of superior men, The Master said "He cultivates himself so as to give rest to all the people." (*Analects* XIV.42)

To overcome the human tendency to act expecting personal benefit, Confucius recommends to merely act without expecting anything in return. Just doing what is morally correct precisely because it is morally correct will help us attain interior serenity and detachment from things we have no control over. This is one of the reasons for the importance of following ritual propriety (*li*), meaning to follow the established conventions which set out value distinctions and prescribe activities in response to those distinctions.

From an external perspective, both the actions of a sage and the actions of a man that follows the ritual look the same; but the actions of the sage are the reflection of someone who has interiorized his behavior and no longer pays attention to it. Normal men concentrate on following the rituals, since this discipline will help them reach the state in which moral action has become natural and spontaneous.

Thinkers from Hinduism

Hinduism is a complex philosophy, made up of a large number of texts and movements that cannot be defined as a single unity of thought. Following Stevenson and Haberman, the foundational work that can help understand the fundamental principles of Hinduism thinking is the group of texts known as the *Upanishads*, written by meditation teachers living in the forests with their disciples around the eighth and seventh centuries BC.

Recognized as one of the principal intellectual creations of humanity, the *Upanishads* describe a highly speculative set of reflections on the true nature of reality. They do not constitute a unified body of thought, but rather a variety of writings that are often contradictory to each other. The main global theme is *the ontological understanding that all things are connected.*

The oldest Upanishad is the *Upanishad Brihad Aranyaka*, which deals with the true reality of the world and the true identity of human beings. (Stevenson and Haberman 2004, pp. 27–29). The basic understanding of human nature is the idea that the original unity is not lost, it just has adopted the appearance of a multitude of forms. In this way the *Upanishad* recognizes the simultaneity of unity and diversity. The goal of the *Upanishad* is to transcend the identity from the transitory ego-I associated with the body, to the eternal-I that is not different from eternity and from the whole of creation.

The ultimate problem of humanity resides in a serious identity problem. We identify ourselves with the fragmented and unconnected phenomenological world of diversity instead of identifying ourselves with the *Braham,* the universal spirit. We are infinite creatures attached to finite personalities, blinded by the limited projects of our ego. Human experience is thus an experience of fragmentation and isolation. Human beings are trapped in a cycle of psychological dependency to the desires of their ego.

Human development thus consists in crossing the bridge over the gulf that exists between the theological and psychological approaches to reality.

The basic feature of this process is to discover the self through our own knowledge, once we realize that the reality of anything is the reality of everything.

Therefore, knowledge is to transcend the partial look and reach a complete vision. But knowledge means experimentation not theoretical thinking. Meditation thus helps in the way towards knowledge and contributes in the way towards the liberation of the self from its limited and fragmented state.

The first individual: Socrates (470–399 BC) and Greek philosophy

Pierre Hadot, in his beautiful book on ancient philosophy, clarifies in a revealing manner the practical meaning of philosophy, which for the ancient Greek thinkers meant a combination of self-development, experimentation, and theoretical guidance (Hadot 1995).

Today, the representation we have of philosophy and the philosophers is based on people who built abstract systems to explain the universe. Out of these theoretical systems came doctrines and morals that imply certain consequences for men and society. Men are invited to follow it as a life-choice. However, whether this life-choice is or is not effective is secondary, and does not fall into in the scope of philosophical discourse. Yet Hadot proves that, contrary to general belief, in ancient philosophy and particularly since Socrates, the life-choice that the ancient philosophers made did not come at the end of their theoretical discourse, but at the beginning. The choice of a certain behavior meant a way to see the world which in turn determined their philosophical discourse. Therefore, the origin of the theoretical discourse came from a life-choice and an existential option, and not the opposite. Ancient philosophers after Socrates opted for an existential choice that demanded a total change in their way of living, a total conversion, and a desire of being and behaving in a certain manner that implied a certain vision of the world.

The famous saying of Socrates "I only know that I know nothing" shows us that Socrates' wisdom was an awareness of his own ignorance. In the image we have of Socrates from Plato's *Dialogues*, he does not try to teach anything. He tries to help others find the contradictions existing in their conventional knowledge, and thus help them to empty themselves of formal knowledge and become capable of detachment from themselves. Only with an effort of detachment could human beings find the true knowledge in themselves.

Such wisdom does not consist in the possession of information about reality. Instead, it is a way of life that corresponds to the highest activity that human beings can engage in, and which is linked intimately to the excellence and virtue of the soul. Wisdom itself is a way of being, or transcendent ontological state (Hadot 1995, p. 220).

This knowledge of value is taken from Socrates' inner experience – the experience of a choice that implicates his entire self. Here once again, the only knowledge consists of a personal discovery that comes from within.

According to Hadot, at the end of the banquet in the *Eulogy of Alciade to Socrates* is the appearance for the first time in history of a *representation of an individual* as having a unique and unclassifiable personality. It is the extreme individuality of Socrates that gives rise in the interlocutor of a consciousness of his own individuality. Socrates can transcend his own individuality by reaching the universal, represented by the *logos* held in common by both interlocutors. Thus, Socrates harassed his interlocutors with questions, and obliged them to pay attention to themselves and to take care of themselves. By this process the interlocutor was then able to also discover his own true self.

Things considered bad for conventional humans, such as death, poverty, or illness, were not considered bad by Socrates, since material things were not good or bad per se. He was detached from material demands and followed only his true inner nature. For him, moral qualities are the only real ones; and thus since they are the inner nature of humans, they are the only guide for human development. Human transformation from the external demands on the inner guide is a constant process that is never finished. Human beings need to constantly revise and examine their actions. The way to wisdom would be to undress oneself in search of the right way, meaning the moral or just way.

However, Socrates' detachment from himself did not imply that he renounced the world. Quite the contrary, in the Plato's dialogues Socrates always appears as a *bon vivant*, enjoying drinking, friends, and the pleasures of family and ordinary life (as in the "Dialogue of the Banquet," where he drinks more than anyone, although without ever losing his sobriety, and, once the morning comes, goes back to his daily affairs). Socrates claims that men need to pursue their development process in their daily life. He represents a messianic as well as a popular spirit that refuses to avoid its destiny and accepts the death penalty to show the absolute value of moral intentions.

The ideal that Socrates represents is not a man outside of the world, but a man who acts in the world and yet manages to transcend his own reality. This is a man who performs the daily matters of his reality and is at the same time detached from external demands as well as the demands of the ego (Hadot 1995, p. 67).

What happened to ancient wisdom?

In his work on ancient philosophy, Hadot's main goal is to analyze how Greek philosophy that started as a guide for self-development ended up in the western world as a theoretical science far away from transcendental experimentation. In his research he found that the disconnection of philosophy from its speculative component and its attachment to a practical method was a slow process that began in the Middle Ages and continued through the Enlightenment until today.

After Socrates, all four Greek schools[3] followed his understanding of philosophy as a life-choice and were dedicated to teach wisdom (defined as a certain state of inner peace, a therapy that liberates the human being from the problems and anguish of daily life). Humans insist on making value-judgments of external things. But since we do not have control over these things, it is up to us to detach ourselves from external worries and take things as they come, without judgment, and use them in our self-development. The process was different in each school: for the Cynics it was becoming indifferent to external influences; for the Epicureans it was managing their desires; and for the Stoics it was following the way of virtue. But the purpose of philosophy for all of them was to change human mentality and thus expand the life options available.

In its process of assimilation of Greek philosophy, Christianity slowly but inexorably broke philosophy apart. The ancient schools that had not disappeared (Platonism and Aristotelianism, and in particular the synthesis of neo-Platonism after the third century BC), were removed from the ways of life that inspired them and reduced to conceptual material to be used in theological arguments. Philosophy was made to serve theology and became merely theoretical. Aristotelian logic for example, furnished concepts that were indispensable to the formulation of dogmas such as the Trinity, but Christianity itself, as a way of life, had little use for the practical elements of the ancient philosophical discourse.

The break from philosophy, from a theoretical discourse that was inseparable from practical life, was further aggravated by the rise of European universities in the thirteenth century. At that time, Aristotle's rediscovery had spread among the universities, with a lasting effect on the thinking of the Middle Ages. Faculties in medieval universities were divided mainly between theology and the arts, both of which were strongly influenced by Aristotle's writings. In Theology they used mainly his *Dialectics*, with his distinction of substance and form, to solve Christian problems of reason and dogma. The commentaries of Aristotle's works were gradually integrated into the liberal arts curricula. The increasing efforts to discuss

Aristotle's works and attempt to solve potential problems of interpretation lead to the development of scholasticism.

So when philosophy emerged into its own again many centuries later to breathe the air of the Enlightenment, it considered itself a theoretical science because the existential dimension of philosophy no longer had any meaning from the perspective of Christianity. Hadot concludes that philosophy, stripped to its conceptual content, became the impoverished thing it is in today's universities. There is a radical opposition between the Greek schools that addressed each individual in an attempt to entirely transform his personality, and universities, whose only mission is giving diplomas that correspond to an objectified level of knowledge. Philosophy today is made to serve theology or scientific research, and the professors of this subject today do not teach individuals to become persons but to become philosophy teachers (Hadot 1995, p. 390).

The trend of placing a theoretical discourse into a practical experimentation in the quest for self-identity, was also influenced by the rise of the Newton's scientific method in the seventeenth century. The success of Newton's method set the basis for scientific knowledge by which the understanding of the world was based on a careful and monitored observation of the phenomena studying question.

Following Stevenson and Haberman, the question that is still unresolved today is to what extent the scientific method that has proved to be successful with non-animated entities can also be applied to human beings. Until recently only two answers were put forward. Either human beings were considered to be of the same material as the rest of the world, and thus follow the same physical laws; or humans were perceived as a combination of soul and body in which the first is assumed to be of a different material and thus does not have to follow the same physical principles (Stevenson and Haberman 2004, p. 152).

Today, these two main trends described by Stevenson and Haberman in the study of human behavior and motivation are still valid. For example, neuroscience takes the first position and observes some characteristics of human behavior, in particular neuronal connections found in the brain, that can be observed under objective physical laws. On the opposite side, transpersonal psychology "is concerned with the study of humanity's highest potential, and with the recognition, understanding, and realization of unitive, spiritual, and transcendent states of consciousness" (Lajoie and Shapiro 1992, p. 91).

During the last decades of the twentieth century new discoveries began to confront the scientific method. Several new developments in quantum physics raised some doubts on traditional certainties, among which are what is the real material make-up of the world, and the fact that an object could not be observed without being affected by the observer.

Perhaps, after all, humans are made of the same fabric of the universe, but then the real question is: What is in fact this fabric that the universe is made of?

Lonely stars

Significant exceptions, however, continued the ancient path of Greek philosophical thinking according to the purpose of its first originators. Holistic thinking includes a theoretical discourse that can be applied to a practical inner experimentation, and also a practical experimentation combined with a solid theoretical discourse.

The first group includes Kant, Erasmus, Montaigne, Goethe, Nietzsche, Schopenhauer, Kierkegaard, and Wittgenstein. These thinkers, just as their ancient counterparts, looked for a life of equilibrium, an inner peace that will enable us to connect beyond our ego and desires with our fellow humans and the universe. These philosophers have perceived their work as a concrete and practical activity that can transform the way of life and the way of perceiving the world (Hadot 1995, p. 407).

At the opposite end to the experimental side we can also find exceptional individuals who combined their experimentation with a theoretical discourse. The works of the greatest mystics of Judaism, Islam, and Christianity represent a perfect combination of thinking and practical self-transformation. Ibn Sina, in the eleventh century, is probably the best illustration of the combination of science and the mind with a vision of self-transformation. As mentioned in the works of Henri Corbin (Corbin 1999), the Epistle of the Bird by Ibn Sina, was not a conventional recite; rather it is a visionary recite in which the reader is called upon to situate himself in the place of the hero and re-live his experiences, experiencing a mimetic role. In Judaic mysticism, Maimonides in the twelfth century is a magnificent exponent of theoretical thinking applied to the search for the inner self. This is true of all the Cabalistic work in the Jewish tradition found in the *Sephirotic Tree*. In the Christian tradition of the sixteenth century the works of Saint Teresa de Avila and Saint John of the Cross are some of the best illustrations of Christian mysticism, showing a path of transformation tied together to solid theoretical thinking. Also, the traditions in Hinduism and Confucianism continue the old tradition of combining theoretical models with practical experimentation.

The greatest thinkers in human history achieved a perfect combination of a mental process with emotional experimentation, which they used as a way to explore the inner capacities for harmony. Modern humanity has conquered far more difficult frontiers in the domination of the physical world, but a sense of wholeness has been lost in the way. As Hadot suggests, there is no discourse which deserves to be called philosophical if it is separated from the philosophical life, and there is no philosophical life unless it is directly linked to philosophical discourse (Hadot 1995, p. 422).

3   Self-identity in contemporary science

The self in Humanistic Psychology

At the start of the twentieth century people were hungry for a practical philosophical approach for their everyday lives. Western societies were undergoing a secularization process, and had lost the guidance of a religion in their search their identity. Therefore, many young people during the second half of the century began to look towards the east, finding in the old eastern traditions (specially within the Hinduism of Advaita Vedanta of Sankara) a guide for happiness and self-development that they could no longer find inside their own culture. Practices such as Yoga, Transcendental Meditation, or Chinese Tai Chi, have become the methods chosen by an increasing number of westerners in their efforts to find peace of mind and a connection with their inner self.

However, with the increased development of science, exceptional individuals found new ways to reconnect science with personal experimentation, as a means of self-development. In the western tradition, a new scientific discipline, psychology, took over the role of healing the inner troubles human beings. After the second half of the twentieth century, figures like Carl Jung and Abraham Maslow opened the door to a new approach to a psychology that moved its focus away from illness and opened new paths for the holistic understanding of individuals and their identities. These new pathways made the theoretical discourse an important a personal effort to experiment, with the hope that they could lead to happiness and a fulfilling life.

Carl Jung (1875–1961)

A pioneer in what was to be later called Humanistic Psychology, Jung's quest for human self-development led him to believe that psychologists should go beyond curing pathologies and help individuals in their self-completion process. In his views the process of self-development had a turning point in what he called individuation. Jung clarifies that our individuality is constituted by our self and not by our ego, since our ego is only a temporal structure in life, while the self is our essence is what constitutes our individuality. In order to connect with our true self, our essence, each needs to follow his or her own process of individuation. The process of individuation was for Jung a way for individuals to complete themselves by integrating their consciousness with their unconscious demands.

Individuation is the process of becoming aware of oneself, one's make-up, and the way to discover one's true inner self. Hence, it is the process whereby the innate elements of personality, the different experiences of a person's life, and the different aspects and components of the immature psyche, become integrated over time into a well-functioning whole. Individuation might thus be summarized as the stabilizing of the personality. In the words of one of the collaborators of Jung:

> The individuation process is more than a coming to terms between the inborn germ of wholeness and the outer acts of fate. Its subjective experience conveys the feeling that some supra-personal force is actively interfering in a creative way. One sometimes feels that the unconscious is leading the way in accordance with a secret design. It is as if something is looking at me, something that I do not see but that sees me – perhaps that Great Man in the heart, who tells me his opinions about me by means of dreams. (von Franz 1964, p. 164)

Abraham H. Maslow (1908–1970)

Maslow was a renowned psychologist and professor in various universities. In 1958, in the prologue to one of his best-known books, he described the emergence of the new tendency in psychology. Against the two psychology schools accepted at the time, Freudian psychoanalysis and behaviorism, Maslow affirmed that there were a growing number of small groups that were creating a third way, called human psychology, that was resulting in a new conception of man (sometimes labeled transpersonal psychology, holistic-dynamic psychology or self-psychology). He included in the group Adlerians, Ramkians, Jungians, writers like Marcuse, Wheelis, Marmor, Szasz, Schachel, Kurt Goldstein, and also Gestalt therapists and personality therapists such as H.S. Murray, J. Moreno, and G. Murphy among others (Maslow 1958, 1968, 1999, p. 5).

Maslow highlights his common ground with these emerging new psychologists: they all share a basic understanding of the human being and its inner nature, as well as emphasizing a focus not only on illness, but

on a general path to help individuals to achieve to the best of their possibilities and thus achieve a meaningful life. Maslow's main contribution
to human thinking has been the theory of the hierarchy of needs, which
has enhanced the understanding of human motivation over the past few
decades, and as such is taught in most business schools.

Due to its relevance for modern schools of psychology, it is worthwhile
to review some of the main tenets of Maslow's theory, which in summary
can be described as follows:

- Every action we do we is host to one motive or another; moreover, as
  soon as a motive is satisfied another immediately pops up and take its
  place. These different motives do not succeed one another at random
  but they build in priority; human motives are hierarchically structured,
  and their arrangement within the hierarchy is defined by their respective levels of urgency (intensity, priority, or prepotency). All motives are
  present rooted deeply in the very core of human nature, but heretofore
  they have been eclipsed by the more biologically urgent needs.
- The first levels of human motivation are characterized by deficiency.
  These are all needs for something, from the basics of hunger and thirst
  to the more distinctly human needs for love or self esteem. Looking at
  the world through these deficiencies, is like seeing with clouded lenses.
  "It has by now been sufficiently demonstrated that the human being has
  as part of his intrinsic construction, not only physiological needs, but
  also truly psychological ones. They must be considered as deficiencies
  which must be optimally fulfilled by the environment in order to avoid
  sickness." (Maslow 1958, 1968, 1999, p. 169)
- Those persons whose basic deficiency needs (from the biological to
  the higher human needs) are satisfied will no longer make deficiency
  demands on reality, and thus will no longer be driven by deficiency-
  motivated fears and suspicions. The interactions between their self and
  others, and with the world at large, will change. This person is at the
  stage of self-actualization. This term refers to what human nature really
  is behind the surface. Self-actualized persons have a more efficient perception of reality and more comfortable relations with it; in other words,
  a whole new kind of motivation emerges in the life of the person.

  The consequence is that they live more in the real world of nature than
  the man-made mass of concepts, abstractions, expectations, believes,
  and stereotypes of most people confused with the world. They are
  therefore more far more apt to perceive what is there rather than their
  own wishes, hopes, fears, anxieties their own theories and beliefs,
  or those of their cultural group. ... [Self-actualized people] have the

healthy quality of detachment that will allow them to remain above the battle, undisturbed of what produces turmoil in others (Maslow 1958, 1968, 1999, p. xii).

- Self-actualized persons live in the conventional world and act as conventional people but with a higher degree of freedom in their actions. If you are striving for food, your concentration will be on the next meal; but if your food is secure the need for food would not be a priority and your energy can be used towards other goals. Or if you do not need the approval for others, then your actions would not be shaped to conform to the requirements of approval and would thus have more creativity. This same inner freedom allows the self-realized person to develop a strong creativity which is different from the special talent-based creativity of the Mozart type. This other creativity is potentiality given to all human beings at birth. Self-creative people still can enjoy food, drink, love and external appreciation, but they do not need them in the conventional sense of the term.

It is through self-actualization that people reach their real identity. "My feeling is that people in peak experiences are most their identities closest to their real selves, most idiosyncratic, it would seem that this is an especially important source of clean and in contaminated data; i.e. invention is reduced to a minimum and discovery increased to a maximum." (Maslow 1958, 1968, 1999, p. 115)

The goal of identity (self actualization, autonomy, individuation, authenticity) seems to be simultaneously an end-goal in itself and also a transitional goal, a rite of passage, a step along the path to the transcendence of identity.

Maslow affirms that men have the lower needs in common with his fellow humans but their higher qualities are unique for men. Just as trees need sun, water, and foods from the environment so do all people need safety, love, and status from their environment. However, in both cases this is just where real development of individuality can begin, for once satiated with these elementary species-wide necessities, each tree and each person proceeds to develop in his own style uniquely using these necessities for its own private purpose. In a very meaningful sense, development then becomes more determined from within rather than from without (Maslow 1958, 1968, 1999, p. 39).

However, in his opinion less than 1 percent of the population is self-realized, since most people are either reluctant or afraid or unable to do so. On the other hand, self-realization is not a permanent status.

Even if someone has achieved realization, that does not means that regression cannot happen, quite the contrary, since higher values are hierarchically integrated whereas lower values rest one upon each other. In all stages, safety is a precondition for love, which in turn is a precondition of self-actualization ... our Godlike qualities rest upon our animal qualities. Our adulthood is not a renunciation of our childhood but rather it includes it and builds upon it.

Maslow's contribution linked human self-development with ancient thinkers such as Socrates, Confucius, Christ or the mystics. But the ancient path seemed to be an all-or-nothing gamble; either you had the inner potential to transcend or not. Maslow described a path for all, fit for the men and women of the twentieth century, not just based on personal efforts but also in a logical sequence of resolutions for specific needs.

Maslow and Jung were seeking to help human beings in the process of finding their own identity, their true essence, not only to heal a pathology but to help people in achieving their highest potential and unleashing their inner capabilities.

Happiness and the self in the twenty-first century

We in the twenty-first century still want to be happy, and we keep looking for practical methodologies that can keep us away from suffering and daily sorrows, as illustrated by the number of books in the self-help section of every bookstore. Eastern philosophies and its meditational guides are still very popular, and even older traditions like Indian Shamanism, that connect us not only with the self but also with nature, are increasingly popular.

Also, science has been following the path of Maslow, Jung, and other humanist theorists, by searching for new ways to help individuals in their self-development and in their search for a meaningful life. Some of the most relevant tendencies in psychology are described below.

Gestalt therapy

Groups related to this movement organize different therapies and workshops that help individuals in their process of self-knowledge. Most of these therapies are no longer centered on healing pathologies, but are applied to individuals who want to improve and advance. Many of these workshops are now used by corporations to help their employees in their process of self-development.

Enneagram

Some psychologists with different backgrounds have shared the idea that individuals are integrated by mental, physical and emotional impulses in their functioning. The different shares of each one of these three elements lead to different typologies of personality, each with its dark and light aspects. Understanding each personality typology will help individuals in their self-development process. Enneagram, in its different variants, constitutes a useful and practical methodology to know one's self by discovering one's weakness and strengths, and in turn using this knowledge to better understand others.[4]

Briggs Myers Personality Test:
Myers-Briggs Type Indicator (MBTI) Assessment

The Briggs Myers approach is based on Carl Jung's four basic functional types: *Sensation* (the perception of the senses); *Thinking* (applying the intellectual faculty in order to orientate oneself); *Intuition* (which tells you whence it comes from and where it is going); and *Feeling* (value judgment of what we do and do not like). Following the functional types of Jung, Katharine Cook Briggs and her daughter Isabel Briggs Myers created an indicator to measure preferences in how people perceive the world and make decisions based on the following types: Extraversion–Introversion; Sensing–Intuition; Thinking–Feeling. Their indicator is offered free on the internet and is used widely in corporations and schools to assess the personality of their members and to form different teamwork strategies.

Positive psychology

With its search for human happiness and living a meaningful life, positive psychology has become a popular trend in psychology during the last decade. Positive psychology began as a new area of study within psychology in 1998 when Martin Seligman, considered the father of the modern positive psychology movement, chose it as the theme for his term as president of the American Psychological Association.

> The exclusive focus on pathology that has dominated so much of our discipline results in a model of the human being lacking the positive features that make life worth living. Hope, wisdom, creativity, future mindedness, courage, spirituality, responsibility, and perseverance are ignored or explained as transformations of more authentic negative

impulses. ... Positive psychology discusses such issues as what enables happiness, the effects of autonomy and self-regulation, how optimism and hope affect health, what constitutes wisdom, and how talent and creativity come to fruition. (Seligman and Csikszentmihalyi 2000, p. 5)

Researchers in positive psychology indicate six relevant virtues that the majority of cultures find positive, the pursuit of which helps on the way towards living more fulfilling lives: 1) *Wisdom and knowledge*: curiosity, open mindedness, innovation, creativity; 2) *Courage*: bravery, persistence, integrity, and vitality; 3) *Humanity*: love, kindness, social intelligence; 4) *Justice*: fairness, citizenship; 5) *Temperance*: forgiveness, mercy, humility, prudence, and self control; 6) *Transcendence*: appreciation of beauty, spirituality, hope, and gratitude.

Following the logical trends of positivism, this group of psychologists seeks empirical evidence to find what makes people happy, in terms of personal attributes, family or cultural environment that nurture positive outcomes. They based some of their research on neuroscience, attempting to find ways of measuring the physiological correlations to happiness. In the same way that Nobel laureate Eric Kandel has found that depression can be diagnosed by looking at brain-scans, positive scientists believe that science can use brain-scans to tell us more about the different ways of being happy as well as finding significant genetic traits.

4   The quest for self-identity in today's business world

Self-development and the search for a meaningful life are also present in the business world. The choices we make in finding a job or consuming certain products and services have a fundamental connection with our search for happiness and self-development.

The influence of the drive of self-development can be best illustrated by the increasing number of people who are searching, in addition to a salary, for a meaningful job. Following the pyramid of needs, many people in the west who have had their basic needs covered are no longer motivated by an increase in salary; often, these people seek higher motivations that could help them in their development process and thus make them happier.

As an illustration we can look at the attitudes of the employees in the case of "JAK Medlemsbank, Sweden: A Different Mindset for Community Lending" (see Case 1, p. 22 below). In JAK Bank, most employees stated in their interviews that they had given up on the possibility of obtaining higher salaries in order to have more fulfilling jobs. They represent normal people in the process of self-development who need to cover their basic needs but who also need a job that will allow them to fulfill other personal aspirations. For them to work at JAK is to work in an environment that they feel can help in their self-development, which means different things for each of them: quality of life; relationships with social groups; believing they are contributing to a better world; freedom to research; or feeling that they are being heard.

In addition, some of the bank's clients choose products that identify with their self-development aspirations. Clients of JAK, mostly those contributing to social projects, were happy to leave their savings with JAK not because of the remuneration but because they felt recompensed by the possibility of contributing to something they believe in – a fair trade shop, a mosque, or whatever project they feel is good for their communities. The lack of satisfaction from a lower reward in their savings is compensated by the inner satisfaction of helping others and feeling they are contributing to a better society.

Finally, most entrepreneurs also tend to reflect their personal self in the companies they create. Many entrepreneurs, in addition to being self-employed and making money, have a desire to contribute to whatever they think is a good idea. For example, the founders of JAK truly believe the world would be better off without interest and wanted to prove it in a practical way. In fact, many worked without any remuneration from the project for years before they could begin to make a living from their work.

Therefore, decisions as to where to work, or what to buy, have a direct effect on the self-development aspirations in each one of us. This is not new, but what perhaps *is* new is the level of consciousness people put into their decisions – the consciousness of a need for a general improvement of living conditions in many areas of the world. When we are free from worrying about covering our basic needs, we become free to move up in our scale of motivation-based needs; and accordingly, we begin to change our life-choices and in particular our business choices.

This self-development process can of course change its priorities, as in the case of a crisis or a shortage of liquidity in which lower-level personal needs once again take priority.

5   First movement: Identity and the self, a continuous process of development from the ego to the self

The quest for the self represents a movement from using the external world to feed our basic physical, emotional or rational needs, towards contributing to the external world beyond our ego needs.

I do not pretend to treat in detail 3000 years of incredibly rich and diverse human thinking. A simple work like this one cannot cover it entirely. But my intention is only to point out some striking similarities within the human quest to understand self-identity, and its relationship to human happiness through the process of self-development. Whether it is the intuition of the greatest thinkers in human history, the faith of religions, or the method of scientific research, there are coincidences in some basic aspects of their understanding of human nature in its quest for happiness.

Most thinkers in all cultural backgrounds had a basic idea of human nature and human purpose, and felt that a theoretical discourse should go hand-in-hand with experimentation. Most argued that individuals in the pursuit of happiness should choose a life that transforms their vision of the world and helps them find their true nature, free from material dependencies.

Most agree that the human being is composed of a higher and a lower nature, both real and necessary, and they also agree that the lower nature is integrated by three basic components: physical, emotional, and mental. Each one of these components produces desires that normally are ranked from the most physical to the most subtle.

Most cultures and movements agree that the lower nature needs to be transcended in order to reach a superior stage, but they disagree on the ways to transcend these desires. Some think the only way is suppression, for others it's the satisfaction of the desires, or focusing only on the positive attributes ignoring the deficiencies, or even developing pharmacological products to help us focus on the best qualities.

Once the lower nature is transcended or satisfied, individuals can fully enjoy themselves, develop higher capacities and even fully enjoy both their higher capacities as well as their lower. A necessary condition of self-development is to be free from desires in order to be able to enjoy them without becoming their slave, as shown by Socrates, drinking and enjoying his everyday life.

When the individual has transcended his or her lower nature, it is then possible to contribute to the fullest to the community. It has been proven that an individual who does not concentrate on their ego frees up energy that is spent on other higher, more altruistic and more creative purposes, and can also better connect with his or her environment and fellow human beings. Those few who manage to detach themselves from lower demands are called self-realized, individuated, superhuman, or *Rajul kamil* (a completed man in Sufi terminology).

For ancient thinkers the process was more an all-or-nothing venture, whereas modern psychologists take a more gradual approach following a slow process such as the pyramid of needs, in which the basic harmonization of the physical nature with the emotional and intellectual needs is gradually achieved. However, most of us are not self-actualized, according to Maslow at this time only 1 percent of humanity is. But most of us are struggling in this process of harmonizing our mental needs with emotional and physical ones. And most importantly, there is an increased consciousness of behavior in our approach. Most people are aware of their needs and understand that material needs alone do not satisfy our human aspirations (see Figure 1.1).

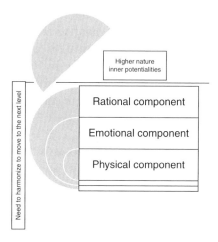

Figure 1.1 The quest for self-identity: understanding the true nature of human beings

In summary, more than ever in the history of humankind, there is a large and growing number of individuals pursuing more meaningful lives and who are thus aware of their own process of self-development. More than ever in history, a large number of people has overcome the satisfaction of basic needs and is now looking to develop higher capacities. For that reason employees, clients or entrepreneurs seek in their market relations something that might have meaning for them, under whatever is meaningful to each within their self-realization process.

Case 1   JAK Medlemsbank, Sweden: A different mindset for community lending

Introduction

Miguel has just finish his Skype conversation with Jay Standish in Seattle on potential synergies between his project www.symbionomics.com and JAK Medlemsbank in Sweden. Miguel is really pleased with the growing interest that JAK is provoking all over the world. He is not surprised: JAK and its interest-free banking model is a really good idea, and, after the financial crisis, more and more people around the world are looking for new ways to change traditional financial patterns, and achieve higher degrees of economic emancipation from the fixed world financial system.

When he first arrived in Sweden from Spain seven years ago, Miguel was quite interested in the system of popular universities, "*Folkhögskola,*" that, following the tradition of community education, are found all over Sweden. That is how he heard about JAK for the first time, and now he cannot believe he has already worked in the cooperative bank for five years, and he likes it more and more every year.

He likes working for the international development of JAK, although for him is very clear that his role is to support members to spread JAK idea in the world, "Not only because of the fact that we own a cooperative bank together, but also because we try to avoid a 'culture of expertise' and instead try to stimulate all our members (ourselves) to participate in the cooperative, in its development, in the decision-making and growth." That is the reason why in most of the occasions when JAK is presented abroad it is done by a voluntary member and by one of the 26 full-time employees of JAK.

That is how Miguel Ganzo, Consultant and International Relations Coordinator for JAK, explains the bank's differential approach in reaching new customers. The organization supports 550 local representatives and 28 local groups throughout Sweden. JAK totaled 36,300 members during 2010, with a 12 percent yearly growth rate. During the same year, members' savings amounted to €111 million, of which €99 million was granted as loans.

JAK (*Jord Arbete Kapital*) Sweden is a cooperative, member-owned financial institution based in Skövde, whose main function is to provide members with interest-free savings loans. JAK has been operating since 1970 and became a full bank after having received a banking license from the Swedish Financial Supervisory Authority at the end of 1997.

JAK's banking activities occur outside the capital market, as its loans are financed solely by member savings through the "Saving Points System," in which members accumulate savings points during saving periods and use these points when asking for a loan.

The Foundations: Jord Arbejde Kapital (Land, Labour, Capital):
From a discussion group to a practical solution for non-interest lending

"We like to think of ourselves as a movement for a better world."

Eva Stenius (member number 79 in
JAK cooperative, JAK's founding member
and member of the elections committee)

JAK's foundation has its roots in the aspiration of a group of Swedish university students in 1965 close to the Green Party, looking for a sustainable financial credit lending formula in order to achieve "economic emancipation." Inspired by the example of the cooperative society *Jord Arbejde Kapital*, founded in Denmark during the Great Depression in 1931, the founders of Swedish JAK believed that economic instability was the result of interest, and that, in turn, caused unemployment, inflation, and environmental destruction. Personal loans, but also pension funds and investment funds, made individuals as well as society as a whole dependent on a system based on interest over which regular people and even societies had little control.

The group of Swedish university students was firmly convinced that interest-driven transactions moved money from the poor to the rich, and favored projects which tended to yield higher profits in the short term, instead of aiming for stability and long-term results. The founders supported Aristotle's idea that making money from money did not favor society's advancement.

Eva Stenius remembers when in 1965 she, along with other university friends, were very attracted to the original JAK's ideas and success in Denmark and decided to go to a conference on the founder of Danish JAK, Halfdan Kristiansen.

The cooperative *Jord Arbejde Kapital* (Land, Labour, Capital: the three pillars of classical economics – abbreviated to JAK) was founded in Denmark during the Great Depression in 1931 by Halfdan Kriestiansen. Close to the Christian Socialist movement, he believed that interest was one of the main causes of economic instability and, as a consequence, JAK started three interest-free projects to prove that there could be practical ways of finance without having to take interest.

Their first project was the issuance of an interest-free local currency in Sønderjylland. These notes were backed by real wealth (farm property) in contrast to the national currency and they were enthusiastically accepted by the cash-starved population. At the peak, JAK currency amounted to 1.5 percent of the total Danish note circulation. The Danish government prohibited the experiment in 1933.

A second experiment, started in 1934, was an interest-free savings-and-loan system (*andelskassen*). By saving together without taking interest, they were able to give interest-free loans in turns to all participants which were used to pay off expensive bank loans. This venture also became quite popular. Certain defects in the system, together with strong opposition by the media and authorities, forced the *andelskasse* to liquidate in 1938.

The third experiment was also started in 1934. It is what would now be called a LETS (Local Exchange and Trade System) – an interest-free checking account system / clearing house whereby members traded goods and services with each other without cash. The accounts were simply adjusted up or down as the case may be. Money lying unused in the system was loaned out at low cost to members. (This second experiment, served as the chief inspiration for the business barter exchange system WIR Bank in Switzerland currently used by more than 60,000 companies.)

Though these systems were forced to close, the savings and loan system reemerged in 1944. JAK started up a new interest-free savings-and-loan system with different rules and this time it grew steadily. In 1958, JAK became licensed as a bank, beginning a ten-year period of rapid growth. At its zenith, JAK was among the 20 largest banks in Denmark. The system promised loans at a level of 3.2 times one's savings. For example: If one deposited 1000 DKK per month for two years, it resulted in a savings of 24,000 DKK. One could withdraw this sum and also borrow 76,800 DAK to be repaid over two years. This worked quite satisfactorily when the growth rate for funds entrusted was over 35 percent per year. In 1968, however, the growth rate began to fall, due, possibly, to a high inflation rate. No changes were made to the system, however, until it was too late. The loan demand became increasingly difficult to meet, reserves dwindled to fatal levels and the board saw no choice but to fuse with Bikuben Bank in 1973.[5]

Eva Stenius, together with some friends and supporters, including her husband at the time, Per Almgren, a mathematician, initiated a dialogue with the Danish JAK to analyze the system, and shortly after created *Jord Arbete Kapital – Riksförening för ekonomisk frigörelse* (National Association for Economic Emancipation) in 1965 as a nonprofit organization in Sweden. As in Denmark, the primary purpose was, and still is, to relieve people from interest debt through mutual cooperation, and to spread information about the effects of, and alternatives to, interest.

For many years JAK in Sweden was registered as an association, not as a bank, to discuss economic issues and ways to achieve economic emancipation. However, Eva Stenius and her group realized that the early success of the Danish formula greatly depended upon attracting new members, therefore they searched for a more stable and sustainable formula, that also included small groups. As a result, Per Almgren developed a mathematical system based on saving points, called the "Balanced Saving System," which created the foundation for the JAK Members Bank's system.[6]

JAK's business model: The Balanced Saving System[7]

The system works by allowing a member to take a loan in the same measure he or she allows other people to have loans, in other words, by saving into his account. For this reason, to ensure sustainability, when asking for a loan, earned savings points must be equal to spent savings points.

The amount of savings that each member has in the bank ultimately determines the amount that can be borrowed. The goal is that every borrower has to achieve a balance between their saving and their borrowing. When a member opens a savings account, instead of interest the account accrues savings points, which gives the right to borrow without interest. The savings points formula depends on whether a member is in presaving period (i.e. prior to receiving the loan) or in a postsaving period (i.e. repaying a loan). Savings points are "used up" or consumed during the loan period.

The first step for a person to acquire a loan from JAK is to become a member. The annual membership fee is 250 Swedish Crowns (SEK: 250 SEK ≈ €27) for the primary member in a family. Other members in the same family pay 200 SEK and children (up to 18 years old) do not pay a membership fee.

The second step is to open up a deposit account. If the member does not want a loan at that moment, he or she can build up his or her presavings account and start earning what is called presavings points. If he or she decides to obtain a loan, then throughout the repayment period the member will accumulate after-savings.

The Savings Point System

As previously mentioned, the members' deposits finance all loans. There is no external refinancing; hence the stock of loans cannot exceed the members' deposits plus the equity of the bank. To achieve a balance between savings and loans on the individual level, the following Savings Points System was created:

To save one Swedish Crown in JAK during one month generates one positive Saving Point (= +1 SP).

To have a debt of one Swedish Crown in JAK during one month generates one negative Saving Point (=−1 SP).

The following basic rule applies in order to reach a balance between savings and loans:

> Every member who takes a loan has to reach a minimum balance of 0 Savings Points before any bound savings can be repaid.

In order to reach a positive balance of points when a member takes a loan in JAK he/she usually has to make parallel savings (bounded), as well as repayments, during the repayment period as is shown in Exhibit 1.

If, thanks to presavings, the member has enough positive saving points when he/she takes the loan, then parallel savings are not necessary. When the balance of savings points is ≥ 0 then the member can withdraw his/her savings.

JAK uses the Savings Points System in the after-savings scheme as well, as a way to measure the savings and the loans of its members. We observe in Exhibit 2 that the light grey area is exactly the same as the dark grey area. At the end of the eleventh month the saving point's balance is zero points.

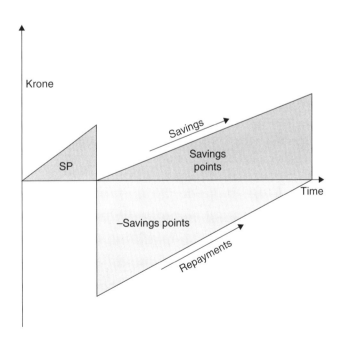

Exhibit 1 Saving vs. repayment

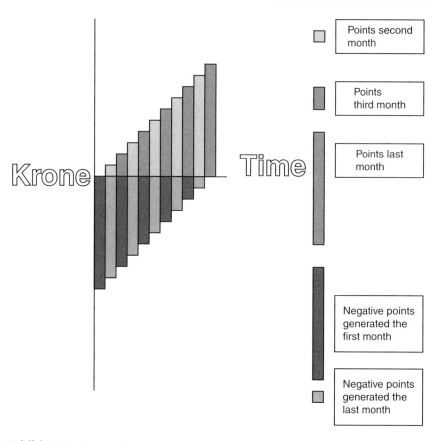

Exhibit 2 Savings points

Loan fees[8]

Every loan generates a fee worked out as a fixed charge for borrowing each Crown for each day it is borrowed. For example:

> For a loan of €10,000 taken over 10 years the fee would be:
> 10,000 × 10 × 1.5 percent = 10,000 × 10 × 0.015 = €1,500
> So €1.500 is the cost of the loan (which is paid back during the 10 years).

There are thus two kinds of fees in JAK: membership fees and loan fees. In 2008, the membership fees covered 20 percent of the operating costs whereas the loan fees covered 70 percent. The rest of the operating costs are covered by the interest received from the money that is placed in Swedish Bonds.

JAK's equity deposit

When a member takes a loan, he or she has to provide the bank with an amount equal to 6 percent of the loan, to be held by JAK as an Equity Deposit. The bank legally owns this deposit and uses it as a reserve, thereby meeting its regulatory reserve requirement. This provides JAK some security against potential loan default. Seven to nine months after the last repayment on the loan, the member's loan equity deposit is refunded.

How is the individual profile selected to be part of JAK system?

The process of credit risk and profile determination is very similar to any conventional bank. Therefore the amount of borrowing will depend on the promptness of loan repayment, money available in the pool of loans as well as the member's saving performance – credit history, reputation, and the collateral he/she can provide.

Stakeholders at JAK

One of the key successes of JAK is the fact that its stakeholders feel all part of the same community, and therefore show strong links with the organization and its development.

Among other stakeholders the following acquire significant relevance:

- **Owners/Clients.** Within the organization, member shareholders hold the same position as clients do. Voting is subject to a strict, carefully supervised, democratic process. All decisions and policies follow extremely transparent procedures, including regular changes of board members to avoid inequality and unfair practices:

    As CEO of JAK my duty is to listen to our members, it is up to them to decide in a democratic manner the strategy and the way forward for JAK. They have to feed me with their ideas and their needs. It is not up to me to decide any new project. Members are the shareholders as well as the clients, and it is my obligation to always listen to them. (Johan Oppmark, CEO of JAK)

- **Employees.** The bank has entered a professionalization phase: the CEO, as well as other employees, all come from the private financial sector.
    Although not required, most employees are bank members. Many of them have conventional commercial banking experience and decided to work in JAK, mostly for personal reasons, with the idea of offering to

society more than a mere banking service. Annika Norström profoundly believes in JAK ideas:

> We make money since we need to do it to pay our salaries, but policies are driven by something more than profit, and I believe it is a humane bank and I identify with that. Although I had to lower my salary I do feel much better; I have time, the environment is open and friendly, we help each other, and everyone is heard at meetings.

- **Members.** Many members feel a part of the bank and thus act as volunteers to promote the idea in the different localities in which they live. Cecilia Andersson, a member from Boden, says, "I became a member many years ago, and believed it was such a great idea that I wanted more people to know. ... Here in the north region we organize, through an ad in the local newspaper, at least four meetings a year, during which we have coffee and talk about JAK. Also, by being a member, I was able to innovate. At one point, a business project opportunity came up, and I could not find any savings to finance it, therefore I proposed a common savings product to have the municipality put in the savings. This has been a great way for JAK to offer loans to entrepreneurs."

Community innovation: The Support Savings Account

Balanced Savings is the main system behind the two main products at JAK.

The Balanced Savings Loan (best suited for individuals)

JAK's original loan, offered since 1970, designed for people who are saving in order to get a loan for themselves, for a relative or a friend. All loans have to be balanced by savings. A certain amount of savings points that are borrowed have to be balanced out by an equal amount of savings points that are saved. The saving can be done before the loan is taken out, and during repayment, but the bank and the saver/borrower enter an agreement that the balance will be reached three months after the payment of the last installment. Then the money that is saved during the loan period can be withdrawn.

The Support Savings Account (for small companies and associations)

A new instrument introduced in 2001 designed for small companies and associations who can afford fee and installment payments. These loans have to be balanced by savings, just as the ordinary savings loan.

When a need arises to finance an important community project, there are people willing to do the saving. First, they open a Support Receiving Account at JAK, enabling the volunteers to open Support Savings Accounts, depositing money in support of the project. (Volunteers do not have to be JAK members an are free to withdraw their money if needed). If the Support Savings Loan Fund becomes smaller than the actual loan, JAK asks the volunteers to increase the fund. If unsuccessful, JAK will require full loan repayment within a year.

An association or company can ask for a Support Receiving Account for a project. The bank assesses the character of the applicant before granting a loan. A loan will be maximized to equal the sum of deposits in the Support Savings Accounts intended for the recipient of the support savings.

The Support Savings Account has proved to be an innovative way to channel resources for community development. All kinds of projects can be supported, for example a church or a shop. Each of the projects has a loan-holder, who is the one ultimately responsible for paying back the loan; however each of the projects has a "support system," meaning individuals who decide to support a particular project feel a personal connection to it and therefore make a deposit from his or her personal savings into the account of the project. The savings account is completely risk-free, since the risk is always borne by JAK. Furthermore, no time-commitment exists for the support savers and they can remove their deposits at any time.

Since "savers" are free to take out the money any time they want, it is possible for the positive savings points to move below the required level for savings support. If this occurs, the savings points have to grow over time, in order to balance with the loan at the end. Therefore JAK employees will alert the loan-holders that the savings have decreased below acceptable levels, so they know they will have to find new supporters and/or extend their support for a longer time in order to balance out the positive savings points with the negative.

Small companies and associations that find it difficult to borrow money in conventional banks can open a Support Savings Account. For example, a group of small companies and associations in the countryside might want to buy a building to house their activities. They are members of a community association that buys the building. The association can afford to pay the amortization and the loan fee but does not have enough liquidity, hindering the possibility of accumulating savings points. Therefore, any individual or association can open Support Savings Accounts where they can save money and automatically give away their saving points to this community association, thereby enabling their building project.

A specific Support Savings Account example for fostering entrepreneurs is the project developed by the municipality of Boden, in the north of Sweden. The municipality approved a total amount of 3 million SEK for seven years to finance various projects of entrepreneurs in the area. In those seven years the municipality will not receive any interest; however they do not have to bear any risk since the risk of the operations is supported by JAK. Furthermore, the municipality can withdraw its money at any point in time given JAK does not oblige the Support Savers to save.

Conclusions: Identity and belonging in community lending

JAK's community lending methodology embodies one of the basic characteristics for stability in the twenty-first century: balancing individual responsibility with community belonging. The system maintains the bank's stability given the loyalty that bonds the members who can identify, with their multiple identities, within a larger framework where all identities can find their own space.

JAK has proved that a bank can participate in the banking system while providing an alternative service unrelated to the system: interest-free loans. However, JAK plays in a difficult field, since being part of the system provides the bank with the legitimacy it needs to operate openly in the market, but as a player in the system it must follow its regulations and standards, More difficult during a time when the financial system in Europe is adapting to new banking regulations.

In the past, JAK has always had innovative solutions for the challenges that came its way, and today it has a newly added asset, a young generation of people committed to helping the banking face the new challenges. "We at JAK believe that our duty is raising consciousness in crucial issues for today's humankind. Now we are too small and our impact is limited. The impact will be stronger if we grow bigger while maintaining the main features that distinguish us." (Johannes Kretschmer, Member of the board)

CHAPTER 2

Identity and community

> Do I belong?
> Second movement: Identity and community: from communities of origin to communities of aspiration

1 Do I belong?

The first thing that is said about us, even before we are given a name, is whether we are a boy or a girl. It used to be the first words we heard when we came into the world, nowadays they are said even before arriving. Soon after birth we are registered as members of a particular country, then we go home after a few days in the hospital with a particular family, and after few months many of us take part in a ceremony to become members of a religious faith.

So before our first birthday, without having any say in the matter, we already belong to a number of groups, each of them with their particular assumed-behavior norms and obligations, as well as rights.

Most of us keep on adding new identities, such as our school or town, and we increasingly have more say in our choice to join our next set of memberships: university, sports club, workplace, hobby, organization, etc. ... Moreover, today, with the possibilities offered by the internet, we can find a community anywhere in the world that happens to share our passion for collecting butterflies, or any other strange thing we may be interested in.

Years ago, individuals had very limited possibilities in choosing their social identities, because not only their gender, family and religion, but also their companion in life and the type of work they would perform was decided by the community, and the individual had to either accept it or leave. Today we increasingly have a choice, we can decide to move from *our identities of origin to our communities of aspiration*; and now when these two coincide, it is for the most part a matter of choice rather than of imposition. For example, I can choose to be part of a women's group as my aspirational community, or I can choose to put my energies elsewhere, since the fact of being a woman does not necessarily force me to be active in the women's community.

Today, our choices are limitless, and some people may decide to reject their given identities, even the primary ones such as gender or religion. Others will just keep those identities together with their new one; but in any case we all have many identities with which we conform our lives. It is the multiplicity of identities and their flexibility that make us healthy, even if our identities may conflict with each other, or some take priority over others, depending on the circumstances of our lives.

But the fact is that in addition to connecting with ourselves, we need to connect with people outside of us. Paraphrasing Hannah Arendt, while thinking is a solitary activity, action requires other human beings (Arendt, 1978).

In fact, the path of separation from society in order to connect with the self in solitude, and then coming back to act and contribute to the community, is one of the oldest myths, and is present in every culture. Every tradition includes the tale of an individual hero who, for a variety of reasons, is forced to get away from the group, and then after difficult tests – which he overcomes thanks to his inner strength – he becomes the real person he is inside, with all his potential developed. Only then does he come back to his community and lead it into greatness. This myth manifests in many different ways and is, in fact, the basis of most of the coming-of-age rituals still present in many societies. Myths represent primitive archetypes that are part of all of us. Since in our western society rituals are not as prominent as before, we have transformed them into stories, novels, and films that keep telling us over and over how Neo, Skywalker, Frodo, Jake Sully, or the regular middle-class guy goes through difficult tests that make him a real man (the myth is normally embodied by men), and once he has connected with his true self, he can go back to his community and save it.

The myth can also be seen from the perspective of the community and not of the individual hero. In order to develop the community needs the energy of its individual members, who must first leave the group to grow and then come back and contribute, having achieved their potential, to the growth of the collectivity.

However, it is difficult to distinguish when we act as self-identities and when we do it as part of a group. Often, we cannot distinguish whether our ideas and behavior originate from a reflection of our selfhood or if they are merely a reflection of the group behavior to which consciously or unconsciously we have conformed. To better understand the differences between personal identity and communal identity, it is important that after having analyzed some of the humanistic approaches to the idea of personal identity in the previous chapter, we now move on to analyze some of the humanistic approaches to the idea of social identity and the ways scientific thinking can help us in the study of communal identities.

2   Identity and community

Community and belonging

Community it is not an intellectual invention, it is a powerful everyday notion in terms of which people organize their lives and understand the places and settlements in which they live and the quality of their relationships. As such, community, following Jenkins, is among the most important sources of collective identification (Jenkins 1996, 2004, 2008, p. 133).

In addition to regulating our everyday lives, belonging to a community has a strong emotional component. In Bauman's words:

> words have meanings: some words also have a "feel." The word Community is one of them. It feels good; whatever the word "community" may mean, it is good to "have a community," to be in a community. ... The meaning and feelings the words convey are not of course independent of each other. "Community" feels good because of the meanings of the word "community" conveys – all of them promising pleasures and more often than not the kinds of pleasures we would like to experience but seem to miss. (Bauman 2001, 2008, p. 1)

Most of us are attached to a certain number of communities; however, whether this attachment is a product of our own imagination or is genuinely a reality that links us together is a question debated amongst experts. In other words, the popular saying that "the group is more than the sum of its individuals" is for some thinkers a living entity, meaning that a group is a reality beyond its individual members and, as such, it has its own patterns of behavior that differ from those of its members.

One of the first postulants of this theory was Durkheim, one of the fathers of sociology, who affirmed that the "collective consciousness" is a fact, and that the whole is indeed greater than the sum of any of its individuals, and that it consists of shared beliefs and moral attitudes that operate as a unifying force within society. The collectivity thus functions as a living organism with firm boundaries, complex internal functional relationships, and higher and lower systems.

Taking Durkheim's principles further, some anthropologists who have studied the phenomena of primitive shamanism have found, besides a common consciousness, a common unconsciousness that binds a group together and can be manipulated and transformed by the shaman at the subconscious level in order to bring about a transformation in the consciousness of the community, and thus to the individual members of the community themselves (Fericgla, 2000, 2006).

At the other extreme, some scientists stress the fact that there is nothing beyond ourselves, that there is not such a thing as a collective identity. Following a positivist approach, they believe that identity is only a product of our imagination, a cognitive construction, and thus they affirm that identity it is not real but an imagined constructions (Brubaker and Cooper, 2000).

In between the two approaches, Jenkins states that although collective identity is a symbolic construction, nonetheless it is real, since it does have an impact in our everyday life. "The internal and external moments of identification loop in and out of each other in the unfolding of individual and collective identities. And although those identities are imagined they are not imaginary." (Jenkins 1996, 2004, 2008, p. 158) Individuals make a selection from the available possibilities, collective identifications with which to identify, and in the process they contribute to the production and reproduction of the collectivities with which they are identifying, evoking and constructing intragroup similarities and intergroup differences.

Everyday life would be impossible without classificatory systems. Scientists affirm that symbolization permits the necessary abstractions for individuals and collectivities, and for relationships between them, thus it is the constitutional basis of the notion of society.

Identity as a two-way process

The word "identity" comes from the Latin *idem* meaning same, and *entis* meaning entity. Therefore it is the movement of becoming identical to some entity, implying a process. This process can have two directions: I might decide consciously or unconsciously that I do belong to a certain group, and thus identify with it, meaning that I follow certain patterns of behavior to conform to the group; or the process can being outside of me because "They" have decided to categorize me into a certain group, which implies a certain pattern of behavior which people expect me to conform with accordingly, which nevertheless I may or may not identify with.

Therefore, it is commonly assumed that there are two distinct processes of identification: one is self-identification or group identification, which is the process through which an individual decides to identify with a certain group; and the second is that of categorization, when the process is external to the individual and he or she has no choice in the matter. The categorization process can be illustrated by a process described in the famous book *Orientalism,* by Edward Said (Said 1979). In it, the author describes how during the process of European colonization, individuals in the Middle East ended up conforming to the patterns of behavior that the orientalists (European experts on the Middle East) expected of them, even if those expectations were false. In other words, we are first put into a category and then we may consciously or unconsciously identify with the norms of behavior contained in said category.

The identification process can be very deeply rooted, since it might have been established in the earliest stages of development, and thus difficult to modify. With this in mind, Jenkins categorizes humanness, selfhood, and gender as the primary identities. Other identities, such as ethnicity or kinship that are also rooted in the early stages of human development, are more dependent on external circumstances according to Jenkins:

> Unlike human-ness, selfhood and gender are not universal primary identities. Kinship or ethnicity may be salient early in the individual experience of identification, they may be enormously consequential, they may be entailed in selfhood. That both involve embodied criteria of identification-family resemblance, physical stereotypes, and race – is likely to reinforce this. But neither ethnicity nor kingship is necessarily a primary individual identification, depending on local circumstances and individual history they may be more negotiable and flexible that human-ness or gender. (Jenkins 1996, 2004, 2008, p. 88)

Social Identity Theory

In the 1970s investigations conducted by the psychologist Henri Tajfel in the University of Bristol became very well known. His ideas, known generically as *Social Identity Theory* and some of its experiments in group behavior, became highly influential.

Tajfel, together with a group of psychologists from Bristol University that included his collaborator John Turner, conducted what are called

Minimal Groups Experiments – placing people in groups totally at random, where the scientists observed that the subjects ended up developing connections and preferences as individuals influenced by the groups they were placed in.

The scientists' observations led them to assume that people have an inbuilt tendency to categorize themselves into one or more in-groups, building a part of their identity on the basis of their membership of that group and enforcing boundaries with other groups. Therefore, Social Identity Theory suggests that people identify with groups in such a way as to *maximize positive distinctiveness*; groups offer both identity (they tell us who we are) and self-esteem (they make us feel good about ourselves).

Social theory assumes that we do not act as isolated individuals but rather as social beings who derive part of our identities from the human groups and social categories we belong to, and therefore we act in accordance with this awareness. The theory provides a framework for concrete analysis, studying the interplay between psychological functioning and social structures, and it proposes theoretical models to study this interplay.

Social identity theory, understood as the study of the role of self-conception in group membership, group process and intergroup relationships, was initiated by the personal drive of Tajfel who was inspired by his experience as Polish Jew during the Nazi era. His past led him to research the causes of prejudice, discrimination and intergroup conflict. He did not believe that the causes were rooted in personality, individual differences or interpersonal relations; instead, he believed that social forces configured social action. His challenge as a psychologist was to understand how this was being done (Hogg 2006).

Tajfel defined social identity as the individual's knowledge that he belongs to certain social groups, together with holding a certain value and emotional significance towards group membership (Hogg 2006, p. 112)

Tajfel defined social identity theory as a tripod with three legs:

- The first is the sequence of people that have an unsatisfactory group identity and will change their status by restoring a positive distinctiveness to their group.
- Second, the complex set of processes that change behavior from interpersonal to intergroup level, and the psychological consequences of such a shift.
- The third is the social contextualization of psychological dynamics, understanding the social context in which these events occur (Robinson 1996).

Within social identity theory, each individual is seen to have a repertoire of identities open to them (social and personal), each identity informing the individual of who they are and what this identity entails. The fact of having a concrete identity that is more prominent than another can also be influenced by social context. A concrete social situation may lead an individual to attach to different self-identities that may cause some of the other identities to feel marginalized; thus this individual is traveling between different groups and self-identifications. These different selves lead to constructed images dichotomized between what people want to be (the ideal self) and how others see them (the limited self). Educational background, occupational status and social roles all significantly influence identity formation in this regard.

The generic concept of social identity theory and its further developments into self-categorization theory or intergroup emotion theory, has been very influential not only in the field of social psychology but also in political science and economics, including identity economics.

Social identity theory is often criticized in terms of its methodology since some scientists (mostly from the fields of anthropology and sociology) believe that studies based on minimal laboratory experiments investigating microlevel situations should not lead to generalizations about large-scale collective processes. But also, some scientists criticize the fact that social identity theory focuses on an individualistic perspective where groups are taken for granted, arguing that the actual interaction among groups is not well documented, since identification appears mostly inside people's heads. (Jenkins 1996, 2004, 2008, p. 118)

The work of other scientists, and in particular anthropologists in the field of identities, has focused more on the processes of group interactions that help explain patterns of social form, studying collectivities as such not as the sum of the individuals in them, but as collectivities which have intrinsic norms and processes regardless of individual membership. Studies conducted in this way also focus on the identification processes taking place during the discourses amongst groups. Frederic Barth is one of the most important anthropologists in the field of collective identities and the process of their formation. In 1969 he edited *Ethnic Groups and Boundaries* (Barth 1979), a collection of different works by anthropologists that indicated how collective forms are not fixed but are formed into being by interaction. Barth argues that ethnic collectivities are independent of the individuals whose membership constitutes them. Members come and go, however, the collectivity survives.

Ethnic identity *becomes* and is maintained through relational processes of inclusion and exclusion. Rather than taking identities and boundaries for granted, Barth is concerned with understanding how difference is organized during and arises out of interaction. Collective identification and its boundaries are generated in transaction and interaction, and are at least potentially flexible, situational and negotiable; thus, collective identification is inherently political.

Whatever the specific focus of the study is, regardless of different methodological approaches, most scientists dealing with group identification and categorization, whether from the fields of sociology, anthropology, or psychology, will agree on the basic premise that identity constitutes a process that has some of the following features:

- Identification is rooted in basic and generic human processes; it is part of the specific nature of our species.
- Personal identity, which differentiates the unique self from all other selves, is different from social identity, which is the internalization of collective identifications.
- The identification process reflects the interplay between identification of similarity and difference.
- Group membership is meaningful to individuals because it confers social identity and permits self-evaluation. (Jenkins, 1996, 2004, 2008, p. 120)

3   The rights of communal identities in the political debate

As we have seen, the process of social identification illustrates an interplay between similarity and difference. The matter of policy action is relevant since the basic question is: are communal identities able to make claims to possessing certain rights? Or are the individuals that form these collectivities the ones that have rights? Are legislators ruling for the individuals or for communities?

Here the famous words of Margaret Thatcher become relevant: "and so they are casting their problems on society, and who is society? There is no such thing! There are individual men and women and there are families, and no government can do anything except through people and people look to themselves first." (Thatcher 1987)

The controversy reflects two extremes of a cultural model, labeled in cultural studies as the dichotomy between *Universalism* and *Particularism*. Universalists apply the standard rule to all without exceptions, they look for a general solution regardless of the particularities of each case.

Particularists on the other hand, discriminate in favor of personal commitments and group alliances even to the detriment of general rule. Both positions are in fact two sides of the same coin of the defense of individuals: Particularists believe in group protection, since it is only in within a group that the strong can support the weak; on the other side, Universalists believe that everyone will have more fair opportunities if rules are uniformly applied and no one will be then left out, or judged by his or her communal identity.

The controversy is a complex one, since although the positions are not as extreme as is sometimes perceived (most Universalists will accept the need to make an exception for someone with special difficulties, and even the most relativist of the Particularists will prefer to have certain security provided by a general law that applies to everyone). However, there is an implication for policy actions, and as such the debate has been quite active in politics: often Universalists are found in the ranks of liberals and Particularists in the ranks of leftist movements.

To try to better understand the controversy we can follow some of the main approaches in each position: Appiah in his *Ethics of Identity* (Appiah, 2005) describes how liberalist ideas need to be understood in their true flexible framework, wherein individualism is not opposed to the right of each individual to belong to as many collectivities he or she wants, in fact quite the opposite, since collective identity is a fundamental part of individual development. He does not intend to defend liberalism as such, but "to defend the proposition that certain values which are now associated with Anglophone philosophers help our ability as individuals to live an individual life that includes our multiple identities, without being constrained by collective claims (Appiah 2005, p. xi).

> What has proved especially vexatious, though, is the effort to take account of those social forms we now call identities: genders and sexual orientations, ethnicities and nationalities, professions and vocations. Identities make ethical claims because – and this is just a fact about the world we human beings have created – we make our lives as men and as women, as gay and as straight people, as Ghanians and as Americans, as blacks and as whites. Immediately, conundrums start to assemble. Do identities present a curb on autonomy or do they provide its contours? What claims if any can identity groups as such justly make upon the state? These are concerns that have gained a certain measure of salience in recent political philosophy, but, as I hope to show, they are anything but newfangled. (Appiah 2005, p. xiv)

The debate can be seen in the light of a tension between those who view the entrenchment of social identities as a precondition for autonomy and those who view it as a threat to autonomy. Appiah claims that partial autonomy between the two positions cannot be a solution. Therefore, the two points of view cannot converge and necessarily end up being superimposed one over the other. The problem is in the views of most liberals, who feel that upholding differences amongst groups will normally result in uniformity within the same group, and therefore may end up in a state of tyranny.

Liberalism, according to Appiah's understanding, is concerned with moral equality: the state is to display equal respect towards its citizens. "Where we go wrong," he believes, "is to suppose that individuals should be subject to the same constraints. Social justice might require impartiality of fairness or neutrality, but social justice is not about individuals, but about citizens. As individuals we are entitled to our differences, as citizens the state has to guarantee equality." (Appiah 2005, p. 55)

Appiah affirms that identities of the self and collective associations have been there since the beginning of time and have been accepted by all. However, two points of view are being confronted: on the one hand, the idea of reflective self-direction as it runs through Locke, Kant, and Mill, as well as through much of the recent liberal thought; and on the other hand, the communitarian emphasis on a social matrix that not only constrains but constitutes ourselves. The latter reflects the *Particularist* approach which, according to Appiah's analysis, was first developed in German Romanticism with its embrace and enthusiasm for the difference, and this discourse of *the difference* was once again adopted by social scientists in the 1950s, who worked on the social identification of minority groups following Max Weber's analysis of bureaucracy and its impact on working life (Appiah, p. 65).

Max Weber's concept of bureaucracy, was highly influential through the twentieth century, and has been widely used in the diversity debate. For that reason it is convenient to expand his views in further detail in the following box.

Max Weber's concept of bureaucracy

Sociologists in the 1950s were very influenced by the works of the German sociologist Max Weber (1864–1920), who had produced an influential analysis at the beginning of the century to explain the move in western society towards rationality and individualism away from the kinship motivations of former times. This new form of organization, based on a set of rules, was for Weber the result of the growth of capitalism and bureaucracy. Weber described bureaucracy as the most efficient form of organization, characterized by a set of rules and principles for all to follow, regardless of individual differences. Procedures and rules facilitate central decision making, as well as specialization and planning, and thus bureaucracy helps organizations to achieve set goals (Weber 2001).

While recognizing the value of bureaucracy and its importance for the modern state, Weber also saw negative effects, since bureaucracy tends to generate oligarchy by concentrating power in the hands of a few, and those few can easily control resources in pursuit of their own personal interests. Bureaucracy also limits individual creativity, since labor is being sold to someone who is in control, instead of individuals being artisans and craftsmen and benefiting from their own labor (Weber 1991, p. 412). Another negative side-effect of bureaucracy is the fact that specialization makes society more interdependent and reduces its common purpose, and thus there is a loss in sense of community because the purpose of bureaucracies is to get the job done efficiently, regardless of particular interest.

The ongoing bureaucratization and increasing rationalization of human life traps individuals in a system of rule-based rational control referred to as the Iron Cage, by which capitalists' care for material goods and the demands of rational conduct and bureaucratic organization diminish the human spirit to a point beyond despair (Weber 1976, p. 181).

Weber's analysis of the impact of modernization in working life inspired the work of social scientists in the 1950s on social identification, identity crisis, and minority groups' identity. The work of social scientists also inspired the works of politicians and other social activists who defended the right of communities to be different and to preserve their difference, including women's groups, and LGBT and other minority groups. The protection of minority cultural rights owes much to the American liberation movement against slavery and the work of pioneering intellectuals who promoted the rights of blacks, women and Native Americans, such as Frederick Douglass (1818–1895), an important former slave turned social activist. Later, in the 1970s, a political shift occurred with the Civil Rights movement that drove subsequent legislation in favor of minority rights to include actions of positive discrimination.

Many multiculturalists' ideas go beyond the protection of minorities' rights, and embrace the "right to difference." These thinkers believe in winning individual rights for members of minority groups, but also assert the rights of the group to be recognized by its differences. Trotman, for example, states that multiculturalism restores a sense of wholeness by raising consciousness about the past and giving voice to the voiceless. The acknowledgement of the specificities in each community dignifies their members and enhances their lives as individuals and as members of a collectivity (Trotman 2002). The liberal system, say multiculturalists, does not allow for fairness, since a subtle uniformity is promoted against any claim for difference, and thus people cannot fully express who they are within a society or an organization, but often need to accommodate to the "majority's value system." Often, this accommodation ends up in unfair treatment and discrimination. Therefore, for supporters of multiculturalism, the right to be different and the protection of minorities and their different lifestyles and behaviors has proved to be a useful tool to combat racism, protect minority communities of all types, and undo policies that had prevented these minorities from having full access to the opportunities for freedom and equality promised by liberal society.

Multiculturalists consider that cultural differences enrich society as a whole and as such they should be preserved; therefore, cultural rights are included in most international systems such as the United Nations or the European Union, and incorporated in specific legislation like the International Covenant on Social, Economic and Cultural rights (1966) as well as numerous national codes.

A recent approach to the same debate is a discourse often conducted by social scientists who, although denouncing the liberal approach, take a different approach to that of the multiculturalists. These thinkers are opposed to the liberal approach that accepts minority unfairness and discrimination, but they also disagree with the cultural relativists, believing that in the end *the debate is not about abstract identity rights, but in fact, we are talking about a social problem of redistribution of resources.* These thinkers agree with the right to individual development; however, they believe that the history of Europe since the Industrial Revolution has formed a class of people that is socially deprived and has not had the chance to enjoy the privileges of self-development. In developed countries this class comprises the so-called minorities, while in developing countries it is the majority of the population. These thinkers state that the universal rules that liberals claim to be made for everyone, are in fact much more fit for some privileged minority than for the excluded majority.

For example Bauman, in his book *Community*, states that the trademark of European modernity is an individuality that was in fact a trade-off in which freedom was exchanged for security, although not all were granted the freedom side of the exchange. "The chance to enjoy freedom without paying the harsh and forbidding price of insecurity was a privilege of the few; but these few set the tone of the emancipation idea for centuries to come." (Bauman 2008, p. 2)

Following Max Weber in his analysis of individualism during industrialization, Bauman traces the breaking-up of community supports back to the pre-industrial period. At that time, traditional community links were broken to transform workers into isolated and lonely beings first, and then into a mass made to fill the new factories. This fact allowed workers to make a living free from the web of the moral and emotional bonds to their family and neighbors; but by the same token it also emptied such actions of all the meanings they used to carry before, and also took away the dignity attached to doing one's work well.

> The work ethic of the early industrial era was an attempt to rebuild through a punitive regime the self workmanship which in the dense network of communal intercourse came to craftsmen, artisan and tradesman matter-of-factly ... it was no longer clear to the craftsmen and artisans of yesterday what "work well done" would mean, and it was no longer clear to the craftsmen and artisans of yesterday that work well done would mean there was no longer dignity worth or honor attached to doing it well (Bauman 2008, p. 27).

Since communal structures were destroyed by the demands of new capitalism, something needed to be put in place to substitute people's natural obedience to the rules of their community. Bauman speaks of two tendencies:

- Change the natural understanding of a bygone community to a coercively imposed monitoring routine, culminating at the beginning of the twentieth century with Frederick Taylor's time and motion study, scientific organization, and the assembly line – separating performance from the motives and feelings of workers.
- Model villages of a few philanthropists who associated industrial success with a feel-good factor among workers. A century later this second tendency emerged again in the 1930s with the "human relations school" and Elton Mayo, leading to experiments at Hawthorn enterprises showing that a friendly and homely atmosphere contributed to improved production.

The Fordist factory followed the analysis and attempted to synthesize the two tendencies. In both tendencies, the main understanding behind them was that both social processes and productive work needed to be managed rather than left to their own momentum, and therefore, *social engineering* was the instrument most developed to enhance productivity.

In modern society Bauman distinguishes two types of individuals. First are the *individualists de facto*, those in the privileged class for which individuality is at its most and whose main objective is to preserve their gains. They also resent the lack of community, and so they have built an illusion of community, a community of non-belonging, *a togetherness of loners*. On the other hand are what he calls *individualists de jure,* those who are not benefiting from the gains of the new freedom and are told to resolve their problems by themselves because no one will do it for them. The de jure community seeks an ethical community not an aesthetic one; it wants communities that would imply long-term commitments to help against individual misfortunes (Bauman 2001, p. 58).

For most of the second half of the twentieth century there was a *bourgeoisization* of society in which more and more individuals increased their levels of material wealth, and the state, particularly in European countries, increased the protected rights of citizens. Thus, more individualists de facto were emerging in western societies. However, as Bauman suggests, the process is now reversing into a *proletarization* shift in society, wherein an increasing number of people every year see their levels of material wealth being reduced, and on top of that states are lowering their level of protection; thus more people are becoming individualists de jure and are being told to resolve their problems by themselves.

Bauman believes that identity problems are in fact products of genuine social conflicts and not psychological problems. Since, after all, this is a question of social inequality, the solution should be redistribution more than recognition. We need to talk more about social justice rather than about self-realization. Demands for redistribution are vehicles of integration, while claims for recognition promote division and at the end break down the social dialogue. Against some of the claims in favor of cultural relativism, Bauman calls for a real community, not based on the right to be different, but rather a community that can fulfill its obligations towards its members, which in his opinion are protection and development.

> If there is to be a community in the world of individuals, it can only be a community woven together from sharing and mutual care; a community of concern and responsibility for the equal right to be human and the equal ability to act in that right. (Bauman 2001, p. 150)

Bauman states that the debate should be positioned as a truly economic debate, away from the claims of some intellectuals for the right of groups to be culturally different and follow their difference. For Bauman this debate is a new form of racism, aiming to placate moral scruples and produce reconciliation with the fact of human inequality, either as a condition beyond the capacities of human intervention or as a plight in which humans should not interfere with, lest sacrosanct cultural values be violated; therefore, the right to be different is equated to the right to indifference. (Bauman 2001, p. 107)

The controversy is still open and at the heart of our political debates, as shown by the recent public controversy over the "quota laws" on women in higher decision-making positions that countries such as Norway, Spain, and France have recently launched (de Anca 2008).

The solution is not easy, since each position has valid arguments. Most likely, all the different positions will agree on the unfairness of being discriminated against by reason of belonging to a group; however, they will disagree on how equality should best be promoted. For some, past records of unfairness can only be redeemed by positive discrimination measures that will effectively correct the position of minorities; yet many, including members of those same groups, will debate against positive discrimination measures since they believe it will end up stigmatizing the very same populations they try to help.

On the other hand, the consolidation of particular values or behaviors as a trait of a particular group might frustrate the members of that group who do not feel identified with those particular values. By being categorized in that group they are thereafter forced to claim their own minority rights within that group. For example, a woman who does not identify with the assumption of sensitivity held to be characteristic of womanhood often needs to defend herself against outside criticism. As stated by Virginia Woolf, "... And I thought how unpleasant is to be locked out ... and I thought how it is worse perhaps to be locked in." (Virginia Woolf 2004, p. 28).

4   Communal identities in the twenty-first century

New tribes

In popular speech "tribe" carries both a positive feeling of warmth and protection and at the same time a strong fear of limitation and individual constraint. That is the reason for the general surprise when at the end of the twentieth century a new form of tribalism became very popular. In

European thinking, the individualism that had marked European history since the seventeenth century was the most superior stage in human evolution; therefore intellectuals observed with surprise the new phenomena of emerging communitarism.

Sociologists attempted to describe and analyze these new tribes, and Michel Maffesoli was one of the first to name the "new way of being together" neotribalism. At the end of the 1980s, he stated that the microgroups that dominated the landscape our societies were not residuals of former traditional social life but the key social fact of our experience in everyday living. These new organizations represented a new way of living everyday life based on a communal as opposed to an individual basis (Maffesoli, 1988).

The previous paradigm was based on a rational element and on the principle of individuation and separation, whereas the emerging one is based on the principle of empathy and is marked by the lack of differentiation, the "loss" in a collective subject. A person in this new form of society can only find fulfillment in its relations with others, with an emphasis on that which unites rather than that which separates. The community is characterized less by a project oriented towards the future than it is by this being together, the emotional warmth of companionship.

Maffesoli sees a movement in our society coming from the undifferentiated masses, characteristic of the former paradigm towards microtribes, where individuals seek to transcend their individualities by playing a role in open and free tribes that provide them with temporary identification.

He distinguishes the individual who has a *function* in society with this new form, *sociality*, in which the person (persona) *instead of having a function plays a role* – as many different roles as his or her different affiliations allow. Therefore, ideology is not involved in these new forms of organization, unlike the movements of the 1960s in Europe and the USA. It is not so much a question of belonging to a particular ideology or movement; rather it is about switching from one group to the other. In fact, in contrast with classical tribalism, neo-tribalism is characterized by the fluidity of occasional gathering and dispersal, both of which are fragile, but for that very instant they become the object of significant emotional investment.

That flexibility makes individuals free to choose and change from different groups, and act upon them in temporary ways of identification, and therefore these new forms of tribalism refuse to identify with any political project whatsoever, to subscribe to any sort of finality and their sole raison d'être is a preoccupation with the collective present. (Maffesoli 1998, p. 75)

What really matters is the feeling of belonging, the joy of being together, expressed by customs and rituals: having a few drinks; chatting with friends; the anodyne conversations of everyday life.

> Thus a pertinent study on secondary groups points out that single mothers, feminists and homosexuals are not seeking a "temporary resolution of individual situations"; it is rather an overall reconsideration of the rules of solidarity that is at issue. Gain is secondary; it is not even sure that success is desirable, since it risks draining the warmth of being together. It is to share warmth. (Maffesoli 1998, p. 99)

In the new volatility he sees the rediscovery of a holistic perspective in which nature and ecology play a great role, moving beyond the divisions imposed in the nineteenth century, with the arbitrary division between the physical and the psychical. Ecology in its largest sense ("*oikos*" – house; "*-logia*" – study of), as the relation of living organisms with each other and their surroundings, where individuals are not any longer separated but just part of the system.

> In a single word, the economy of the political order, founded on reason, the project and activity, is giving way to the ecology of an organic (or holistic) order, integrating both nature and proxemics. (Maffesoli 1998, p. 69)

The phenomena that Maffesoli described at the end of the 1980s as just beginning and still in its early chaotic stages, twenty years later has fully exploded, and now social groups are the DNA of our times. With the help of technology, they have defined the new structures within which our society is being transformed. Increasingly, these new forms of organization constitute not only forms of being together but also of working together, and are thus building emerging forms of organizations in which production and consumption is co-shared, co-organized, and co-created.

Social networks

If one thing illustrates the possibility of freely choosing our own communities, it is the social networks in their modern internet manifestation.

Enrique Dans, one of my colleagues at IE, is a world-renowned expert on social networks who often helps explain to my students the importance of having a digital identity and being part of the world of virtual networks. One of the students recently checked the number of followers that Dans had online, and found he had 120,000 on Twitter and 22,103 on Facebook. He is of course a guru in the field, has always loved it, and he will be the first one to find a use for any new instrument of social technology. It is unthinkable to me to consider 120,000 followers, I would not even expect 12 people would follow me on anything! And what is worse, just thinking that so many people would expect something from me every day makes me panic with stress!

I am from another generation and probably of another profile; but I have to admit that my opinion on social networks radically changed when I was in Cairo last year during the Egyptian revolution and when the latter movements on the internet also exploded in the May 15th Movement in Madrid. The so-called Facebook revolution made me realize the power of these networks, the power of communication definitely, but above all the power of organization, especially in countries not famous for their organizational skills. But, also, the Facebook revolutions have proved that the new tribes are not only "communities of belonging" in an emotional sense, but rather, places *to act temporarily* in companionship with others that you identify with. These kids felt a strong membership to the different groups they created; but their importance lay in the opportunity those groups gave their members to participate and contribute, to change their countries and their worlds.

The multitude of microgroups described by Maffesoli in the 1980s have now formed a multitude of networks that cross-feed each other, and which, while being totally independent from each other, can also act for a common goal. Information about the network of networks characterizes our society and shapes new ways of interacting in our social lives as well as in our economic lives, the effects of which we will examine in Chapter 4.

Scientists from the fields of sociology, anthropology and psychology have all described a new paradigm characterized by a new way of being together. *These new communal identifications are roles that people play and not permanent forms of associations.* According to Bauman, these new communities will not play the traditional role of a community since their liquidity is their main characteristic, as well as their changing nature. Looking for shelter and protection from individual misfortunes is not one of the characteristics of these new forms of collectivities. Instead, they are a place to act in the *theatrum mundi* as described by Maffesoli.

... The person (persona) plays roles, both within his or her professional activities as well as the various tribes in which the person participates. The costume changes, as the person, according to personal tastes (sexual, cultural religious, friendship) takes his or place each day in the various games of the *theatrum mundi*. (Maffesoli 1988, p. 76)

5 Communal identity in today's business context

Understanding community has been fundamental for business transactions in any given period. Segmentation has been a key tool in marketing for decades. Segmentation and market studies allow companies to understand preferences in their various target groups and thus set strategies of product, price, place, and promotion for each segmented group.

However, the difficulty today is to target the communities according to the choices of their members and not by their origin. People are increasingly conscious of their multiple identities, and these might coincide or not with the identities they have at birth. After a long period of social engineering in which the categorization of people defined their position as workers and as consumers, people today want to choose. Therefore, developing a product for a targeted community can result in reaching some enthusiasts but also creates the same number of detractors. Likewise, the organization of a specific program for employees of a particular group, will probably meet equal number of enthusiasts as it does of detractors.

In the case that illustrates this chapter, "Brazil: Communal Identity and Networks at the Bottom of the Pyramid," we can see two very different approaches to understanding the same community. The two companies described in this case were created by lower-middle-class women from the Afro-Brazilian community, one from São Paulo and the other from Rio de Janeiro. Both women have a strong drive to help their communities; however for Adriana, the founder of *Feira Preta*, her community is clearly defined by color, whereas for Leila the community is defined in socioeconomic terms in which color does not play a part.

Feira Preta is an organization that wants to dignify the black community by emphasizing the positive elements of being black; thus the exposure to products such as music, culture, or ethnic arts and crafts represents a way to dignify the community. On the other hand, Leila Velez and her partners insist that *Beleza Natural* does not target the black population but people with curly hair, from whatever origin and color they may come from.

Interestingly, the participants of both *Feira Preta* and *Beleza Natural* are for the most part of Afro-Brazilian origin and from the lower or lower-middle class. However, the clients of *Feira Preta* for the most part consume products to reaffirm their blackness, and they participate in the different events and activities as a way to be active in the Afro-Brazilian community. The clients of *Beleza Natural* do not particularly want to be active in the Afro-Brazilian community, but rather aspire to belong to a community that is escalating socioeconomically from lower class to emergent middle class, which is represented by the founders and the clients of the salons.

Both examples relate to an ethnic community in Brazil; however in the same community there are those who identify with it and make it their aspirational community, and there are others who although they belong to the same community of origin and do not reject it, do not particularly want to make it their community of destination.

I believe this is one of the most important challenges for business organizations today: how to target communities of aspiration, both in terms of their employees as well as their clients.

6 Second movement: Identity and community: From communities of origin to communities of aspiration

Therefore, in the second movement we see a shift from a community or origin, where affiliation is outside of the control of the individual, to a community of aspiration that is chosen by the individual. The choice is a conscious one; this is not so much a new emotional community as it is a community that individuals consciously want to be part of and to contribute to. There can be emotional links: however, they are not a strong emotional attachment. It is, of course, evident that being able to choose a community of aspiration is only possible if basic needs are satisfied. If the individual is looking for basic security, food or emotional security, his or her priorities will be somewhere else, because a community of aspiration, in the forms that are present in today's society, will not satisfy these needs. He or she could find shelter, emotional warmth and even help in finding a job or even creating a new job, but this is not the main purpose of these communities; in any case, the flexibility and volatility that characterizes them would not provide for long-term shelter and they would therefore not be a reliable source to satisfy his or her basic needs. Becoming conscious of these larger aspirations is possible only if the basic needs are covered.

With this in mind, the movement within the trends of personal development that we have seen in the previous section is parallel with the movement of communal identity in which the individual looks for a community in which to act and contribute. The movements in personal development

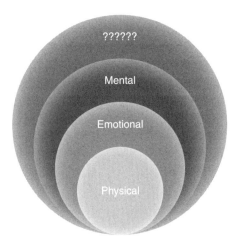

Figure 2.1 Mental, emotional, and physical

and communal identity are parallel; they both represent a movement in which the individual is increasingly becoming conscious of who he or she is and wants to be, and where he or she wants to participate in the community and contribute to the best of his or her capacities. In Figure 2.1 we can see that the levels interact with each other, showing that one movement does not eliminate the other, instead it is integrated with it into a larger framework of options. Therefore, all needs, whether physical, emotional or rational, need to act in harmony with each other within the individual as well as at the collective level.

Case 2   Brazil: Communal identity and networks at the bottom of the social pyramid

Instituto Feira Preta, São Paulo[1]

Introduction

Today is December 20, 2010. Adriana Barboso, 33 years old, a pretty young black girl, is really exhausted after the hard work of the past three days. She is having breakfast at her flat while reading journalists' comments on her "*Feira Preta*" (Black Fair) that closed the day before. She likes the way one journalist described the event: "the ninth *Feira Preta* took place on December 18 and 19, 2010 at the *Exhibition Center Imigrantes*. The figures confirmed the success of the biggest event for Afro-Brazilian expressions and diversity: 14,000 visitors, 100 exhibitors, 170 attractions, more than 270 direct and indirect jobs created, and approximately R\$700,000[2] in business generated. In addition, the event has united generations and shown, once again, it is the most important initiative of its kind in Latin America."

She can hardly believe this is already the ninth fair, a long journey since the informal conversation she had nearly ten years before with her friend Daisy in a packed São Paulo metropolitan bus in May 2001. She remembers it as if it was yesterday. Adriana and Daisy were quite devastated after their incipient, small, informal business of selling used clothes in street fairs was ruined when its inventory was almost completely stolen after an *arrastão,*[3] kind of mass robbery. For her this was the second blow in only 4 months! First she had lost her job as marketing assistant at Trama Records, a prestigious Brazilian music company, which the Brazilian economic crisis of 1999 had forced to reduce costs by cutting labor. Sadly, leaving the job meant also leaving the university since she had no way to pay for it any more.

After losing her job, Adriana decided not to despair and, as always, found ways to support herself. So she began selling her own clothes in popular fairs in the streets. She had too many clothes anyway, and she did not need them anymore to go to work at an office. Thus, she began to frequent the popular street fairs, and that is how she met Daisy. They formed a good tandem, Adriana selling her own clothes and Daisy her own home-made cakes. Things began to work and she managed to save some money that she reinvested in buying more used clothes, this time only to be sold at the fairs. She finally was looking at the future with a little optimism until that day of May 2001 when the *arrastão* ended up with most of the merchandise she had managed to acquire.

Going back home on the bus with Daisy, they began a conversation on their precarious situation and the difficulties of making a living by selling on the streets. On top of that, in all the fairs they visited there were hardly any people like them, young Afro-Brazilians. "Let us create a fair for black people!" Daisy said. "A fair where black producers can sell their products and black youngsters can have a space where they can feel proud of their culture, their music and their difference! A *Feira Preta*!" "*Preta* relates to identity, to a reaffirmation of the Afro-Brazilian culture," states Adriana.[4] Adriana knew immediately that the concept would work; it was only now a matter of putting the pieces together and making it happen!

Nine years later, the *Feira Preta* is consolidated and well known in São Paulo. However, the road has not been easy. To begin with, she had to overcome the barrier of her looks, "being women, black, young and poor, no one really took us seriously, we had to work twice to be respected by suppliers, donors or sponsors."

She also recognizes having many weaknesses at the start:

> I am not a manager, I know how to make things happen, but I do not have the capacity of a good manager to plan and set strategies, for that I had to struggle double. On top of that I never managed to go to the university and so my knowledge on how to make business was very limited... All these barriers made me insecure and I could see this insecurity was showing in the negotiation process with suppliers, donors or sponsors. Also, I identified so much with the idea of the fair that any rejection I took it personally as a rejection to my personal self and my identity, and that has caused me some psychological difficulties.

However, she also found along the way people and opportunities that helped her overcome her barriers and navigate through her journey, among which has been getting all the training she could obtain in order to enhance her management skills:

- The first opportunity in 2002 was found in a public institute to help entrepreneurs SEBRAE.[5] The facilities she found there and the books found in its library help her and her partner in developing their first written proposal.
- From 2006 to 2007 Adriana Barbosa competed in a training competition at Artemisia,[6] one of the main Brazilian NGOs supporting the development of social entrepreneurship.
- In 2009 she was selected to participate in a 10,000-woman initiative supported by the Goldman Sachs Foundation;[7] this was an important step in her personal and professional vision on how to conduct a business.

She proudly affirms that every single year she has managed to accomplish her objectives, and that the fair has been organized for the last nine years, without interruption. Also, *Feira Preta* today is a much broader concept, since now, in addition to the fair, other activities are being developed to help her community including monthly festivals, permanent exhibitors at Casa da Preta, training and educational activities in partnership with SEBRAE as well as their own brand of clothes, Marca Feira Preta, in partnership with Bruna Battys.[8]

Social impact

Since its conception, the fair had a clear social mission with two concrete objectives: reinforce the Afro-Brazilian identity, and enhance ethnic entrepreneurship and improve its standing in the national economy.

The Afro-Brazilian identity: Is there one?

The attendance for the 2010 Fair was 97 percent black and 3 percent white, although this was not intended and was something that happened over time, since during the first fair in Vila Magdalena in 2002, the composition was 40 percent black and 60 percent white. As for the exhibitors, ever since the beginning the ratio has been constant, approximately 70 percent black and 30 percent white.

The *Feira Preta* intends to develop, reinforcing the identity of the black community and thereby raise its self-esteem; however, as Adriana Barbosa states, the Afro-Brazilian community, unlike other communities such as the Japanese, Koreans, Lebanese, or Jewish, does not form a unity but rather is made up of very fragmented tribes. The people who participate in the *Feira Preta* mostly come from the tribes of Samba, Hip Hop, intellectuals, and street boys, and most of them are young. The exhibitors are also of the same tribes, young and urban with a taste for urban looks and music.

"I was proud of belonging to this community, I love the music and the spirit, the dances of so many people in the fair makes me really proud of what I am," says Henrique Oliveira, a visitor to the fair.

Visitors have mixed feelings on the question of identity, for example, Reynaldo, a young visitor:

> I normally do not like this type of affirmative race event, but most of my friends like to come so this year I did go. I did like the music and the culture, but not so much the exhibitor's products. A fair should also exhibit other products of higher quality beyond handmade, precarious arts and crafts; this is not how I want my community to be perceived. On top of that my white girlfriend came with me and she did not feel comfortable at all.

Zelia, one of the older visitors to this year's fair, says:

> I love to come, the first year I came with my son, and this year I came alone with my granddaughter. She loves the fair too, the music, the arts, and she always makes me buy her some necklaces or a black Barbie that she adores.

Adriana believes that the fair is breaking many stereotypes people have against blacks, "now they see we can also have our own culture in a very reputable space in which other national fairs also take place."

Enhancing ethnic entrepreneurship

Adriane reflects:

> I was able to develop myself partly because I was born in a middle-class neighborhood; if I had been born in the periphery, I am not sure I would have found the strength and courage to leave the dump and try to raise my economic condition. This is why *Feira Preta* is so important, because most of the visitors are from the periphery and they can see there are ways of improving themselves and that they are part of a community that is proud of their culture and their legacy.

To qualify as exhibitor, merchants either need to be of Afro-Brazilian origin or sell products focused on the black population. Out of the 100 exhibitors there is a large range, from small producers of T-shirts up to Banco Santander. However, the fair only has around seven big companies, among them Petrobras and Natura. Among the small exhibitors, the majority will be young Afro-Brazilians from the periphery, from classes C and D: most of them are female. Many young people from the periphery, after visiting the fair, have realized that they could also start their own business. That was the case for Helena:

> The first year I just went as a visitor; being there made me realize that I could also make something and sell it. So the second year I developed some stylish shirts to be sold at the fair, but since I did not have money to pay for the stand, I asked Adriana Barboso to let me sell the shirts with her own brand. She allowed me to do it. And so the third year I was able to pay for my own stand and now after three years I have opened a shop.

Other exhibitors have some concerns about the visitors to the fair, as stated by one of the founders of *Preta Pretinhia*,[9] a shop that makes hand-made inclusion dolls:

> We have always exhibited our inclusion dolls since the fair was here at Vila Magdalena. We do not only have black dolls, we have all types of inclusion dolls: a blind doll, one with Down syndrome, a doll with cancer, also an Arab doll, an obese doll and a Chinese doll. Each costs

aprox R$ 70. Here at the shop, the bohemian whites like to buy our dolls but we do not sell them any more at the *Feira Preta* because visitors do not buy. So this year we asked Adriana to exhibit without paying for the stand, but she said she could not afford to allow such an exception so, although we like the idea, I am afraid we can no longer exhibit there ... the fair should be more white, so that more white people will engage with us; and also, white people adore some of the ethnic arts and crafts products sold in the fair.

Where to go from here?

Adriana knows that her Instituto Feira Preta has potential; she is convinced of it because the instituto coordinates a network of 14,000 Afro-Brazilian members, and more than 8000 people are regularly active in its digital social networks. She knows that many challenges are still ahead but she now know what she is capable of and that her inner strength will lead the way as it always has. On top of that she knows she is working for her community and thus she will find in her community the support she needs to make *Feira Preta* a success.

Instituto Feira Preta is a business and so needs to generate enough revenue to be sustainable, but its main raison d'etre is developing an inclusion process for the black, low-income community.

The case of Instituto Beleza Natural, Rio de Janeiro[10,11]

Beleza Natural (BN) has become very popular in Rio de Janeiro over the last decade as a chain of beauty salons for low-income women, utilizing an innovative treatment that transforms rigid curly hair into softer, more moisturized hair with clearly defined curls. According to the CEO, "We are not just selling a product but a concept; a process by which women with curly hair from low economic classes can afford a very good treatment and a personalized advice to improve their self esteem."

The first center opened in 1993 in the neighborhood of Tijuca in Rio de Janeiro. Currently in 2011, the Instituto Beleza Natural has 11 salons, more than 80,000 clients at month, sales that exceed $75 million US per year, and more than 1300 employees.

Leila Velez, co-founder and CEO of Instituto Beleza Natural:

70 percent of Brazilian women have curly hair, many, like me, so rigid and dry that looked very much like the hair of Michael Jackson. And

no matter what I did, it grew wild and to the sides. It was a real frustration to me during my childhood: I needed it to either be combed very tied up to my scalp or cut very short! I have always dreamed of having long hair down to my shoulders with clear defined curls, just as I have now, thanks to the product and the method invented by my partner Zica.

Beginnings

Heloisa Assis, popularly known as Zica, was a hairdresser from a low-income family. For years she was determined to find a solution for her excessively curly hair that grew wild in every direction. She was convinced that a formula could be developed to fix curly hair, and thus could benefit a lot of women in Brazil and their different degrees of curls.

Zica could not understand the lack of segmented products for the type of hair of most the women in Brazil. Specifically, about 20 percent of the population had the typical afro-hair that in the humid conditions of Rio de Janeiro grew wild; as result, a high degree of frustration was common to quite a few women and even caused a huge lack of self-esteem. Like many others, as a child, Zica tried make her hair straight; yet she thought that the results did not look natural because her hair turned dry and was not particularly nice. She wanted her curls hanging down, not puffing out sideways, so free hair with firm curls would be the ideal for her.

Zica then decided to commit herself to finding a product that could really help her and others. She was not a chemist and never had any education; however, she had been a hairdresser for a long time and knew most of the available products quite well. So in 1983 she began to systematically mix different products to find the right one. She tried the combinations on herself and her friends, and in particular with her sister-in-law Leila Velez, married to her brother Rogerio. After ten years she had not despaired, and finally her efforts paid off – in 1993 she found the perfect formula. She could see it in her own hair, and in that of her friends. Leila was so impressed that she was convinced they need it to turn it into a business for women with curly hair, and that they could do it cheaply enough so people with a low income could afford it.

Leila Velez, knew how to do business, having worked in McDonald's since she was 14 years old, even winning the award for best employee at 15. She thought she could incorporate some of the features that impressed her in McDonald's into her own business.

"In McDonald's, I did learn how to work in teams, the quality patterns, and their emphasis on customer service. I admire the way the business was structured in well defined stages, so as to make a really efficient process. This I believed had to be the structure for our own beauty salon," says Leila.

Zica, her husband Jair (a taxi driver), her brother Rogerio (also a service attendant at McDonalds) and his bride Leila, opened their first beauty center in 1993 in the neighborhood of Tijuca, where they lived. Tijuca hosted different segments of the Rio population, from lower-class people that lived in *favelas*, up to a solid middle class. All four partners were of low-income status and thus they had no hope of receiving any funding from a bank, or any investment from any of their family members. However, they strongly believed in the potential of what they had in hand, so they invested all that they had in it. Rogerio sold his old car, while Leila and the others used the little savings they had.

Their first clients were family members, friends, and neighbors, and soon friends of friends. The word of mouth worked so fast that in less than three months they could not satisfy the demand in their first small salon.

The business model, from McDonald's to Disneyworld

"We have a unique product and a well developed methodology to apply the product in different types of hair, and the business skills we learnt by my work at McDonald's. Therefore, right from the start we knew it would be successful."

The product

Zica's invention was more than a product: it was also a methodology to make the product efficient for different hairs' needs. Thus, right from the start they did not sell merely a product, but a personalized hair treatment.

In addition to the original *super-relaxante*, Zica has developed a whole range of products for the treatment and care of curly hair.

The organization

The treatment needs to be applied regularly, which is why it is important to sell it at a reasonable price, so more clients can afford it. If at the time a trip to the salon cost around R\$ 200, BN would do it for R\$ 45.[12] To sell at such a low price however, BN needed a large volume of clients as well as a very efficient business model.

The business model, as well as the organization, was inspired by McDonald's: an affordable product, sold to large number of people by an efficient chain of well defined processes. Based on that experience, Leila developed processes in four different stages, each conducted by a professional. In the first stage, personal advice is given, so the concrete needs of each customer will be defined, and advice given on capillary structure, eating habits, etc. ... The next stage is to divide the hair in strands, the third stage is smoothing the strands, and finally the product is applied to each strand.

This process has been maintained since the beginning, with some important modifications that were introduced in 2005. When Leila won the Endeavour prize, she was asked to go to the Florida to collect the award. Since she had some free time she decided to go to complete one of her childhood dreams, to go to Disneyland. And there waiting in line she suddenly realized the improvements she need to include in the process of her salons.

> In Disney world, you wait in long lines. However, the waiting is not boring since you keep moving to different waiting rooms, each with some entertainment. Finally the excitement arrives for a few seconds, and then you end up in a shop.

This is exactly how she then reorganized the business processes of her beauty salons, having a circuit with entertainment in each of the waiting rooms. The different stages of the process remained the same, but, instead of having everyone waiting together, she divided the salon into different well decorated rooms, each with different entertainment, videos, etc., and then, once the process was finished, customers moved into the shop, where they could buy other products for maintaining the care of their hair.

The clients

Service to the client was of paramount importance in the company business model. Indeed, low-income consumers usually desire an excellent service, since they are used to serving people in their jobs and in their own moments of consumption they want to be served well. However, Leila and Zica always believed that, more than anything, they were helping women improve their self-esteem. Low-income women could feel different, well-respected, and could afford a personalized service as good as higher income people had.

This was so important that they included this idea in their vision, which is: "Make people happier, promoting beauty and self-esteem." As Leila always says: "Beauty comes from the inside and BN is a place where customers can feel valued and respected, independent of their social class."

BN's understanding of the needs and desires of low-income population has always been a competitive advantage. Examples of this can be seen in details such as the many full-length mirrors in their salons. Low-income people usually have only small face mirrors in their houses but at BN they can see their whole appearance.

The majority of BN clients come from the low-income population; mainly class C, which represents 46 percent of the clients and class B, 27 percent of the sales. For Leila this is the perfect composition:

> There is one person born in class A for every 10 born in class C; this class is thus very interesting to any type of business. Previously, every company ignored the base of the pyramid, or just sold them low-quality products. Now they realize they are good potential customers and that it is very interesting to make segmented products for them. Our objective is to expand the business to other places in Brazil, or outside Brazil but always with the same segmentation of clients.
>
> Although many of our clients are of Afro-Brazilian origins, our segmentation is not based on race but on the type of hair and by income class. We have some Caucasian clients and even clients with straight hair who also like our products.

In any case, in Leila's opinion there are no longer racial frontiers; in Rio de Janeiro it is difficult to see who comes entirely from Afro-origins since there is a large mixed population with different variety of skin colours from very dark to very light.

The employees

For BN products to function efficiently it is crucial to use the right methodology when applying them. Therefore, the partners soon realized that they needed to employ more people and to teach them how to apply the product correctly. They first began to employ friends, mostly former clients. Indeed, even today, of their 1300 employees 70 percent are former clients, many of whom have been in the business since its beginnings. BN also hired other personnel, mostly for managerial tasks.

New employees are not required to have previous experience in the field. Working in BN has been very popular among low-income young girls. Each new recruit to the company is trained and has the chance of promotion. The starting salaries for hairdressers are in the range R$2,000 to R$ 3,000, which in 2011 was a very good salary for beginners in Rio de Janeiro. This salary can go up to R$5,000, and there are also many opportunities in the business. The staff turnover is about 10 percent, low when compared with other beauty centers in Brazil.

The research and innovation process

They soon realized they need to create their own products, and in 1998 they managed to open their own factory. In it a group of scientists research constantly into including innovations in the Extreme Relaxante' main formula as well as the rest of the range of products. The formula is registered and has been changed since its original appearance, BN are always finding ways to improve it.

The turning point: Reaching out for external support

BN has had many difficult moments since 1993. On the personal side, Leila had to balance her personal life with two kids while being the main provider for the whole family. Moreover, as a low-income black woman, she had to overcome many prejudices, such as, for instance, building trust among suppliers.

The business had also important challenges: in 1998, BN opened the factory and most of their working capital was spent. Also, the company suffered from all the bureaucratic processes required to obtain the necessary licenses as well as a struggle to win approval from health authorities to open the company. At that time, says Leila, they had to negotiate with some suppliers as well as with some employees for delays in payment. Their trust and loyalty helped in that difficult moment.

In 2002, the business was growing and the Leila's business experience was not good enough for the new needs of the business, so she began to take different business courses in order to find how to improve BN's operations. Her first training was at SEBRAE.[13] During this process, Leila heard of Endeavor[14] and their competitive program to help entrepreneurs worldwide. At that time, she visited Endeavor's website and saw that they were looking for innovative entrepreneurs in Brazil, so she applied. After a tough and extremely competitive selection process, she was selected. From that moment on, everything changed. Over five months Leila was interviewed by different specialists in different areas who helped her to understand her business better and to reconcile all these different visions. Then she went to the final panel, which included some of the most admired and successful Brazilian businesspeople like Jorge Paulo Lehman and Carlos Alberto Sucupira. Moreover, Leila had the opportunity to do a one year part-time business course in Columbia and a business specialization at Harvard, constantly meeting other entrepreneurs like her as well as some of the world best specialists in different business fields.

Social impact

BN is much more than a chain of beauty salons. The company aspires to be a network to help women from low-income backgrounds to improve their status and self esteem.

The clients come from the base of the pyramid: maids, receptionists, supermarket attendants ... people who may have never had the personalized kind of service they get at BN. Customers feel special. The rooms, the lighting, being listened to by hair advisors: many feel that they don't deserve such a special treatment, that this is only the privilege of the wealthy. "It is not only the hair, it's the belonging to a community that drives many clients to come here," says Leila.

A client said:

> I have been coming here for the last five years. I heard of BN from a colleague at work. At first, I couldn't believe it, but once I saw her transformation I decided to give it a try. For me, it was a total transformation. My self esteem really improved, I felt more confident. Now, I can go to a meeting or a party without worrying, since my hair is always fine!

Another client adds: "I love to come here; it is like coming to a club. I love talking to other clients; to the hair stylists. It is not like going to a regular hair salon. It is like having a personal advisor all to yourself."

Moreover, the company is able to develop loyalty among its employees, as it can be perceived by this statement from Silvana Oliveira, an employee:

> I used to work as a maid, which was the only job I could have since I really had many complexes. I felt ugly and was not happy to be seen in public. So, to be hidden in a kitchen I thought was the best place for me. One day I decided to come to BN after my employer had recommended

it to me, and I could not believe it. I actually started to find myself pretty. The advisors helped me with my image and I found my identity. I began to put some make up and I really felt I was someone different. And then they gave me the opportunity of working here. Now I can do to others what they did to me and I love that, I can see new clients coming with their insecurities and they remind me of who I used to be. So I encourage them the way I had been encouraged. Also, I loved the training center and to be close to Zica and her personal strength. I really feel identified with her, as many of the employees do. Her story is a bit like mine and that of many of us. She managed to succeed from nothing, to become a successful businesswoman, and now she is a model for others to follow as I did and many others do. I love being part of the BN family!

The challenges ahead

The company now is at a crucial point. BN is a very successful business and is enjoying a growing demand, but the decisions to be made at this moment are crucial. They are preparing the business to present it to venture capitalists to be able to expand. But the question is how to replicate the model. Will a franchise will be a good model? The network they have in Rio – can it be replicated elsewhere, where in Brazil? Outside, perhaps in the USA? They have had offers to commercialize the product as a product, but Leila insists they are not selling merely a product but a whole process for improving women's self confidence. Or, as Leila puts it: "My obsession is to find a way to expand without losing the soul of the business."

Communal identity and networks

Both cases are different, and as business examples they cannot be compared; however, both help us to understand social identity better. These cases represent the efforts of young Afro-Brazilian entrepreneurs born and raised in lower-middle-class neighborhoods, who want to make a living while helping their community at the same time. However, Instituto Feira Preta focuses on community in terms of race, while for Beleza Natural race barriers do not exist and economic barriers are the ones that need to be tackled. In both cases though, improving meant raising the individual self-esteem of members of a deprived community.

Both have made extensive use of their networks in the different stages of the entrepreneurial venture, to better understand the needs of their potential clients in the information phase, and to make good use of the suppliers, clients and employees found in their original network, in the execution phase. And it is precisely in these networks that both businesses have found loyalty and support during difficult moments. In both cases it was also the network that gave the businesses legitimacy, since they represented a real need. At a given moment, Leila and Adriana also reached out for external support, and they both managed later to obtain management skills, training and support from international organizations.

Their businesses are different, of course. Instituto Beleza Natural offers a basic service for hair treatment, and Instituto Feira Preta offers a network for promoting Afro-Brazilian culture and ethnic entrepreneurship. However, a basic contrast, besides their business and company models, is the difference in their aspirational community. Both communities are made up of people with low incomes and, for the most part, Afro-Brazilian origin. Nevertheless, the aspirational community of those involved in Feira Preta is the same as their community of origin: the Afro-Brazilian community in its highest cultural expression. In the case of Instituto Beleza Natural, the aspirational community is not the same as the community of origin. Women going to their beauty salon aspire to integrate into what they perceive as a higher social class. The community they want to be a part of is made up of young and beautiful middle-class professionals from Rio.

Both cases help illustrate the long and complex debate on racial integration and communal identity described in this chapter. For the members of both networks, belonging means something different, although their origins are very similar. Both want to integrate and develop within a community but in different ways. The beauty of both cases is that what they are offering is totally voluntary. Belonging to a community is a personal decision that may or may not represent the community one is born into. Companies need to understand that communal identity is free and that their clients may be born into one particular group but not always aspire to belong to that same group in the future.

Annex: Culture and stereotypes in business – Morocco and Spain

In Chapter 2 we have described how people are categorized into different groups which individuals may or may not identify with. In this annex our goal is to try to describe how categories are formed, whether they are the result of real and proven differences or built on false assumptions.

Understanding this is of paramount importance since overly simplified categorizations lead to stereotypes, and these prejudices soon begin to inhibit relationships, especially in the business world.

Trying to find some answers to the development of stereotypes and their effects on business, the Moroccan foundation ONA and the Spanish foundation IE created a think tank in 2005, in which during three separate sessions an international group made up of 20 academics, practitioners, politicians and journalists, discussed issues of cultural diversity. Their discussion was influenced by a research study of cross-cultural perceptions – from Moroccan businessmen to Spanish businessmen – that was conducted over a three-year period.

The think tank helped clarify how stereotypes form and developed a model that could be used to reduce false stereotypes and smooth out business relationships in different cultural contexts. Some of the conclusions are described below.[15]

How stereotypes form:
A practical Moroccan–Spanish example

Our common knowledge of a culture in which we do not have a direct experience, is normally based on two sources positioned at either end of a line that goes from the most concrete to the most abstract.

- Descriptions of second-hand sources, at the concrete end; and
- cultural universal models at the abstract end.

We can use a simplified example to understand the two forms by which stereotypes can be formed, either as a result of a concrete experience that has lost context, or as a result of using an abstraction to classify a given community.

Among the prejudices found in Spanish–Moroccan business deals, two popular ones are that according to the Spanish, Moroccans do not work hard; and from the other side that Spaniards are arrogant. Let us see how these two general stereotypes might have been formed.

Perceptions that became common that are based on the direct experience of some individuals. A Spaniard who has never gone to Morocco may ask friends for information, and probably someone will tell him something like: "I have a friend who had a friend working in Morocco who told him that Moroccans spend hours drinking coffee and do business only for two minutes." The person who had the first experience had a context, perhaps the business was not very clear and the Moroccan partner wanted to find out some more information first, or the Moroccan partner was not very sure of where to go with the deal and wanted to gain time. Whatever the reason, the fact is that there was a context for the story and now the context is lost.

At the other end, a Moroccan wanting to do business with a Spaniard may ask his friends whether anyone has ever had relevant experience, and someone will tell him something like: "I had a friend who had a friend who had some business with a Spaniard and found that he really was arrogant and only worried about short-term deals and not interested in the relationship." Again we have lost the context. Perhaps the Spaniard might not have been very fluent in French and thus the distance was made by the language and not by the person, or the Spaniard might not be too convinced of the business in particular and wanted to call the deal off. Whatever the reason was, there was a context and the context now is lost.

Therefore, stereotypes can be formed by descriptions that have lost their original context. When descriptions are converted into common perceptions and therefore into stereotypes, they lead to prejudices and imprison the members of a given community, limiting it to a set of specific and closed parameters.[16]

Both our characters now have prejudices based on stereotypes that would make them act upon them in such a way that, probably, both will end up behaving as expected, thus confirming the stereotype in what is often called *a self-fulfilling prophecy*. Individuals would not have had a chance to be themselves but would have been perceived in a category, through the lenses of prejudices that would impede seeing the real individual behind them.

Therefore, the first condition of understanding prejudices is to accept that second-hand descriptions will often have lost their original context, and therefore are not objective tools on which to base expectations of the behavior of a particular community.

Cultural models are universal, archetypical descriptions of human ways of behavior. At the other end of the line, in the abstract world, we do have universal ideas behind human cultures. They lack context, they are abstract and impersonal, and they are reached not by direct experience but through introspection.

Cultural models have been studied since the 1950s by leading scholars such as Edward Hall, who define the different behaviors in culture based on different models of perception of the use of time, and of individualistic or collectivist tendencies, among other categories (Hall, 1990). Fons Trompenaars stated that culture was the way in which communities resolved a range of universal problems, and that these problems could be divided into three types (Trompenaars, 1994):

- those arising from relations with other people (individualistic vs collectivist);
- those arising from the passage of time (monochronic vs polychronic); and
- those related with the environment (activist vs fatalist).

These models are extremely useful instruments to understand cultural behavior, but only if understood within their limits. They are not "realities," but tools to help individuals in their own process of cultural understanding. One individual might follow the monochronic pattern (a linear concept of time) and thus behave in a sequential manner; someone whose conception of time is more polychromic, or circular, can be perceived as a multitasking person, able to do many things at one time. In between the two extremes exist a large range of behaviors, and by culture or circumstances individuals might have been educated more towards one model or another. In any case, people may change their behavior depending on the circumstances – people can be multitasking in times of stress, and monotasking when they need to be (in fact this would be the ideal for everyone, to not use the different cultural modes as dichotomies but learn how to use all human capacities and apply them differently at different times).

In our last example, in the Moroccan–Spanish business context there are abstract modes of culture that define the two cultures. Europeans are generally labeled as individualists, as opposed to Moroccans who normally are labeled as collectivists. Therefore, a Moroccan is expected to behave in collective ways, socializing more, and behaving emotionally and with a polychronic use of time. Spaniards working with European values would be perceived as having rational behavior, detached in business and being time-oriented.

The result will be the same as before, the Spaniard will classify the potential Moroccan partner using his own cultural mode. Or if the Moroccan classifies the Spanish potential partner using his cultural mode, both will end up acting upon the expected behavior they have of the other and it could end in a self-fulfilling prophecy. None of them would have had the chance to be themselves and be perceived other than through the lenses of prejudice.

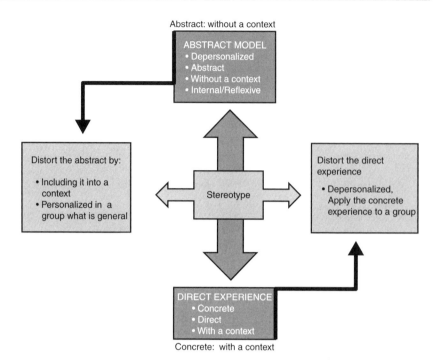

Figure 2.2 Formation of stereotypes

The second condition in understanding prejudices is accepting that abstract models applied to individuals because of their membership to a particular group will also lead to prejudices, and so imprison a given community by limiting it to a set of specific and closed parameters.

In Figure 2.2 we can see that stereotypes are formed in a movement from the concrete to the general or from the abstract to the concrete; either by a distorted direct experience that moves up into a general assumption, or the opposite, as an abstract general quality that gets distorted by being applied to a whole group.

In both cases the effect is the same, the assumed behavior is applied to a concrete individual before giving him or her the chance of a clear and direct experience that could confirm or deny the given stereotype, and thus distort any potential communication.

Dynamic cultural understanding

Whether the stereotype has an underlying basis in reality or not, Figure 2.2 shows how having a correct perception can be a dynamic process, taking the simplified version of the stereotype into its correct dimension.

The process implies three steps:

- first, have a real and direct experience, free of prejudices;
- next, move from the direct experience to trying to find the abstract cultural model that can explain a particular and concrete behavior;
- finally, go back to the direct experience and make the appropriate adjustments.

Let us take our former examples: The Spaniard of our story goes to Morocco and sees that his potential Moroccan partner spends more time engaging in social conduct that doing business.

Instead of accepting the stereotype, and assuming that Moroccans are lazy, he can ask the Moroccan partner to explain why he likes to socialize in business and he can have an answer that will give him a different understanding of this particular behavior: for instance,

> In order to perform well in business, it is necessary to be calm and relaxed, to be able to observe, to take the time to think, to take the time to listen to the other person. All these elements can help to develop efficient and productive and long term business relationships.

The Spaniard can then try to find a cultural model in which personal relations have more importance than strictly business processes, and then observe effect that such a model will have on the different use time.

After analyzing the value of social relations and the emotional component in business transactions, the Spaniard can then go back to the business deal and try to see whether those elements could be helpful for the relationship or the success of the business, and act accordingly.

The same applies to the Moroccan; he can meet the Spaniard, see that he is looking at his watch all the time and ask him why he is in such a hurry. The Spaniard may say something like this:

> In business it is better not too get too personal since the emotional component may distort the correct vision of the objective business.

Then the Moroccan, with his cultural understanding, can find a model in which the rational takes more importance over the emotional, and thus he can go back to the concrete relationship and try to find out whether these new elements help in the success of the business.

In any case both will better understand the real reason once they move away from simplifications. This will help their relationship by initiating a dialogue that could prevent a potential misunderstanding.

Cultural understanding can help us to re-direct our actions, never to plan them.

Another very likely possibility in our example is the fact that in this particular case, neither the Moroccan nor the Spaniard conform with the expected image. The Spaniard can go to Morocco with his preconceptions, expecting to socialize and he can met a very time-oriented Moroccan who does not fit at all into the preconceived model, and any attempt to force socialization may have a negative effect on the relationship. Likewise, the Spanish partner can be a very social and warm individual that would love to socialize and deepen the relationship with his potential Moroccan potential. In any case, a direct experience free from prejudices will help find the most appropriate behavior.

Applying re-directional elements

These examples show a practice termed *"applying re-directional elements."* An active approach consists of observing behavior based on our direct experience and free from preconceptions. Next, we need to think whether this particular behavior can lead to some abstract archetype. Then we must try to understand its purpose – whether it is in relation to the community or to time, etc. Last, we need to evaluate if that specific behavior can be managed in such a way that can result in a competitive advantage for the business.

Of course not all cultural differences can be transformed into a competitive advantage; but being conscious of the possibility that they *can* be, will open up new opportunities and will set in motion the kind of cultural behavior and cultural dialogue that should always guide our experiences in international business.

CHAPTER 3

Identity and gender: Between the self and the social

> Why do girls not want to be princesses any more? Snow White revisited
> Third movement: Resolving gender archetypes: Rediscovering the meaning of giving by learning how to receive

1 Why do girls not want to be princesses any more? Snow White revisited

> Then the prince's tender heart filled with compassion as he saw the sun-kissed hair, the rose-red lips and the pure white skin of his princess. With love in his heart he knelt and gently kissed her. And that was the very thing, the only thing, that could break the Queen's bad charm! ... So, once more, the forest rejoiced and was glad again as Prince Charming lifted Snow White on to his splendid white horse and took her away to be his bride (*Snow White* 1936, p. 14).

Girls do not want to be princesses any more; most would be repelled by the idea of Snow White waiting passively to receive a kiss from her prince. Girls today identify more with strong independent women like Lara Croft, who can actively face whatever challenge is in her way. Boys also do not want to play the passive role; they prefer to identify with the strong courageous man who also actively overcomes any challenge in his path. It seems that both boys and girls want to play the active role, the character of the hero – so who is left to play the passive role?

Passivity is not very appreciated in our society; all of our movies, slogans commercials, keep telling us to move, to be active, to go and aggressively pursue our goals. And so we all run in pursuit of our goals. Therefore, it is normal that no one, neither boy nor girl, wants to take the passive role. But, why is it such a bad thing to be passive? Are there some positive qualities to being passive? Is there no perceived benefit in standing still and waiting? Can we find the utility of receiving?

Perhaps it is worthwhile exploring the myth in an attempt to grasp a different interpretation that can help us better understand both the passive and active roles.

Myths are a fascinating field of research. The greatest explorer was Carl Jung, who stated that the western world, as it moved towards rationalism, needed to eliminate any element that could not be rationalized, and so relegated to the level of the unconscious a series of archetypes that were rooted in our primitive collective consciousness. The relationships of men and women to nature, to the unknown, to rituals, among other elements, were all removed into our unconscious world and only allowed to reappear in the form of dreams, symbols or myths (Jung 1978).

The problem of having lost the link with the unconscious world of our primitive relatives is that there is no-one left to ask! The symbol, having lost its real meaning, is now open to interpretation. Thus, myths are reinterpreted over and over again, each time with a different angle, because all interpretations are probably true but only partially so, part of a fragmented and simplified reality. Every society sees myths from the perspective of their time; and yet myths still influence the society in which they are embodied. Therefore, myths do not only represent a hidden reality that is part of our identity, but they also represent a source of values upon which societies are built.

Archetypes are difficult to describe using conceptual thinking since, as Jung stated, they are both images and emotions and their real significance is experienced differently by different people.

> They are pieces of life itself, Images that are integrally connected to the living individual by the bridge of emotions. That is why it is impossible to give an arbitrary or universal interpretation of any archetype. It must be explained in the manner indicated by the whole life situation of the particular individual to whom it relates (Jung 1978, p. 87).

Therefore, I do not think I could manage to give the correct interpretation of the tales of princesses and princes, since I do not know which one is true; however, as in the previous chapter, I believe the myth of the hero can help us to understand the movement from personal to social identities. In the effort to understand gender, I believe that the myth represented by Snow White may help us to explore three concrete areas of relevant to understanding women and the feminine gender in our society.

Gender as a process of self-identity

Comparing the myth of Snow White with other similar and older myths that emerged in different parts of the planet can help us to grasp some of the hidden meanings of feminine and masculine genders, conceived as abstractions within human understanding. I believe that in this sense, gender is a part of our self-identity, since similar myths are found in the collective unconscious of humanity. In other words, the feminine as well as the masculine myths are part of each one of us as men and women.

Gender as a part of our communal identity

The elements found in the myth of Snow White and others like it help in developing gender as a social identity within the two sides we saw in the previous chapter: social identification, a process by which individuals adhere to a certain pattern of behavior; and categorization, a certain pattern of behavior that society places upon those born into it, whether male or female, which leads them to perform concrete roles in society.

The feminine qualities in our society

But Snow White can also shed light on one of the most important problems of our society today: the lack of feminine qualities in the development of the public space. I say *feminine*, not *women*, since we do indeed have women building the world and present in the public space. However, as shown by the bad reputation of Snow White as compared to that of the Prince, women and men both have ignored and even despised one of the most profound qualities in our humanity – the capacity to receive. Receiving in its deeper meaning, is not a useless and passive act; it is a dignified and conscious mechanism of total openness. Stopping to be quiet and still so that we can receive is a fundamental quality of movement, since giving can only be brought about if we are able to receive first, both for men and women. In today's world we are constantly on the run to produce; we have forgotten how to stop and receive, and as society we have been running on empty for far too long.

Therefore, in my opinion, gender identity does not exist as such, and should be located between personal identity and social identity. It can be understood as an important part of social identity since it is rooted in most of our traditional patterns of education as a human society. But gender identity can also help us to better understand *ourselves* and the way each one of us resolves the archetypes within us. In Jung's terminology, this is the action of completing ourselves with the shades of our unconscious, as part of the individuation process.

2   Mother Earth and Father Spirit: Reconciling primitive archetypes in human experience

Following Jung, in our rational development we have ignored the emotional component, and that is the reason why we have excluded some strong images in our communicating: images that, although irrational, have existed for primitive human beings since they developed real psychological energy. In our movement towards rationality, useful primitive instruments that represented hidden emotional energies were taken out from our conscious mind; understanding nature, connecting with animals, among other abilities, were relegated from our conscious rational mind to hidden parts of our unconsciousness. Thus, *raison* began to dominate our human conscious, eliminating in its struggle the emotional energies that for centuries had helped humanity in its understanding of the world. The gender images of our ancestors, the Great Mother and the Great Father, were more than mere rationalizations, they were part of a leaving emotional attachment to deeper parts of our psyche as described by Jung:

> Today for instance we talk of "matter." We describe its physical properties. We conduct laboratory experiments to demonstrate some of its aspects. But the word "matter" reminds a dry, inhuman, and purely intellectual concept, without any psychic significance for us. How different was the former image of matter – the Great Mother – that could encompass and express the profound emotional meaning of Mother Earth. In the same way, what was the spirit is now identified with intellect and thus ceases to be the Father of All. It has degenerated to the limited ego-thoughts of man; the immense emotional energy expressed in the image of "our father" vanishes into the sand of an intellectual desert (Jung 1978, p. 85).

The male and female principle in ancient wisdom

The male–female principle, labeled as active–receptive, positive–negative, Yin–Yang, is probably the first of humanity's opposites within the complex set that according to Jung make up the real life of an individual (others being day–night, birth–death, good–evil).

The principle of positive–negative, male–female, is active in all religions and traditions, and it represents the principle of life and also the path to reconcile matter with the spirit. We can recall a few maxims of ancient wisdom in which the principle is described in all its different levels, the physical but also the emotional and mental, and many times also in the spiritual plane.

The Kybalion: Sayings attributed to Hermes Tremegistus, "Gender is in everything; everything has its Masculine and Feminine Principles; Gender manifests on all planes."[1]

Dao De Jing: Probably the most popular concept in today's new approach to ancient eastern wisdom is the idea of Yin and Yang as described by Chinese Daoism, specifically in verse 42, written in the sixth century BC (Addiss and Lombardo 1993, p. 42).

> Tao engenders One,
> One engenders Two,
> Two engenders Three,
> Three engenders the ten thousand things.
>
> The ten thousand things carry shade
> And embrace sunlight.
>
> Shade and sunlight, yin and yang,
> Breath blending into harmony.

The principle of Yin and Yang represents the first movement that exists in the universe. The Daoist universe is one, but infinitely diverse. Its unity is implied by the fact that all dimensions of existence, from the budding of a flower to the orbit of the stars, may be denominated in terms of Qi (ch'i) the fundamental energy-matter of the universe whose dynamic pattern is a cosmic heartbeat of expansion (Yang) and contraction (Yin). Its diversity is a function of the complex interaction of the myriad cosmic processes both light and fluid, and heavy and dense. The universe is a single, vital organism, not created according to some fixed principle but spontaneously regenerating itself (Miller 1998).

Yin–Yang is illustrated in the well-known Tai-Chi symbol, found in the I-Ching, (see Figure 3.1 in the last section of this chapter). The Yin, representing the dark, passive and female, is the black area, and the Yang, representing the active principle, the male, active and extrovert, is the white area.

Christian tradition: As in other traditions, in the west the female and masculine principle is illustrated by the metaphysical union of the spiritual and the material, and not in the actual division of the earthly sexes.

As Sylviana Agacinski remarked in her interesting work on the metaphysics of the sexes, the principle of masculine and feminine is shown in Plato's *Timaeus*, as well as in the biblical book of Genesis, to be the result of the removal from the divine, and not the effect of a human division. The masculine and feminine division is found within the mythical hierarchy of heaven and earth, where the soul and the body belong to their respective worlds of the intelligible and the sensible (Agacinski, 2005, p. 35).

Following Agacinski, the image of the fecundity of the soul is associated naturally with the metaphor of Theaetetus, where Plato attributes to the philosophical dialogue the characteristics of a delivery; philosophical education is revealed as the art of giving birth to human souls. In the *Timaeus*, Plato describes how human souls are built of the same material that the universe is built of. However, once souls are implanted in the bodies, a mortal soul is adhered to the immortal soul. It is the mortal soul that deals with mundane passions and material needs. This mortal soul is identified with the feminine, and as Agacinski describes, the metaphor slowly turned the masculine towards heaven and the feminine towards earth.

The process of mystical union in the Christian tradition is often referred to as the union of the feminine (the individual mystic) receiving the masculine spirit in a sublime union, often described with clear physical metaphors. For example, one of the greatest mystics in Christian tradition is Saint John of the Cross; in his poems he described his mystical experiences, referring to himself as feminine and to the spirit as masculine. He used these ideas in his most famous poem, "The Dark Night of the Soul," to describe his peak spiritual experiences as the union of the masculine (spirit) with the feminine (his soul).

> *En una noche oscura,*
> *con ansias en amores inflamada,*
> *(¡oh dichosa ventura!)*
> *salí sin ser notada,*
> *estando ya mi casa sosegada...*[2]

Jewish mysticism: The Qabalah of the Jewish mystics[3] also describe the sublime union of the feminine and masculine as a mystical experience. The two central books of Cabbalistic wisdom are the *Yetzirah* (book of formation) and *Zohar* (book of splendor), and they both stress the importance the female counterpart of God. The *Zohar* implies that it is through the union of the male and female within ourselves that we can truly mirror the cosmic Deity, which is a complete synthesis of masculine and feminine energies (Parfitt 1991, p. 13).

The Spiritual tradition of Islam: As with other monotheistic religions, the core values of Islam are deeply spiritual. The mystical traditions are mostly embraced in the concepts of Sufi mysticism, holding the widespread belief that the Holy Quran has deep inner symbolism beyond its literal interpretation, and that the Prophet Mohammed was the first Master, who passed his teachings to his followers. Among the greatest Sufi Mystics we can mention Ibn Al 'Arabi, born in Murcia, Spain in the twelfth century, who wrote some of the most beautiful and highest expressions of mystical love. Ibn Al 'Arabi, describes how when in love, seeing deep in the eyes of his beloved one, he could see as in a mirror, his own Divinity reflected, and thus how true love between men and women could help us understand higher manifestations of Divine love (Ibn Al 'Arabi, 1990).

What I believe is crucial in all ancient understanding of the male and female principle is that it consisted in an abstract understanding of a transcendental development of the human being, not a description of real men and women. Ancient wisdom stressed the union and not the separation.

It is important to highlight, as Agacinski implies, that the metaphysical union of the feminine and masculine in its transcendental meaning, did not imply the equality of men and women. As she notes, in ancient Greece as well as later on in Christianity, only men were entitled to have the sublime union of masculine and feminine; women were reserved for more mundane tasks such as dealing with cooking and physical love. As mentioned in the *Timeaus*, man is defined by his relation with the Divine, and woman is defined by her relationship to man. However, this is a different story that implies the categorization of men and women into different social groups that are entitled to play different roles in society. What I want to stress here is that for ancient wisdom, the female and male principles were abstractions that could be found in everything, both in the forces of nature as well as within each human being, and also in the concept of mystical union.

Masculine and feminine attributes

In addition to the general and supreme Male and Female Principle, all traditions have described concrete female and male attributes, that also refer *not to concrete women and man*, but to abstract qualities embodied in humans, what are normally labeled as male and female qualities. Of particular influence has been the male and female qualities embodied in the Greek gods and goddesses.

The Greek gods and goddesses

Greek traditions give a clear representation of the basic human attributes of the feminine and masculine, embodied by the representations of gods and goddesses. We can analyze them by a brief and partial description of the story of Greek deities and its main characteristics.

Hierarchy of gods

Primordial gods: Chaos gave birth to Gaia (Mother Earth, mother of mankind and nature), and some traditions also state that Chaos gave birth to Uranus (god of the sky and atmosphere) while others attribute his origin to Mother Earth.

Titans: Gaia and Uranus gave birth to Chronos, god of time and age, as well as Rea, goddess of fertility.

Olympians: Chronos and Rea gave birth to the Olympian gods (with the exception of Aphrodite daughter of Uranus).

Principal feminine Olympian deities and their qualities:

Aphrodite: beauty and sensual love
Artemis: nature and purity
Athena: wisdom and warfare
Demeter: the love of motherhood
Hera: marital love
Hestia: the hearth and cooking

Principal masculine Olympian deities and their qualities:

Zeus: king of the gods, commands, law and order
Apollo: music and poetry
Ares: war, courage and civil order
Dionysius: wine, parties and pleasures
Hades: death and the hidden wealth of the earth
Hermes: travel and diplomacy
Pan: the lower instincts
Poseidon: the sea, rivers, floods and droughts

Qualities of both the feminine and masculine gods were equally appreciated. Likewise, wisdom was not a quality reserved only for women, or courage only reserved for men; the ample range of the superior qualities of humanity were embodied in different gods and goddesses.

All of them had good and bad qualities related to their main attribute: courage has its reverse in a lack of compassion; love has dependency as its dark side; law and order have tyranny in their shade. The gods and goddesses represent the qualities that all of us, male and female, have inside of us with all their lights and darks. The fights, exploits and miseries of all the Olympian gods help as guides for the troubles of humanity, advising humans on how to overcome our weaknesses by following the paths of the deities.

For example, Hera represents marital love with all its good and its bad qualities. Hera is tenderness and stability, but also dependency and insecurity, as illustrated by her sick jealousy and her taking revenge to its cruelest extremes. After a life of suffering because of her jealousy, Hera resolved her dark side when she finally decided to separate from Zeus, and she thus completed herself in the loneliness of her home. In her solitude she acquired independence and detachment, and once she had moved away from dependencies she finally could take back Zeus as a companion. In modern psychological terminology, Hera completed her individuation process by integrating her masculine side within herself and thus as became a complete woman who was now free to continue a more self-fulfilling life.

Other gods also resolved their internal contradictions through a similar process of completing themselves, which is coincidentally very much in the line with the individuation process Jung described many centuries later as described in the following section.

The Animus and the Anima: The process of individuation and self-realization in each individual

Carl Jung believed that the feminine and masculine attributes were present in each one of us, but that for different reasons (historical processes, education, specialization, etc.) men have moved their feminine into their unconscious self, while women have moved the masculine into their unconscious self. The process of individuation takes the portions relegated to the unconscious into the conscious and thus we become complete individuals. The woman inside man is referred to as his *Anima,* while the man inside woman is referred as to her *Animus.*

> The anima is a personification of all feminine psychological tendencies in a man's psyche, such as vague feelings and moods, prophetic hunches, receptiveness to the irrational, capacity for personal love, feeling for nature and his relation with his unconscious. (von Franz, 1978, p. 186).

> The male personification of the unconscious in women, the animus, exhibits both good and bad aspects, as does the anima in man. The positive side of the animus can personify and enterprising spirit courage, truthfulness and in the highest spiritual profoundness. (von Franz 1978, p. 198).

For Jung, the process of individuation is when individuals take their shades from their hidden and forgotten self out into the surface; this process can be brought about by becoming aware of one's dreams and unconscious symbols. However, the problem with symbols is that they mean something different to each individual, since although many of the human problems are similar, they are never identical; therefore, it is difficult to summarize the infinite variations of the process of individuation, since each person has to do something different that is uniquely their own. Therefore, as Von Franz states, many have criticized Jung since because did not present psychic material systematically; however, as he explains: "when dealing with the process of individuation, the material itself is a living experience charged with emotion, by nature irrational and ever changing, which does not lead to systematization except in the most superficial fashion." (von Franz 1978, p. 167) "The process of individuation can be seen as the stages through which the anima helps men, and the animus helps women, mediate between the Ego and their Self." (von Franz 1978, p. 207)

There are four stages in the process of individuation where the Anima acts as guide for a man in his process from the ego to the self (von Franz 1978, p. 194):

- The first is best symbolized by the figure of Eve, representing purely instinctual and biological relationships.
- The second can be seen as that of Faust's Helen, where she personifies the romantic and aesthetic level.
- The third is represented by the Virgin Mary, an example of a figure who raises love (eros) to the heights of spiritual devotion.
- The fourth is symbolized by Sapientia, wisdom transcending even the most holy and the most pure.

The animus, just like the anima, exhibits four stages of development as it guides a woman in her process from the ego to the self:

- He first appears as a personification of mere physical power – for instance, as an athletic champion or muscle man.

- In the next stage, he posses the initiative and the capacity for planned action.
- In the third stage the Animus becomes the "word," often appearing as a professor or clergyman.
- In his fourth manifestation the Animus is the incarnation of meaning at its highest level (much like the Anima), and it becomes a mediator whereby the religious experience acquires new meaning. He gives the woman a spiritual firmness, an invisible inner support that compensates for her outer softness. The Animus in his most developed form sometimes connects a woman's mind with the spiritual evolution of her age, and can thereby make her even more receptive than a man to new creative ideas. It is for this reason that in earlier times women were used by many nations as oracles and seers.

If an individual has wrestled seriously enough and long enough with the problem of the Anima (or Animus), he or she has fully identified with the unconscious and become individualized – very much like the *Rajul* and *Kamil* of the Sufis, the supermen of Nietzsche, or the self-actualized person of Maslow. The self with a renewed life has found a new spiritual orientation, a creative *élan vital* for which everything is full of life and enterprise.

The integration of the combination of masculine and feminine qualities inside each individual often results in higher creative capacities. Virginia Woolf, for example described some of the greatest writers of all times, such as Shakespeare, as having both masculine and feminine sensibilities, and that is the reason they could appeal so much to both men and women.

> But the sight of the two people getting into the taxi and the satisfaction it gave me made me also ask whether there are two sexes in the mind corresponding to the two sexes in the body, and whether they also require to be united in order to get complete satisfaction and happiness? And I went on amateurishly to sketch a plan of the soul so that in each of us two powers preside, one male and one female, and in the man's brain, the man predominates over the women, and in the women's brain, the women predominates over the man. The normal and comfortable state of being is that when the two lie in harmony together, spiritually cooperating ... it is when this fusion takes place that the mind is fully fertilized and uses all its faculties. (Woolf 1928, p. 113)

Projections: From abstract attributes to concrete men and women

Women and men have both masculine and feminine qualities, (or psycho-logical tendencies); however the masculine qualities are buried in women's unconscious, while in men the feminine resides in the unconscious. Because they are hidden they are not recognized, and thus they tend to be projected outside on to an external object. As Jung describes, the process of projection is when an unconscious content is transferred to an outside object, so that the content a man does not want to see appears to belong to the object and not to himself. This is how the Divine Couple is transferred to the idea of mother and father, or to the actual literal couple. Therefore, the primordial archetypes of the masculine and feminine wound up being transferred to the qualities of the mother and father, the attributes of men and women as significant others. The anima is only one aspect of the unconscious material that is not recognized as the self, because since the self is masculine, the unrecognized aspects must represent the feminine. And since it is not recognized as being part of self, therefore the Anima has to be external to the self. For that reason, Jung argues that for men, the image of the Anima is normally projected on to real women, and the reverse occurs in the case of women (Jung 1970, p. 55).

3   Nature or nurture? Men's and women's brains

The masculine qualities of the Greek gods tend to be projected by society upon men, while the feminine qualities or attributes of Greek goddesses tend to be projected on women. And because of this, many women iden-tify with these womanly qualities and many men identify with the manly qualities. The question is whether this general tendency is the result of education or if it is rooted in human nature.

The debate over the behavior of men and women has served in different moments in history to develop arguments that have defined the roles that women and men should play in society. If women have internal attributes that are different from those of men, then their roles in society should fit those attributes – or so has been argued by many theorists throughout the years.

Do women behave differently than men?

If so, is the difference rooted in genetic differences or in education?

Simone de Beauvoir was one of the first exponents of the idea that the educational process was the most significant factor in explaining the differences between men and women. "One is not born, but rather becomes, a woman" (de Beauvoir 1953, p. 281). Women as we know them are the product of socialization, not the direct product of biology, Beauvoir's ideas were adopted for many years by a number of activist groups to promote an active campaign of educational changes with the goal of reaching equality in society.

At the other end of the debate we can find the position that defends the biological differences of men and women, mostly in the ranks of social biologists and neuroscientists.

Harvard professor Edward O. Wilson is one of the leaders of sociobiology, a field of research that has evolved in the last 25 years and is closely related to evolutionary psychology. Its focus is understanding human behavior through research on human genetics and neuroscience, drawing on theory and data from both biology and the social sciences.

Wilson's thesis is based on the idea that behavior is rooted in evolutionary patterns; for example, due to the fact that hominid women were subject to the responsibility of bearing, nursing and caring for children, they consequently evolved to be more nurturing than men. On the other hand, hominid men naturally evolved to be more aggressive because they were responsible for hunting and fighting. Evolution and specialization can thus explain the relevance in women of some specific qualities, such as empathy, verbal skills, social skills and security-seeking, among others, as well as the relevance of other qualities in men, including higher independence, dominance, spatial and mathematical skills, rank-related aggression, and other characteristics (Wilson, 1992).

These arguments lead to the idea that the human mind is shaped as much by its genetic inheritance as it is by culture, and therefore there are limits on just how much influence social and environmental factors can have in altering human behavior.

The defenders of the evolutionary postulates have based their thesis on neuroscience studies of male and female brains, and the now-popularized arguments of the left vs. right sides of the brain and their effect on certain human tendencies and attitudes.

Some of the most relevant studies include:

- Scientists working at Johns Hopkins University have discovered that there is a brain region in the cortex, called inferior-parietal lobule (IPL), which is significantly larger in men than it is in women (Rederikse *et al.*, 1999, p. 86).

- Another study, led by Dr. Godfrey Pearlson, has shown that two areas in the frontal and temporal lobes related to language (the Broca and Wernicke areas, named after their discoverers) were significantly larger in women, thus providing a biological reason for women's notorious superiority in language-associated thoughts. Using magnetic resonance imaging, the scientists measured gray matter volumes in several cortical regions in 17 women and 43 men. Women had 23 percent more volume than men in Broca's area (in the dorsolateral prefrontal cortex) and 13 percent in Wernicke's area (in the superior temporal cortex) (Schlaepfer et al., 1995).

The anthropologist Helen Fisher, wrote an influential book in 1999 called *The First Sex*. Following the trend of evolutionary psychology, she explained some of the discoveries of neuroscience as the effect of human history and the specialization of primitive men and women, although she also recognized that there is not a clear-cut definition in biology since there is none in the process of formation.

> Even this intriguing amalgam of male and female in each of us is shaped in biology. The fetal brain grows slowly and unevenly. Different parts of the brain become susceptible to sex hormones at different times, levels of these fetal hormones also change continuously. So tides of powerful sex hormones can masculinize one part of the brain while they leave another region untouched. As a result, every human being lies somewhere along a continuum that ranges from superfeminine to hypermasculine, depending on the amount and timing of hormones the individual was doused with in the womb (Fisher 1999, p. xviii).

After being born, culture and education play a significant role in our finally behaving as male or female. Fisher's influential thesis was that the new century needs many of the feminine qualities, including web thinking, collaboration, and communication skills, and therefore women will be playing a fundamental role by being able to exploit their talents in the new society that will be collaborative and equalitarian.

In my belief, the debate of nurture vs. nature is not really important. Whether behavior is rooted in our brains due to a process of specialization built up over thousands of years, or is due to a process of education that has also been rooted in our collective unconscious over thousands of years does not really matter. In both cases, patterns of behavior are imposed and deeply rooted both in our brains and in our common unconscious. However, the key is that these patterns are not deterministic.

In fact, neuroscientists admit that their findings are not deterministic. As Pearlson affirms, it would be an oversimplification to say that the findings of the studies conducted on brain structures mean that men are automatically better at something than women, since, often, individual women excel in math and individual men excel in language skills. In his opinion, the value of their findings is based on general trends resulting from large population samples where slight differences can be quantified. He feels that there is a grain of truth in these studies that underlines some of the ways people characterize the sexes, albeit with plenty of exceptions (Schlaepfer et al., 1995).

Old patterns of social division have always encountered countless examples of individuals fitting the categorization imposed upon them. As Jenkins states: "the human spirit is at the core of the resistance to domination. It may ebb to the point of invisibility, but it remains a consistent thread in human life. It is as intrinsic and as necessary to that life as the socializing tyranny of routine and everyday categorization." (Jenkins 2008, p. 206)

Goleman, in his renowned work on emotional intelligence, opened up a new understanding into this matter by stating that humans are much slower to change than their external circumstances do. He states that some of our physical reactions fit us to escape from lions, not meet the challenges of modern society (Goleman, 1995). By analogy, some of the specializations of men and women were developed to make men hunters and women gatherers. However, modern life does not use hunting much as the main activity to provide for food, and, for that reason, life today needs some of the traditional male qualities but also could use some of the traditional feminine attributes such as holistic intelligence and nurturing – whether or not they are carried out by men or women. Also, our modern "huts" could benefit from some of the traditional male qualities (more so when the value system is fading); for example, discipline and linear intelligence would do a lot of good to many adolescents today, whether these qualities are performed by men or women. Therefore, societal conventions are good as long as society decides that they are good; as circumstances change so do human habits, and in the process of this change there is a liberation of the hidden potentialities that many individuals had repressed because they did not fit the accepted conventions of society.

Science per se is not good or bad, it is the use that humans make of science that makes it a good or bad tool. Washing machines, which in my mother's opinion have been the key to women's emancipation, were developed thanks to defense technology. Thus, I do not think scientific findings are dangerous per se, but the use some people may make of them can be really dangerous. In this particular case overly simplifying the findings of neuroscience about the left and right sides of the brain can be led towards pushing men and women back to medieval discussions of what roles they are fit or unfit to perform.

Science can study how men and women behave as an aggregate collectivity, with interesting findings that can generate discussions and conferences and even light talk about how women cannot read maps and men can only do one thing at a time. But most importantly, science can lead to the cure for specific brain pathologies. Yet, to pretend that because an observation is based on science it is applicable to all of the members of a particular group, without individual differentiation, undermines the basic principle of individual freedoms.

The emphasis of some studies on the fact that women are "better at communication and nurturing," has resulted in assuming that women are better suited to the communication and human resources departments and not for the line, and this is one of the reasons why we see so few women in the higher decision-making positions of corporations. Because *if* we *insist in categorizing all women by what they are good at, someone may turn it around and categorize women based on what they are not good at. One side is dangerously close to the other.*

The European Enlightenment led to great achievements through the development of the scientific method, by which things are separated, fragmented, studied and then put back together. The method has proved ideal for many areas of understanding nature and has taken us to the moon, literally! However, new discoveries of the presence of complex systems lead to the conclusion that fragmented studies will tend to give a fragmented picture of reality. A fragmented truth is obviously incomplete and static, since complexity shows things that are in the continuous process of movement, wherein behavior and attributes change, and the whole can only be understood as a moving process.

What I believe both the ancient sages and privileged minds such as Jung's had right, was not so much the ability to describe what things are, but rather the capacity to understand their movement. The feminine and masculine understood as a movement towards self-development by acquiring new qualities in the process, is in my opinion, the right way to come to terms with the mystery of both of these elements within ourselves and in society as well. Since in movement there is not conflict, we can be something and yet have the germ of something else growing inside. *We are not self-contained final products, but entities in permanent development.*

Yes, we need feminine and masculine qualities in society, in business and within ourselves. Now having said that, no-one, not even scientists, can guarantee that a woman, just because she is born a woman, is going to bring love, nurturing and communication skills to any given position. On the other hand, men can finally study arts and humanities and not worry about being the sole provider in the household.

It took too long for individual men and women to be able to choose for themselves instead of by the guidelines of the role society imposed on them. Let us be careful, since gains can be easily lost and society may decide once again what is best fit for individuals by categorizing them as a group and not by their individual capacities.

4 Social roles and women's fights

The debate over women's role in society, based in assumed women's attributes, has pushed women over centuries into particular functions in society. However, history shows a permanent fight by many individual women who have refused to accepted their assigned role and fought to act in society with their full self, regardless of social conventions, as we can see in the examples of Jeanne D' Arc, Jane Austen, Mme Curie, among many others.

Political liberation was the final battle of women's fight for their rights, it began with women's right to vote, in England in 1919, a year later in the USA, in Spain in 1931 and in France in 1945, and the last decade has seen an impressive number of women at the highest level of political representation in countries such as Germany (Angela Merkel) Chile (Michelle Bachelett), Argentina (Cristina Fernández de Kirchner), Brazil (Dilma Rousseff), and in past decades prime ministers such as Benazir Bhutto in Pakistan or Tansu Çiller in Turkey. The fact is that today it is not difficult to visualize a women president in most parts of the world.

The economic fight has also shown a slow but steady progress; In 1880 England allowed married women to legally possess their own property and, as Fisher describes, economic emancipation speeded up after the Great Depression. The number of women in the workforce doubled between 1870 and 1940, and again during World War II. By 1950 even married women had been pulled into the American workforce, and by 1970 43 percent of women over the age of 16 in the USA were holding paying jobs. By 2010 according to the last Catalyst report, women comprised 40 percent of the total world workforce (1.2 billion out of 2.9 billion).[4]

Yet, although the figures show an impressive development during the twentieth century, equality has not been achieved. Women constitute only 19 percent of members of parliament worldwide, they hold only 10–20 percent of management positions and 5 percent of senior management positions; there are only 15 women CEOs in the Fortune 500 and only 28 in the Fortune 1000, and just nine companies led by women in the *Financial Times* Europe 500. Partly this is caused by external factors, but also women still face internal barriers that hinder their progression in the public sphere.[5]

However, and although the path to equality is not yet reached, most barriers have fallen for western women and progressively in other geographical areas. Women can choose a professional life and, even more important, women can finally occupy the public space, denied to them over the centuries.

To be able to understand the progression it is helpful to overview briefly a few episodes of history and the spaces that women have occupied in them.

Primitive collectivities

The story begins around 30,000 years ago as *Homo sapiens* in Africa began forming communities. By 9000 BC, men and women had settled along the Tigris and Euphrates river basin, and by 8000 BC they had started domesticating animals. Most anthropologists believe that these communities divided work, with men being the hunters and women the gatherers, both of which were crucial functions for survival, and both activities were performed outside the home. (Fisher 1999, pp. 170–176).

The Agricultural Revolution

Fisher highlights how, by 4000 BC, the invention of the plow and intensive agriculture had destroyed the balance between men and women, diminishing woman's productive role and thus her bargaining power:

> As the agrarian tradition took hold across much of the world, men become the primary producers. Soon they also came to own land, the livestock, the crops, valuable commodities they could convert into wealth and influence. With time, the farming men in Europe, North Africa and Asia also become the warriors, craftsmen, scribes, priests, traders, heads of households and heads of state. (Fisher 1999, p. 173).

As cultivated fields spread along the river banks of the ancient world, former gatherers were drawn into new kinds of domestic work: spinning, weaving, feeding cows and pigs, making soap and bread, and rearing a lot more children to help do the chores and defend the property. This situation lasted pretty much up to modern times; women, although less educated in craftsmanship than men, were nevertheless slowly growing into positions of higher productive activity during the Middle Ages, and as Fisher points out, by 1300 some female Londoners were reported to be grocers, bakers, brewers, and hat-makers.

The Enlightenment and the liberation of reason

Another major change that had important implications for the role of women and the space reserved to them in society occurred in the seventeenth century. As Soledad Murillo explains, the age of reason and individual liberation was reserved for men, and in fact only a few of them (Murillo, 2006).

The feudal state was in its final decline, a new society was being built with a new organization based on a centralized state and the return of the public space, which had been lost since the era of the classical Greeks. Along with this new space emerged a new kind of relationship between people and the state, based on the "social contract" that regulated these new spaces through new rules for society. The new contract defined the rights and obligations of free individuals, recognized according to their degree of economic independence and their capacity for reason; and thus women did not qualify, since they could not legally own property and their capacities for reason were presumed to be inferior to those of men.

Take for instance the words of Locke:

> but the husband and wife, though they have but one common concern, yet having different understandings, will unavoidably sometimes have different wills too; it therefore being necessary that the last determination, i. e. the rule, should be placed somewhere; it naturally falls to the man's share, as the abler and the stronger.[6]

The new society that was being developed gave the individual a new legal status of "citizenship." The *Encyclopédie, ou dictionnaire raisonné des sciences, des arts et des métiers* published from 1751 to 1772, is an ambitions work designed to expand the concepts of the Enlightenment that aimed to liberate men and enhance the progress of humanity. It reserved the status of citizen for men only and clearly specified that women and children would only be granted the condition of citizen as members of the family of a proper citizen.[7] Subsequently, the Napoleonic Code of 1804, which was imposed throughout continental Europe, declared women legally incompetent, since responsibility was directly linked to reason (Murillo 2006, p. 47).

The Murillo thesis implies that the ideas of the Enlightenment intended to liberate reason from the powers of nature, and since nature was projected on to women, women needed to be out of the public space. Each gender would find their role in the new society, men in the newly created public space and women in the domestic space, where their assumed character, closer to nature, would be put to its best use; their changing emotional state and their connection with the earth, plants and healing, would be naturally developed by the nurturing of children (Murillo p. 45).

The Industrial Revolution

Women, thus, were assigned to the domestic space where they could develop their natural talents. The domestic space was also shared with men working in different arts and crafts, until the Industrial Revolution moved this type of work from the domestic space into factories. Therefore, as the Industrial Revolution emerged, the domestic space was no longer the main space of productive activity and increasingly its function became the space in which children could grow healthy and be morally educated, and where man could find a private place to think and rest.

However, the Industrial Revolution also witnessed an increase in the number of women working outside of the home. By 1830, American women began to leave the farm for domestic service and low-paying factory jobs, although still in low numbers; for example in 1870, 14 percent of American women of working age were employed outside the home, and most of these were unmarried (Fisher 1999, p. 174). Thus, women began to take on remunerated productive work, and thus their bargaining power in society began to rise. John Stuart Mill was one of the first intellectuals to press for the rights of women to work and act inside the public space, for the sake of their own self-esteem as well as out of respect for their husband, and so that they could help build a more complete society.

After the First World War, women increasingly took on clerical jobs outside the home. By 1920, 20 percent of clerical jobs in the USA were filled by women. The Women's Liberation movement helped to conquer new spaces for women, both in the public and private spheres, moving them away from their former confinement to the domestic space.

The twentieth century, particularly in the west but also in other geographical areas, has clearly been the century of women's liberation and their conquest of the public space, and today a woman has more options to be whatever she wants to be. However as the options increase, so does the difficulty of making decisions, since decisions entail tradeoffs. *No one said it was going to be easy!* Today the fight is changed but women still face difficulties in fulfilling their potentials, as we shall see in the next section.

5   Did something go wrong in the feminist movement?

During the 1990s the famous phrase "Having it all!" pushed many women to the limits of exhaustion as they performed a multitude of roles, leaving them caught between the stress of work and the guilt of not doing everything perfectly. They were afflicted by guilt about not being perfect mothers, perfect wives and perfect executives, as described accurately in the famous book by Silvia Hewlett (Hewlett, 2009) in which the author describes the difficulties of combining high-level work with family.

As a reaction in the last decade we have seen an important move towards more traditional positions, and many young women today do not want to risk the fulfillment of motherhood by taking on too-demanding careers, as the older generation did. Because of that, many young women have opted, if given the economic choice, to stay at home, or work reduced shifts as we see in some countries as Holland or Denmark, in which close to 80 percent of working mothers work part-time. Working part-time is perceived by many as having the worst of both worlds, since, because of lack of time, women still cannot perform their home responsibilities well, and often are passed over at work as they are perceived as not ambitious enough for high-responsibility tasks.

The two opposite models are seen in opposition in women's groups, which can be roughly divided into those that claim equality and those that defend the right to be different (Ramos 2003, p. 8). That is, some movements are still operating from a classically liberal point of view, asserting that women should have equal rights, since they are born equal, whereas, on the other side of the divide are feminist movements in which members, although they still want equal rights, highlight the fact that women are different and thus that it is natural to celebrate the feminine. This latter movement has also evolved to positions of hyperfeminism, looking to primitive theories of women as healers or seers, since they assumed to have a closer connection to nature and spirituality.

Choices for women still are affected by society's pressures. Some women who can afford to choose either to stay at home or have a career still engage in endless fights to justify their choices. If a women does not have children she may often spend countless hours justifying herself in social encounters and even to clients, which occasionally adds to an internal frustration of having waited too long to make the decision about having babies. On the other hand, women who have decided to stay home and to depend economically on their partners often have to fight against accusations of not being complete modern women, and to deal with a constant fear of being abandoned and thus having to start a new working life in a hostile working market, one that does not see women over 40 in a good light.

But, above all, the most important missing factors in women's lives, whatever choice they make, are *space* and *time:* space to be on their own, to be able to reflect in solitude, away from children and multiple responsibilities; and time to be able to pursue their potential to its fullest. Time is the scarcest resource in today's crazy life, and thus is probably also the main problem for men. However, women's free time is normally dedicated to family chores, and her space is still shared, either the kitchen, or the common areas of the house, where she can survey her children.

In her essay "A Room of One's Own" Virgina Woolf famously stated: "... the prosaic conclusion – that it is necessary to have five hundred a year and a room with a lock on the door if you are to write fiction or poetry" (Woolf 2004, p. 121). She refers to a salary as a means, not an end. Financial resources can empower women to free their minds and allow them to develop their intellect as writers or as what they were best fitted to do.

Women still need to to fight to be able to develop their fullest potentiality, and in this fight they can help men who also were limited by society to concrete roles, frustrating in many cases their potentialities. The fight over time and space can only be won if fought together, women and men combining to redesign a society in which both can better fulfill their capacities, developing to their fullest both their female and male characteristics.

The twenty-first century, the time for men's liberation

The roles assigned to women and men are in my opinion, equally restrictive for both. Men probably have more freedoms, and more importantly, they have economic rights and the access to the public sphere; however, they are also trapped in their role of being the sole provider and this also limits their ability to choose.

Virginia Woolf described how society's imposition of roles also limited men:

> True, they have money and power but only at the cost of harboring in their breast an eagle, a vulture, forever tearing the liver out and plucking at the lungs – the instinct of possession, the rage for acquisitions which drives them to desire other peoples' fields and goods perpetually ... watch in the spring sunshine the stockbroker and the great barrister going indoors to make money and more money when it is a fact that five-hundred a year will keep one alive in the sunshine ... And, as I realized these drawbacks, by degrees fear and bitterness modified themselves into pity and toleration; and then in a year or two, pity and toleration went, and the greatest release of all came, which is freedom to think of things in themselves (Woolf 2004, p. 44).

The twentieth century was undoubtedly the century of women, but perhaps the twenty-first will be the century of men's liberation? Men are increasingly demanding their rights to fatherhood and a role in the household not merely as providers of food or helpers in with the daily chores – they are searching for a deeper meaning of fatherhood.

But there are still many barriers to pull down, external and internal. There are not that many men who are staying at home while their female partners work, or decide to quit their careers and follow women as they pursue international positions; and if they do any of these things society still looks down on them, and these men still have to repeatedly hear well-intentioned speeches about how bad it is for children not to have their mothers as their nurturers.

As women have enriched the working space during the twentieth century, men can enrich the domestic space in the twenty-first. The proliferation of emotional intelligence courses for men, especially those that help them touch base with their emotional being, is a good sign that men are headed in the right direction and that they are realizing the need to connect with their emotional side.

We live in a period in transition. If they wish, women can now occupy the domestic and the public space, and, increasingly, the private space as well. Men are also in a process of trying to understand their multiple roles in society and in their private lives. However, the traditional role that was reserved exclusively to men has been lost to them, and yet new roles are still not quite open to them. So in this process we are all suffering: women from stress and the difficult decisions they have to make, and men from the lack of roles to fill.

Hopefully, the twenty-first century will bring the development of a society in which men and women, individually as well as with their partners, will decide the roles they want to occupy: roles that will satisfy them and their families, and thus enable them to carry out more fulfilling lives as individuals who can enrich the society they live in.

6   Gender identity in the business context

As we saw in the previous chapter, communities are not only defined by members' origins but increasingly are made up of members acting on individual choices and aspiration to belong. When a company develops a new product targeted for women there is usually a group of clients who thinks it is a good idea and buys it; however, there is also a large group that will not feel identified with the product. The challenge for companies is to balance the risk of opportunities to develop target-specific products and developing programs specifically targeting women.

All women are categorized from childhood onwards, and this categorization implies certain norms and behaviors. Some not all, choose to act and participate in a community of aspiration of women and a particular gender role which they identify with. And thus from a homogenous community of origin, women have moved into a myriad of communities of aspiration, some of which can also be women's communities, each with a different set of values.

Working in a women-only environment is a rarity in western society, where it is often seen as too traditional. However, in other societies, mostly in communitarian ones, working in a women-only environment can be a great help to the individual effort of self-development, as we can see in the case of Dana women's banking (Case 3).

The case of Dana shows us a situation in which position of both women employees and women clients was due to a choice. A choice that is restricted in a society that still is separated by sex, the categorization of sexes and their roles in society. Many women in this traditional society decided to move up, and they managed to advance in their self-development and independence without breaking the link with their origins and their societies. In this case, the community of origin is very close to the community of aspiration, but it is nevertheless a community of aspiration in which the women advance in their personal identities while they act in a community they truly want to be part of and help to improve.

7   Third movement: Resolving gender archetypes: Rediscovering the meaning of giving by learning how to receive

As philosophers say, truth is everywhere and so in everything said there is a fragment of truth. It is therefore a question of integrating different truths into larger frames.

The myth of Snow White does have some content that is valid today, but to find it we need to reinterpret the myth through our modern perspective. The myth of the hero has not changed over time, but the myth of woman has been totally undermined because the values it represented were not well appreciated in a society where the masculine values were in the ascendant. Therefore, the feminine myths were altered to mirror the masculine ones.

And, thus, this is perhaps a good moment to revisit the feminine myths and understand their hidden values, looking beyond their patriarchal interpretation – I do not want to ask women to stay at home waiting for their gallant prince (our common unconscious is a bit more sophisticated, I hope!). The wait that Snow White goes through can also represent a conscious action, not a passive surrender but an openness to receive and be fertilized by what it comes to us. To receive is as important as to give. Only the one who has been capable of receiving will be able to innovate, because this act will regenerate his or her self with new ideas and new visions.

In a cultural tradition in which giving is always considered a generous act and receiving an egotistic act, we have lost one of the greatest generosities of the human condition, the generosity of accepting the other,

Figure 3.1 Yin and Yang. Yin and Yang Each contains the seed of the other, which is why we see a black spot of Yin in the white Yang and vice versa. They do not merely replace each other but actually become each other through the constant flow of the universe

described often in poetry as the act of giving yourself away to the other and so the other becomes yourself. As in the Poem by St. John of the Cross, "Amada en el Amado Transformada" ("The lover transformed in the beloved").

In our society action does not leave room for reflection, and we only receive something in exchange for something else. If we have lost the capacity to receive, then what is left to give? The remains are an empty container, with only mud and filth left behind, which are better no to share.

I believe the reinterpretation of feminine myths can help men and women to move forward in the twenty-first century.

Case 3   Abu Dhabi: Dana: In the footsteps of Khadijah al Kubra[8]

Women banking at the Abu Dhabi Islamic Bank (ADIB)

Written by Fatimah M. Iliasu and Celia de Anca

Introduction

Salha is very satisfied with her decision to join Abu Dhabi Islamic Bank four years ago. She remembers how when she had just graduated with a degree in economics, she received several job offers to work for different banks in the UAE, including one of the top international banks and the main commercial bank in Abu Dhabi. She did not hesitate to accept the offer from the Abu Dhabi Islamic Bank (ADIB) because of its reputation as a modern and professional institution. She had two other reasons: the first was the fact that ADIB was an Islamic Bank; and the second that she would be working in women-only branches. "Working for ADIB makes me feel closer to my community," she states, "it makes my family happy, and most of all I feel I can live my religion in a complete way." Salha believes that Dana, the women's division at ADIB, positively impacts all aspects of the business:

- **The relationship with fellow colleagues:** "We are like a family here, for example employees can openly discuss their personal problems. When they need some time off, they will have greater difficulties to have these conversations with male managers."

- **The relationship with customers:** "We work within our traditions of hospitality and treat our clients as part of the family, often our women clients bring us breakfast or chocolates and come only to chat with us and to openly discuss their financial queries."
- **The innovation of products:** "We spend so much time with our clients, we know them well and we are very aware of their needs. This is the reason why we are successfully creating new products adapted to our clients' needs, as in the case of Banun."

However, most of all, Salha feels *she can be anything she wants to be* because Dana enables her to fulfill her professional dreams. Salha Omer Dana Bateen, Branch Manager, says: "Muslim women are often perceived wrongly. Dana illustrates that Muslim women can be anything they want to be; they can work, they can became directors or anything they want and show that they can be equal at work with men."

The foundation: In the footsteps of Khadijah, women in business in the UAE

Muslim businesswomen have in their cultural tradition a model for a strong woman in the figure of Khadijah.

Khadijah was a member of the Arab tribe of Quraish. Born in the sixth century to the Banu Hashim family, she was the daughter of Khuwaylid and Fatimah. Her father was a wealthy merchant, a caravan trader of goods between al Hijaz in present-day Saudi Arabia, and other regions such as Yemen and the Mediterranean coastlands of Syria.

Khadijah successfully managed her father's inheritance and became the owner of some of the largest caravans. The Prophet Muhammad was a reputable merchant recognized for his business acumen and his honesty, which is said to have given him the name of al Amin. Khadijah had heard of his reputation and hired him as her agent to take care of her caravans to Syria and to other regions.

Khadijah was 40 years old and Prophet Muhammad was 25 years old when they got married. She was the mother of all his children except one, and the first to accept and believe in the message of the Prophet Muhammad, and thus she is the first woman to convert to Islam.

Khadijah is a role model in the Islamic tradition. Muslim women have always managed their wealth independently.

> Islamic jurisprudence clearly forbids a husband mixing his wealth with that of his wife. Since it is the man's duty to bear all financial expenses of the family, even if he is poor, he is never allowed to take the woman's wealth. Women thus enjoy full freedom to manage their finances independently. (Dr. Osaid Kailani, Global head of Shari'a, Executive Vice President of the Shari'a Division of Abu Dhabi Islamic Bank.)

In fact, there are many recorded cases throughout Islamic history of women resorting to the protection of the law and to judges to enforce their right to manage their own wealth without any interference, not even from their husbands or family members.[9]

It is not surprising or uncommon to see women in wealthy countries such as the UAE contribute significantly to their country's economy as investors and as economic agents. According to a recent BCG report, "women control about 22 per cent of the wealth in the Middle East."[10]

The number of businesswomen in the UAE has increased during the past years, reaching about 11,000 in 2010, which has helped the country's economy grow by pumping huge sums of money, estimated at about 14 billon Dirhams, into the economy. These businesswomen manage about 14 percent of local investments and own 33 percent of the vital projects of the country. Banking sources state that Emirati women own about 25 percent of the private wealth in the country and that their funds constitute 30 percent of bank deposits, while the value of their savings accounts is about $100 billion.

The Current Minister of Foreign Trade, Sheikha Lubna al Qassimi is a model for many young women, and she encourages other women to be whatever they want to be. As most barriers are removed, they need to also find the inner strength to fulfill their dreams and overcome their internal barriers.

Women banking at Abu Dhabi Islamic Bank:

Islamic banking in the UAE

"In Islam, profits are only acceptable if they either come from work or from ideas; anything else should not be rewarded. This is why interest and all speculative practices are forbidden in Islam," says Saeed Al Lootah.

"Therefore, an Islamic bank becomes either agent or partner in any commercial transaction."

Believing in an economy without usury and speculation, Saeed Bin Ahmed Al-Lootah (Saaed Al Lootah) founded the first modern Islamic bank in the UAE in Dubai, in 1975. Now, at the age of 90 he has gone back to the simplicity of life in the desert. He remembers his youth at sea, where he spent four to six months a year searching for pearls with his father, Husain Ibn Naser al Lootah, who was a merchant and a poet. Then in 1956, taking the opportunities offered by the new wealth of oil discovered in his country, he established the first construction company in Dubai, which soon became one of the UAE's most important holdings. After founding the first Islamic bank, he also founded in the 1980s and 1990s a number of Islamic foundations, training and educational centers.

He writes from his experience on the three main stages of life: the first stage of real wealth, since birth until the age of maturity at 15; the second phase of real strength from puberty up to the age of 40, "where humans have the real responsibility to manage life and participate with their community in building the earth"; and third, the stage of real experience, "it is the product gained through the observations and actual experiences during the life of man; some of these experiences are useful and may benefit people and some of them are not."[11] He firmly advocates the need to heal the most urgent problems of society through the true application of Islamic economics and finance.

Saeed's Lootah's Dubai Islamic Bank was the only Islamic bank in the UAE until the incorporation of the Abu Dhabi Islamic Bank in 1997. Since 2000, new Islamic banks have been created through a conversion from conventional to Islamic, or through incorporation of new banks. In 2010 there were eight Islamic banks in the UAE, representing 15.8 percent of total loans, and advances of the banking system equal approximately US$ 43.3 Billion (the UAE banking system is made-up of 23 national banks, 22 foreign banks, and 6 GCC banks).[12]

The majority of Islamic banks operate with women-only sections; some have even branded the women's section as a separate brand (such as Johara in the Dubai Islamic Bank, Dana in the Abu Dhabi Islamic Bank, Al Reem Ladies Banking in the Emirates Islamic Bank, and Amirah in the Dubai Bank). Others, such as the Noor Islamic Bank, operate with women-only sections although they have not created a separate brand for women. Increasingly, conventional banks are also opening women-only sections.

There is no difference between the role of women and the role of men in Islamic economics, finance and in Islamic banking. In fact, I would love to see a bank totally managed by women to prove that there is no difference in their minds and to challenge those who do not believe it. ... From the very beginning when we founded the first Islamic bank in 1975, we opened a section for women clients, run by women employees, separated from men fulfilling the Islamic precepts, separated but not different. (Saeed Bin Ahmed Al Lootah.)

Abu Dhabi Islamic Bank

Abu Dhabi Islamic Bank was established in May 1997. It was listed on the Abu Dhabi Stock Exchange in November 2000 and has a presence in the UAE, Egypt, Iraq and Bosnia-Herzegovina.

The bank's total income is distributed in: Islamic commercial banking (contributing 64 percent, growing annually by 6 percent to AED 2.57 billion (US\$£700 million)); private banking (contributing 10 percent); capital markets, (contributing 15 percent); and real estate, (contributing 10 percent). The shareholders are Emirates International Investment Company with UEA 40.66 percent, Abu Dhabi Investment Council with 7.61 percent, and the public with 51.73 percent.[13] ADIB was awarded the Best Islamic Bank award in 2010 by the Banker Middle East Industry Awards 2010.

> Islamic Banks do not only offer Islamic products, the whole environment of the Bank internally and externally as well as the way services and products are offered need to be as Shari'a compliant as the products offered. It is what our customers expect, and this is why they trust us. ... Both male and female customers will then trust their financial operations to the Islamic Bank ADIB, not only for financial advice, but also to ensure that their financial operations are in accordance with the principles of Shari'a. (Dr. Osaid Kailani, Global Head of Shari'a, Executive Vice President, Shari'a Division of Abu Dhabi Islamic Bank.)

Women employees at ADIB

As of 2011, ADIB has 1568 employees, of whom 576 are women. Women are employed mostly in the women-only sections; however they work alongside men in all central services as well as in the general and top management services. There are currently four women in the senior management team.

Living according to their Islamic faith is common to most of the women employees of ADIB. Working in women-only sections of ADIB enables many female ADIB employees to work with the acceptance of their husbands and family members.

> I feel I am in an Islamic environment by working in a women-only division. I had offers from other banks with higher salaries, but I refused because I send part of my salary to my mother who accepts it because I work in an Islamic institution. If I worked in a conventional bank, my mother would not accept any part of my salary, because she would consider it unlawful. I feel proud that I can help my mother. (Alia Ahmed al Ali, Priority Banking Manager from Al Ain)

Most women employees feel they can really contribute to pushing the bank forward because they feel closer to their clients and their needs. "I feel really comfortable working with women, I feel I understand my clients better, they trust us better than the men, and we can get closer to fulfilling their needs, because they speak clearly and openly to us," says Sheikha Al Qubaisi, Relationship Manager in Priority Banking.

Women clients

ADIB created Dana in May 2010. As of April 2011, the total number of ADIB/Dana female customers is 162,610, divided as follows: 121,000 Classic, 3909 Gold, 960 Diamond, 38,000 covered card holders and financing products.

"The reason I chose a women-only Bank is because of my religious beliefs. I prefer to be in a women-only environment separated from men," says Futoon Riyad Al Masri, ADIB high net worth client.

Young female customers, unlike their mothers, do not mind going to a branch that also serves male customers. However, they still like the idea of women-only branches.

> I opened an account in the regular ADIB section since, unlike my mother, I am not uncomfortable using a branch that serves both women and men; however, now that Dana exists I would probably prefer to open an account with Dana because Dana gives you a sense of identity, it makes you feel special, like a pearl! I believe it is a great idea to create the Dana brand for women only. (A young ADIB client, in the Sharjah branch.)

Women customers often go to the bank for financial advice and for Shari'a advice.

> Our customers feel they can trust us not only to take care of their finances but also to ensure they adhere to their religious values in their financial life. For example, when our customers choose our covered cards, they feel they are protecting their families because the card will not work in places where alcohol or pornography are sold. (Sheikha Al Qubaisi, Relationship Manager in Priority Banking.)

> Customers also ask for advice on whether a certain purchase will be acceptable from a Shari'a point of view. For example, a woman came yesterday asking whether it was Islamically acceptable to buy a cell phone SIM card with a special number for AED 800,000. We asked the Shari'a department and we will give their answer to our client. (Maryam Hamad Al Darmaki, Branch Manager Al Ain Ladies Branch.)

Women use all of the ADIB banking services and products, as depositors, investors and, credit users. Women are increasingly asking for financial resources to initiate their business ventures. Often non-Muslim clients open accounts in a women-only branch of an Islamic bank because they enjoy the atmosphere and the networking activities offered by the women's division to their customers.

Product innovation in Dana

As at 2011, ADIB has a total of 60 branches, 23 of which are women only branches, and or branches that provide women banking services to customers. Women-only branches have the same opening hours as the regular branches, however since 2009, the new brand called "Dana" integrated all the women divisions.

The Dana brand name was inspired by the meaning of the word Dana (pearl) in Arabic. Pearls are very important in UAE culture, because pearl fishing was the first means of living in the UAE before the discovery of oil. Dana (pearl) is a very popular name for women in the region and it is the symbol of the Dana customer used in their branches.

The new brand Dana infused fresh life to the women's division. Before Dana was launched, Nawal Bayari, the business head for ladies banking and a member of the ADIB management team, led a committee that conducted focus groups and research to understand what improvements could be made in the women's banking segment of ADIB. As result of this research, some new services were introduced and new products like the Banun account were created.

Women employees have realized that one of the unfulfilled needs of their clients, especially divorced women, was opening accounts in the name of their children without the signature of their husbands, as required by law. Once this need was detected, managers consulted with the Shari'a division who in turn sought the advice of the Shari'a Board, and after some discussions they agreed to create a special product called Banun. This is a special saving account for children, and Dana will be the first in the United Arab Emirates to offer this special type of account. Banun enables women to open a savings account for their children without requiring the signature of the father of the children.

Nawal Bayari the Business Head of Women's Banking at ADIB has great hopes for ADIB Dana, Banun, and for product development targeted towards women customers:

> The Banun account adds value to women's banking, and it is a great product for ADIB Dana. ADIB Dana will succeed Insha'Allah with the help of the ADIB brand name, and the creativity of the team that is working on developing this segment of product innovation for women.

Conclusions: Identity and belonging in women-only banking

Traditionally, banks in western countries have viewed women as an important but secondary segment for targeting purposes, with segments composed mainly of males at the forefront.

In countries such as Spain, women were only allowed to open accounts without the signature of their husbands well into the second half of the twentieth century. Before then, women needed the approval of a male (husband, father or legal tutors) to open an account, receive their father's inheritance, or travel abroad. Some hundred years earlier, as we see in Jane Austen's books, women could lose their property rights to male members of the family if they were not married.

Although, fortunately, things have changed somewhat in most European countries and in the USA, it is not coincidental that banks still do not target women as primary clients. The perception still is that while women play the lead role in controlling household spending and in influencing family financing decisions, they are not the account holders or the primary targets. Typically men still make the decisions on which bank to take a loan from, where to invest assets and where to buy insurance etc.

A Forte report stated that banks from all over the world, both in the west and in Muslim-majority countries, have discovered that women are an important and undertapped banking niche. Thus, they are reaching out to women.[14] Some interesting cases include:

- **Caixa Geral de Depósitos:** This bank publishes *Caixa Woman*, a magazine with a circulation of 20,000 copies. A section at the end deals with personal finance issues, with emphasis on the ways Caixa can meet the needs of their consumers. The bank attributes their success to issuing more than 2000 new Caixa Woman credit and debit cards and collecting more than €10 million in deposits directly from this initiative.
- **Raiffeisen:** Austria's first bank for women was recently opened. All the employees are female, and they are instructed to thoroughly explain products and services to their customers.
- **Mujer Banorte**: This is the first bank to target the female segment of the Mexican market. The services they provide include insurance for illnesses common to women, including cervical cancer.
- **Legacy Bank:** This is a relatively new start-up bank in affluent Scottsdale, Arizona in the US, which specifically targets affluent women through its business banking and private banking operations.
- **ABN Amro:** have just launched "Lady Delight" in Holland, an investment fund for women, managed by women. Lady Delight invests in three major funds also managed by women: Odin Europa, JP Morgan's UK Smaller Companies and Morgan Stanley Latin America.
- **Eva Capital:** This is a UK-based venture capital firm investing women's funds in women's projects in a Shari'a compliant manner.
- **LADIESFUND®, Pakistan:** was established in 2007 as an initiative to provide financial security to women and to promote and train women entrepreneurs. It aims to integrate the entrepreneurial needs based on the economic and social aspects of the local communities, with respect to greater women participation in the workforce.

As we saw in the Dana case, Muslim women are free to independently use their own wealth as they deem fit. Therefore, it is not surprising to see that once women attain social freedom, they become successful financial agents and become widely recognized as a niche market in their local financial industry.

As the Dana case also illustrates, a strong feeling of identity and belonging between managers and customers can enhance innovation. In Dana, women employees feel they can succeed without breaking away from their tradition and values, which in turn empowers them towards a more active role in product development, because they are fully aware of their client's needs and have the technical and leadership capabilities to transfer those needs to the appropriate departments at the institution.

The challenge for the future is how to serve the increasingly growing number of women entrepreneurs in the UAE, who so far are not fully using the resources available to them in banks.

PART II

Identities in action

CHAPTER 4

Identity and the market

Is there life outside the market?
Fourth movement: Identity and the market: finding an equilibrium between labor, work, and action, in and outside the market

1   Is there life outside the market?

Many of us, particularly those living in urban areas, wake up every morning to go out into "the public space" and find our designated place within the boundaries of our jobs where we perform our productive roles. Production is periodically measured by analytical tools that often have a direct effect on the salary we receive each month, which allows us to "make a living."

After a hard day's work we go home to "our private space" where we consume goods or services: food, television programs, films, computer games and sometimes even books.

Some of us are lucky enough to have some free time at the end of the week that we normally spend in different consuming activities: gym, cinema, theatre, hair salon, restaurants, bars, or the shopping mall, where many families spend a large part of their weekends.

Thus many of us, the lucky ones that have a job and some resources, spend most of our time in the market, either as producers or as consumers. It is increasingly difficult to think of things to do that do not involve producing or consuming. Even if we dream of winning the lottery and thus become free from necessity, most of our dreams of gaining freedom are intimately related to consumption: going to a desert island, taking a tour around the world, etc. As Santiago Alba suggests, the market has become our only public space, and as such it is where our society reproduces itself, where human beings recognize themselves as free, where they exchange their symbols and elaborate the categories of their relationships with themselves and with others (Alba 1995, p. 31).

The market by its common definition is a physical space where merchandises and services are regularly exchanged. The question is: has the market ceased to be a space *we go to* and instead has become our shelter?

2   Where we produce, what we produce, and for what purpose

Where we produce: The confusion between the public and private realms

What is the line between the public and private? Our society certainly is confused about this issue, as illustrated by the number of lawsuits about breaking into the private life that we see in our courts every day. But the confusion gets further complicated when for example, we read some of the tweets of politicians or business people, or even our own friends, where professional opinions are mixed with personal ones, or personal activities get mixed with professional interventions. For many, it is perfectly normal to include in a professional CV their marital status, number of children and sexual orientation, while others refuse to give that information since for them it is a part of "their private lives" that should not be mingled with their professional skills. Who is right? And who is entitled to say what is the right thing to do?

I used to apply an exercise in my class "Women and Leadership" which consisted of separating the activities we perform into the different areas of our lives – public, domestic and private – and then taking a look at the priority we give to each one, as well as the energy and time spent on them. The problem for many students was separating their activities, since for many the domestic, the public and the private are mixed and it is increasingly difficult to decide what belongs to what realm.

As humans, we perform a number of activities, some in the public and some in the private realm, but we are becoming confused as to which of our activities should be seen by everyone (that is the meaning of public after all), and which ones we should keep out from the public eye (which is, of course, the meaning of private).

This issue is really complex because our society has reversed the original meaning of the public and private that has been accepted since the beginning of human civilization, in particular within western civilization and subsequently in capitalist society. For the early Greeks it was clear that only activities that had *a common purpose* should enter the realm of the public, and all the activities related to private affairs should be left outside, including economic activities. "No activity that served only the purpose of making a living, of sustaining only the life process, was permitted to enter the political realm, and this at the grave risk of abandoning trade and manufacture to the industriousness of slaves and foreigners." (Arendt 1958, 1998 p. 37) In the Classical Greek approach, the public space referred to common interest for all, not what they all shared due to their sameness (their private affairs), and the public space was where each man could contribute his uniqueness to the objective of improving the aspects of life everyone had in common. Therefore, the public realm was reserved for individuality, for free men who, existing beyond the urges of necessity, could show who they really were. Being heard and seen by others derives significance from the fact that everyone sees and hears from a different vantage point, and it is that variety of visions that leads to the enrichment of *the common*.

Private space during Classical Greek times was reserved for the performance of activities that served the purpose of maintaining biological life; these activities were thus performed inside the household by women and slaves. That is the reason why only free citizens could participate in the public space (meaning they were men, had property and their necessities of life were covered).

In fact, even during the Classical Greek era, public space began to change when the Agora increasingly started to host more "market activities" rather than the "political life" that in principle it was designed for. With the arrival of Christianity the public space, understood as the place that free citizens share in common, was replaced by the spiritual space, where the community could meet and share a common experience; the public space reserved for "free men" was replaced by the church.

The public space in our modern society has been taken over by the market as the place of common exchange, where we exchange the products of labor and also, breaking with tradition, where we display both our private affairs and productive activities.

In Hannah Arendt's words:

> The emergence of society – the rise of housekeeping, its activities, problems and organizational devices – from the shadowy interior of the household into the light of the public sphere, has not only blurred the old borderline between the private and the political, it has also changed beyond recognition the meaning of the two terms and their significance for the life of the individual and the citizen (Arendt 1958, 1998, p. 38).

What we produce? Human activities

The different uses of these spaces and the changes of the public and private places from Classical Greek society to the mass society we have today can be understood by analyzing the basic activities of people, together with their value in the context of society and the place in which they were performed.

Most philosophers since antiquity have divided human activities by rank, starting with the lower activities whose purpose is to maintain biological life and which we share with other animals, to the higher ones fit only for human beings due to the very fact of being human. As Rothbard suggests, "Plato saw no problem, however, in morally ranking the various occupations, with philosophy, of course, ranking highest and labor or trade being sordid and ignoble." (Rothbard 1995, p. 12)

Not all civilizations had the same disdain for economic activities. Ibn Khaldun,[1] the so called first sociologist, who lived in Tunisia in the fourteenth century, illustrated how the Islamic civilization praised commerce and manufacture as the activities of civilized men, as opposed to the primary mode of making a living based on agriculture and livestock (Ibn Khaldun 1989, pp. 232–237). He considered the capacity for thinking, especially scientific thinking, to be the highest of human abilities; however, he did not include it in the ways of making a living, but rather as an activity that was separate from economic activities.

The basic tasks of keeping people alive, such as domestic chores, were despised by most civilizations and decreed to be the proper activity of women or slaves, and they received little attention in the literature of our greatest thinkers. Of course there were some exceptions, for instance a respect for cooking can be appreciated in some of the great recipes by the philosopher Ibn Rushd[2] on how to cook eggplants (but again, that was more from the healthy perspective of a doctor, rather than as a glorification of the task of daily cooking to keep oneself alive).

Hannah Arendt is probably the theorist who best understood how human activities were perceived by ancient and modern thinking, as well as the different places where these activites were performed. She describes the three human activities in the *vita activa* as opposed to *vita contemplativa* (Arendt 1958, 1998, p. 7).

- **Labor:** the cyclical activity related to the biological process of living; its production is bound to be consumed. Its purpose is thus to keep the biological bodies alive, and therefore does not leaves any traces per se.
- **Work:** that activity whose purpose is either to ease the tasks of labor, or materialize the results of action. The purpose of the production of work is to make *objects*, which are meant to be used (as opposed to being consumed), and their permanence in the world goes beyond the act using them.

- **Action:** that which makes individuals reveal themselves as unique and different from others, its productions being speech and deeds. Its results are shared among a web of humans, and do not leave any concrete product, unless it is materialized by the act of work into a specific physical object.

We can analyze each activity in more detail.

Labor

In my childhood I remember every meal would end by my mother saying how much work she had spent for so little a reward, since every meal would be finished quickly and then what was left was to do the cleaning and prepare for the next meal.

The frustration of labor, whether it is cleaning, making food, washing clothes, or any of the other activities that keep us alive and in good shape, is exactly that its function is to be consumed, to merely reproduce the cycle of nature, to be repetitive and short-lasting. Labor, following Arendt, would also include the cyclical activities keeping humans alive, such as farming or livestock, which are just as frustrating as the activities of the housewife, in the sense that they are cyclical, mechanical, and their results are consumed without leaving any traces per se.

In modern times, after the Industrial Revolution, labor moved from the farms to industrial centers, where the invention of the division of labor grew directly from the labor process, meaning a division of tasks into similar and cyclical moves whose performance did not need any specific skills, their main characteristic being exchangeability – not the distinctive skills of the workers but a sameness. And so, in Arendt's view, the process of labor increasingly substituted for the need for high specialization of workers.

While specialization of work is essentially guided by the finished product itself, whose nature it is to require different skills which then are pooled and organized together, division of labor, on the contrary, presupposes the qualitative equivalence of all single activities for which no special skill is required (Arendt 1958, 1998, p. 123).

Work

The second main activity of human beings, the capacity to produce objects, was held in a higher esteem in ancient times; the objects made by artisans were sold in the marketplace, although as an activity it was also kept secluded in the private realms of the households of different artisans.

The results of work have a more lasting nature, the product will stay in the world for some time independently of its use: its making has thus a larger separation from the biological activity shared with animals, and is closer to what makes us humans different; therefore, it was supposed to have more worldly value.

> The work of our hands, as distinguished from the labor of our bodies – *Homo faber*, who makes and literally "works upon," as distinguished from the *Animal laborans*, which labors and "mixes with" – fabricates the sheer unending variety of things whose sum total constitutes human artifice... Their proper use does not cause them to disappear and they give the human artifice stability and solidity without which it could not be relied upon to house the unstable and mortal creature which is man. (Arendt 1958, 1998, p. 136)

Action

The very highest activity in ancient Greek times, action was the most respected and admired because it was the product of the mind. The capacities of speech and deed were performed in company, having both the qualities of equality and distinction, since action can only be performed among equals, and it is only among equals that each one can be different: "In acting and speaking, men show who they really are, reveal actively their unique personal identities and thus make their appearance in the human world." (Arendt 1958, 1998, p. 179). They do not produce objects; if their stories are being materialized they will need the capacity of reification, and thus would need the assistance of *Homo faber* to transform the story into a book, a painting or any other form of object. Arendt highlights the story of Socrates, about whose life we know much more than we do of the lives of Plato or Aristotle. Although Socrates never wrote anything, his essence was transmitted by his actions into the web of men that surrounded him.

Action needs people, since action is basically made up of two parts: the beginning, comprising a single person; and the achievement, in which others join. This activity is very different from what is now understood as leading, which requires someone who commands and others who execute (this activity was in Classical Greek times closer to the relationship of the master of a household to his slaves). Action in the public sphere was, on the contrary, a set of processes initiated by one free and equal man into which others joined together.

Action has always been considered dangerous by governments, and with good reason, since action has three main characteristics that tend to frustrate society: the unpredictability of its outcome; the irreversibility of the process; and the anonymity of its authors. Once actions begin, they lead to a series of processes that no one, not even the initiator, can have control over, and once they are in the common space the results cannot be predicted by anyone. Also, once they are initiated, actions cannot be reversed, since they have escaped the control of any single actor. Whoever initiates does only just that, and from that point forward the action begins to become an anonymous product of the common human experience.

Due to these dangers, action, and thus the public space, were gradually reduced and then eliminated altogether by different governments because of that degradation of politics to a means of obtaining higher ends (in antiquity the protection of the good man from the rule of the bad, in the Middle Ages the salvation of souls, and in modern times the protection of productivity and progress in society). And so, very soon even in Classical Greek times, action began to be replaced by making. Producing tangible things with the idea of utility, and productivity criteria rather than a meaning being a reason for the making, as opposed to bringing ideas together to move forward a common purpose.

What is the purpose of our activities: work to live or live to work?

It is frequently said that we live in a consumer society, and since labor and consumption are but two stages of the same process, imposed upon man by the necessities of life, this is only another way of saying that we live in a society of laborers.

> The point is not that for the first time in history laborers have been admitted to and given rights in the public realm, but that we have almost succeeded in leveling all human activities to the common denominator of securing the necessities of life and providing for their abundance. Whatever we do, we are supposed to do for the sake of "making a living"; such is the verdict of society, and the number of people, especially in the professions, who might challenge it has decreased rapidly. The only exception society is willing to grant is the artist, who, strictly speaking, is the only "worker" left in a laboring society ... From the standpoint of 'making a living' every activity unconnected with labor becomes a "hobby." (Arendt 1998, p. 128)

The speed with which production has accelerated in our modern society has turned former objects of utility into consumer objects, and the object's obsolescence begins immediately after being bought, thereby guaranteeing an endless growth and hence guaranteeing salaries for increasing numbers of people immigrating to the cities. Producing in order to foster consumption, and consuming in order to enable production, seems to have been the economic logic of the last century. As Arendt explained many years before "planned obsolescence" became a trendy concept:

> The endlessness of the laboring process is guaranteed by the ever-recurring needs of consumption, or, to put it in another way, the rate of use is so tremendously accelerated that the objective difference between use and consumption, between the relative durability of use objects and the swift coming and going of consumer goods, dwindles to insignificance ... So that a chair or a table is now consumed as rapidly as a dress and a dress used up almost as quickly as food. (Arendt 1998, p. 125)

The three activities that Arendt described as being fundamental in human lives – action (mental activities performed in the company of other humans); work (using our sensitivity and imagination to produce useful and /or beautiful objects) and labor (make a living in order to assure physical needs) have been increasingly reduced to the one of making a living – labor. In today's society, action is understood in terms of making, and in turn making is regarded as another form of laboring. The last stage of the laboring society, the society of job-holders, demands of its members a sheer automatic functioning, as if individual life had actually been submerged in the overall life process of the species, to the extent that even kings and presidents *hold a job* today, well paid but nonetheless a daily task in exchange for a salary.

The three activities are considered necessary as part of a human hierarchy. Labor keeps human beings alive but also imprisoned in the ever-recurring cycle of life processes. This activity is redeemed by the superior capacity of men to making lasting things. Work in that sense is what gives labor worth, but in turn work can only mean production, a means to an end, and thus it needs the human capacity to produce a story that will give a meaning to the things being produced.

For the majority of religions, the three activities of the *vita activa* are only the first precondition to the pursuit of higher activities, the *vita contemplativa*. If the spiritual element is eliminated, the human capacity for reflection becomes unnecessary and the ability to think is rendered subject to the ability to make things.

Hannah Arendt's argument ends with a positive observation: the fact that modern man has not lost his capacities; no matter what sociology, psychology, and anthropology will tell us about the social animal, men persist in making and acting, although these faculties are more and more restricted to the realm of the artist, and the capacity for action is more focused on science rather than on building together with other humans.

Human activities in the twenty-first century

Hannah Arendt's writings during the 1950s depicted with incredible clarity what society was transforming itself into, and her depth of vision is evidenced by the different ways that her analysis is still valid today. Most of our lives are being spent in the market, either as part of mass production or mass consumption, and everything that exists does so because of its capacity to be sold or bought in the market. As the anthropologist Aguado suggests, we are at the point that only boredom is left to us to protect our free time from the market: the capacity of standing still amazed at the flight of a fly (Alba 1995, p. 96).

However, our society has gained something that the Classical Greek society did not have: the ideal of equality among people. While it has by no means been completely achieved, the rise of a social middle class in many areas of the world does prove that the ideal of equality is moving forward.

I am personally very glad that society has transformed itself so that women are no longer secluded in the household, performing chores so that men can be free from the burden of necessity, and thus able to act in the public space among their fellow-men. Having said that, I would have preferred a society where men and women could have the possibility of acting together with others in the public space, while still showing their individual essence instead of their sameness. In other words, I would have preferred that instead of increasingly considering labor as the highest human achievement, society would have given human beings a common experience that promoted their highest capacities.

Classical Greek society was by all means unjust, but the basic truth (not its execution) is still valid today. Human activities are divided by the capacity of humans to do different types of things, each human within him- or herself. If not a hierarchy, we definitely need a better balance of these activities: those of the physical body that keep us alive; those where our sensitivity enables us to make things and to materialize ideas into beautiful objects; and those of the mind, with the two meanings of thought as the activity of enacting a dialogue with oneself and the capacity of contemplation and reflection – "the complete stillness, in which truth is finally revealed to man." (Arendt 1998, p. 291)

What I reject from the Greeks, and from most ancient civilizations, is the classification of people by their origins into different degrees of activities: women, slaves and foreigners into labor; free artisans into work; and free citizens into action. What a more equal society such as ours needs are individuals who have a better balance in their shares of labor, work and action. This does not means the same share for all; each one will have to find their own balance, by choice or necessity. For instance, this could mean that the amount of labor is far more important than that of action, but nevertheless, each one of us should have the ability and *the urge* to play in all three levels. We all need to do our share of labor, both in domestic chores as well as in efforts to make a living; yet we all like to leave things behind us, in the form of objects valuable by reason of their usability, and not by their mere consumption – and finally, all of us should also fight for our share in action, since we are all needed to help shape the world.

I believe that the young generation of today understands this much better than its predecessors. The first decade of the twenty-first century probably marks a turning point for the consumer and labor society. An increasing number of young people understand that they need to perform labor activities and make a living, but they also stake a claim to the right to have a meaningful life, and to act inside the communities they have chosen to belong to.

As a good example of how more people are trying to do their share of labor, is the fact that domestic chores are no longer reserved for women but are increasingly shared among all the members of the family. All men and women try to take care of their share in making a living, even the participation in fundamental farming activities meant for human consumption is increasingly being shared. To illustrate this, in the UK a million people are on the waiting list for an allotment (a plot of land that can be rented by an individual for growing fruits and vegetables). And also, when an 1100-square-foot patch of the manicured south lawn of Obama's White House was turned into a vegetable garden, the number of homes growing their own vegetables in the USA increased by over 40 percent (Botsman and Rogers 2010, p. 51). Also, we see a rising urge in people to make lasting things, whether it is paintings, poetry, or household objects. Finally, the active participation of many in their internet communities indicates that action is being increasingly performed. We all need a little share in all of the human activities, and each of them is dignified by its intrinsic value: the products of labor for their capacity to keep us alive and in shape; the products of work because they make our lives more comfortable; and the products of action since they allow us to show ourselves among others as equals, and actively participate in building the common human experience.

Now it is only a question of turning a society of laborers into a society of actors, and I believe that some business activities illustrate a change in the consumption and production habits. We can see this in a few of those myriad communities now active on the internet, where the "public realm" is now being shaped, with the same idea as that of the Greek *polis*, free individuals (now both men and women) who altruistically act with others for a common good, not driven by necessity but by the desire to insert themselves into the world, to be heard and seen.

However, we still need to resolve what should be seen by all and what needs to be preserved for our private eyes. This is probably one of the most difficult challenges of the twenty-first century. If by the public space we understand the sharing of our private lives, we still have to find a place where we can come together as equals and work for the common good. What is shared in the public space should not be only what makes us equal, but what makes us different, only then can we build a richer world by bringing together our different ways of seeing a common problem.

3   Usability vs use value: The value of things as an emerging paradigm

In recent economic and business literature there is a tendency to mix the *use value* in Marxist terms (the production cost), with *the value we obtain from the usability of things*. This second meaning has nothing to do with Marx, since it has nothing to do with the value of production but rather refers to the idea of the utility we gain for using objects, instead of the utility we gain just from buying them (implying that we only obtain utility because something is new and not because it can be used many times). (If you are interested in the old debate of exchange value vs. use value from St. Agustine to Marx, see the endnote.[3])

This increasing tendency is effectively advocating a reversal of consumer habits, and specifically, of the hyperconsumption that has dominated western society over the last decades. The consumption patterns that began in the 1920s and flourished in the 1950s have turned products into consumer goods whose only value is in being consumed, and thus once they are bought (consumed) their value diminishes instantly. Hence we no longer value the object for its capacity to be used.

The usability of objects is increasingly becoming appreciated, partly because the current economic crisis leaves no other option, but also because of the influence of the ecological movement and the pressing need to recycle in order to eliminate waste and save the natural resources of the planet.

It is often said that Spain is always thirty years behind the USA, and it may very well be true. When I went to the States in the 1980s to study, I took with me my little tape recorder, since it was one of the "objects" that really made my life more comfortable. After a few months, the machine broke and so, naturally, I went to look for a repair shop. This turned out to be impossible to find. My friends finally convinced me to forget about my useless tape recorder and buy a new one in the store. At that time in Spain we used to fix the objects we appreciated, and we wanted to use them until they were irreversibly broken and truly needed to be replaced. Yesterday my Blackberry broke and it did not even occur to me that it could be fixed, although I was not very enthusiastic about having to learn to use yet another electronic device. We do not fix things any more. However, an emerging movement that began a few years ago in United States and is spreading fast in other areas of the world, insists on going back to repairing objects so that we can use them longer.

Harvard graduate Rachel Botsman has become widely known in recent times for her idea of collaborative consumption. A book that she and Roo Rogers published in 2010 analyzes some new patterns developing in consumption habits in the west that reverse hyperconsumption by revaluing the usability of objects and sharing them among different people (Botsman and Rogers 2010). They analyze a number of companies that have emerged on the internet whose purpose is to facilitate the sharing of tangible and intangible goods among people, including common ownership of property, such as sharing a car, swapping baby clothes, books or DVDs. Pioneering companies such as eBay,[4] quoted in NASDAQ since 1999, opened a new understanding of the *fulfillment of needs instead of the owning of objects*. If something does not have usability for someone, it may be needed very much by someone else, and so objects can become independent of their owners by virtue of their usability.

Handmade objects are another illustration of a new appreciation not only for objects, but also for how they are made (in Arendt's terminology, appreciation for the products of work). The Etsy company, for example connects buyers with independent creators.[5] We increasingly tend to value handmade work as a luxury product, and because we value it in this way, the price increases. Consumers will value a unique item made by a known artisan much more than an industrial object, which although it is cheaper and functional, it would not give us the same feeling.

In summary, a new trend is emerging, mostly in urban areas around the world, that seems to mark a change in consumer habits, in the sense of stopping the *consumption* of objects and instead promoting the *use* of objects.

Of course, sharing consumption is not new; it has been used mostly by people with low resources in the west, as well as in many other places in the world. Due to necessity, the majority of humans on the planet know very well what sharing means. A great example is the Cuban movie *Guantanamera*,[6] describing a most unusual sharing of a car-ride from the east to the west of the island. For the people who have for many years shared a car, a telephone, a tractor, a computer, or a vacuum cleaner with their neighbors, to be able to own the specific object in question for themselves would probably bring a high degree of utility, and many would be happy to spend all their resources, or get a loan if possible, in order to finally posses this object for themselves without having to share it.

It is not a question of universal values but of proportion and of where we stand. In the case of the west, some indicators suggest we are getting to the limit of consumption: there are now more shopping malls than high schools in America; and it is estimated that Australians alone spend an average US\$9.9 billion every year on goods they do not use (Botsman and Rogers 2010, p. 20).

The hyperconsumption of the west might be the result of persuasion due to marketing campaigns, to the need to keep the production level up, or simply driven by our greed. But lately, some movements are showing some signs of attempting to reverse course and move into a more restrained pattern of consumption, in an effort to avoid the destruction of our habitat. Yet for many others who are just beginning to reach the level where they can buy and own objects, the path will probably be very different. Hopefully they will not have to go through what we did in the west, and they will just move up a bit in their level of consumption without leaving their sharing habits, and we will meet at some point in the middle.

The products of labor, those made to keep biological life in shape and whose purpose is to be consumed, are also being revalorized by these new consumption patterns. Farm-fresh products are increasingly in demand; in the USA more than 2500 CSA schemes operate – people pay a sum of money at the beginning of the year to a local farmer who will deliver a weekly box of fresh produce throughout the growing season – compared to only one in 1985. (Botsman and Rogers 2010, p. xvii) And in every corner in any of the European big cities, organic food shops compete side to side against the regular supermarkets.

These as well as many other examples, show a return to some of the habits of old. My grandfather knew his baker, since he was the only one in town, and every morning the smell of fresh bread from the bakery filled the neighborhood. My mother bought industrial bread in the supermarket and so did I, but now my niece only buys bread from the organic baker, even if she needs to walk 15 minutes to buy it. Many of my Nordic friends make their bread at home, a habit that is becoming increasingly popular all over Europe.

So it seems that two trends are emerging in the twenty-first century:

- Re-valorizing human activities: all three activities are being increasingly appreciated by the effects of their results: labor for its consumption and its effect on our biological lives; work for its usability and how it makes our world more comfortable; and action for its deeds that help us grow as society.
- The reversal of the old division of people into laborers, workers and actors, into a division of these activities inside each one of us, a balance of all three.

Therefore, a higher or lower market price is not what gives utility; the source of utility is the personal use we derive from an object. And for this utility many people will be willing to pay more, as in the case of an organic farming product, or pay less, as in the case of shared ownership. This shift in consumption is already affecting prices in the market.

But this emerging paradigm need new structures, because new wine does not fit in old bottles, as Toynbee used to say. The new emerging habits in production and consumption require new structures. In my belief, the new global networks of chosen communities of aspiration are the incipient structure that will make the production organizations of the near future.

4   Changes in organizations: From multinationals to collaborative networks

The rise and decline of big firms

Probably the most accurate definition of what constitutes a firm was the one given by Ronald Harry Coase in his popular article "The Nature of the Firm," written in 1937: "A firm therefore consists of the system of relationships which comes into existence when the direction of resources is dependent on an entrepreneur." (Coase 1937, p. 394)

Thus, by allowing some authority to the entrepreneur, or to his delegates, to direct resources, the transaction costs that emerge during production and exchange will be reduced.

Outside the firm, price movements direct production, which is coordinated through a series of exchange transactions on the market. Within a firm, these market transactions are eliminated, and in place of the complicated market structure with exchange transactions is substituted the entrepreneur–coordinator, who directs production (Coase 1937, p. 388).

Coase suggested that firms will naturally tend to expand until they reach their limit of marginal returns, when "the cost of organizing an extra transaction within the firm becomes equal to the cost of carrying out the same transaction by means of an exchange in the open market, or the cost of organizing it in another firm." (Coase 1937, p. 393)

And, as he predicted, companies that emerged in the USA and some parts of Europe during the first decades of the twentieth century, expanded and began integrating into the firm new products and activities, since the insertion of these new processes into the firm was cheaper than buying them in the open market. Then the rise of the multidivisional company structure with clear procedures for all staff members began, thus liberating processes from the subjective influence of the entrepreneur. Subsequent organizational structures created by the emergence of management science have enabled firms to expand overseas to cover every corner of the world (de Anca and Vazquez 2007, p. 42). These processes created the corporate giants of today's business world that employ an estimated 90 million people around the globe, among the largest of which are Ford, which employs approximately 213,000 people in 90 plants, IBM, with 400,000 employees in 200 countries, and the Coca Cola Company, with 139,600 staff members. Moreover, multinationals are currently responsible for two-thirds of world exports of goods and services and almost 10 percent of all domestic sales in the world. (de la Dehesa, 2006, p. 73)

However, in the 1980s the trend began to change, and reducing size became the watchword of many organizations as they found new ways of reducing transaction costs that did not require hiring new people: instead they would contract a particular *exchange* in whatever part of the world it was cheapest, as described by Naomi Klein in her influential book *No Logo*:

> by the eighties, pushed along by a decade's recession, some of the most powerful manufacturers of the world had begun to falter. A consensus

emerged that corporations were bloated, oversized; they owned too much, employed too many people and were weighted down by too many things. The very process of production – running one's own factories, being responsible for tens of thousands of full-time employees – began to look less like the route to success and more like a clunky liability. At around this time a new kind of corporation began to rival the traditional all-American manufacturers for market share; these were the Nikes and Microsofts and later, the Tommy Hilfigers and Intels. These pioneers made the bold claim that producing goods was only an incidental part of their operations, and that thanks to recent victories in trade liberalization and labor-law reform, they were able to have their products made for them by contractors, many of them overseas. (Klein 2000, 2002, p. 4)

Manufacturers no longer produced goods and advertised them, as Klein suggests, but rather bought products and "branded" them.

The process of outsourcing that underlines the changes described by Klein, was led by the deregulation and liberalization that took place in most countries during the 1980s, which made companies look for contracts in other countries where wages were much cheaper, and the existence of an infrastructure of telecommunications, information technology, and fast transportation systems provided the technological capacity for the system to work as a unit on a global scale.

However, outsourcing is one of the many results of three separate factors that began in the late 1960s and 1970s which, as sociologist Manuel Castells explains in his trilogy "The Information Age: Economy, Society and Culture" (Castels, 1996, 1997, 1998), not only transformed the nature of the firm but also the whole of our society in fundamental ways.

A new world was emerging originating in late 60s and mid 70s by three independent processes, The information technology revolution, the economic crisis of both capitalism and statism, and the booming of sociocultural libertarian movements. The interaction between the processes, and the reactions they produced brought into being a new dominant structure; the network society. A new economy; the informational/ global economy, and a new culture the culture of real virtuality. The logic embedded in this society this economy and this new culture, underlines social actions and institutions, throughout an interdependent world.

Information technologies let to the networking logic that prevails in all forms of social and economic life. The new economy was dominated by globalism, organizational flexibility and more independent management from labor, weakening the welfare state. And the new libertarian culture leads to an individualized use of technologies, and decentralized forms of organizations. (Castels 1998, 2000, p. 368)

In these changes, the entrepreneurial spirit which was key to the formation of the firms of the 1920s rose to prominence again in the development of the new organizations of the recent era. Entrepreneurs bet on the technologies of freedom to buy their own freedom (or in some cases were forced to gain their freedom by downsizing), and they created their own industries. This shift was accelerated even more in the first decade of the twenty-first century by the youth internet culture and its demand for permanent connectivity, which has forced the migration of the internet on to a mobile platform and that today operates with more than 4.9 billion mobile users.

Following Castells (1996, 2000, pp. 154–62), the radical transformation of corporations has gone through the following patterns:

- The transition from mass production to flexible production:
- New methods of management that resulted in the vertical disintegration of production along a network of firms.
- Inter-firm networking or a "multidirectional network model enacted by small and medium businesses" and the "licensing-subcontracting model of production under an umbrella corporation (p. 160)."
- The transition from vertical bureaucracies to horizontal competition involving seven trends: "organization around process, not task; a flat hierarchy; team management; measuring performance by customer satisfaction; rewards based on team performance; maximization of contacts with suppliers and customers; information, training, and retraining of employees at all levels." (p. 164)

Facilitated by the new technology, network enterprises were able to adapt to the new demands, to build a flexible organization using subcontracts, outsourcing and flexible contracts that in turn enhanced a new individuation of labor, where knowledge and information become the driving forces of the new production process. These new producers are made up of a cooperation between inseparable individual workers.

Social e-networks

Castells states that the resulting "network society" is one where the key social structures and activities are organized around electronically processed information networks. So it's not just about networks or social networks, because social networks are very old forms of social organization.

It's about social networks which process and manage information and are using micro-electronic technologies.

But networks are neutral and do not have personal feelings, it is what people do in the networks that can lead to certain social processes:

But the issue here is that first you start with a network which is equipped with information technology. That's the key. Then what the network does depends on the programming of the network, and this is of course a social and cultural process. As Castells explains:

> ... So, citizens do not trust their governments by and large these days; do not trust, in fact, anyone except themselves and their identity networks, and in some cases, social movements with alternative values. And in that sense, the complexity of our world is that the institutions of governments are crumbling, while networks of technology, capital, and production are organizing our lives throughout the world. As a result, many, many, different alternative sources of values and interests are emerging, because people do not have institutions through which they can process their claims and their demands.[7]

In Castells' analysis, the power of identity in the new e-networks becomes the key driving force for identities whose source lies in three patterns:

- **Legitimizing identities:** Those provide by institutions such as the state, political parties or unions, the church or patriarchal state, that within the network society are weakening as forms of legitimized identity because they have lost their influence over social cohsion. Since legitimizing identities are weakening, two other forms of identity can be found in the Network Society:
- **Resistance identities:** Top-down identities that are built around traditional values such as God, nation, family, enclosed in territorial defense, or built around proactive social movements like feminism or environmentalism.
- **Project identities:** Emerging where individuals link their personal projects together with others for a common good; this identity can be derived from certain resistance identities that have developed into identity forces.

Collaborative net-organizations

e-networks have thus enabled a new form of organizing business through the internet and open networks. However, this new form of being together also represents a new form of working together, and these e-networks are increasingly being turned into new forms of acting in the market as producer and as consumer. Therefore, the new collaborative ways carry along the whole of the economic process, which also underlines new ways of collaboration: co-consumption, co-creation, co-production and co-financing all seem to be new ways of reducing transaction costs. Different individuals bonded by a common project, sharing their different skills to create new goods and services, which in many cases are used and consumed within the same community. Thus, producers and consumers are united by community bonds of shared interests rather than by a division of labor. As the boundaries of boss, employees, clients, and suppliers are blurred, these new organizations have managed to reduce costs, but also to guarantee sales, without needing marketing costs.

We can analyze the main areas by a few examples:

- **Collaborative consumption:** Many of the new networking enterprises began with an idea of *collaborative consumption*. These schemes have led to the emergence of a number of companies dedicated to facilitating exchanges between people.

Examples of collaborative consumption

Collaborative consumption takes many forms: shared ownership, recycling or shares in particular services. The fact that the core concept is sharing does not mean that it is not a good business activity, as some of the following examples illustrate:

Car sharing or per hour car rental is expected to be a $12.5 billion industry. **Zip car** is the world's leading car-sharing network, with more than 560,000 members and over 8000 vehicles located in major metropolitan areas and college campuses throughout the United States, Canada and the UK. In 2009 it made $130 million.

Freecycle: a worldwide on line registry that circulates free items for reuse of recycling. Its website has 7.6m users across 85 countries.

Trend UP: a clothing exchange for kids' clothes. Approximately 12,000 items were exchanged within the first eight days of launching in April 2010.

Couch Surfing: connects people who have a spare sofa with travelers who wish to sleep on it, on the tacit understanding that the travelers will do the same for someone else in the network some day. There are 2.3m registered couch surfers in 79,000 cities worldwide.

Source: Schumpeter (2010).

- **Co-creation:** Collaborative consumption has opened up new forms of collaboration in the entire economic cycle, not only on the consumption side but also on the side of creation. New products and ideas increasingly involve end consumers and the community in the creative process. Examples of co-creation are experiences such as the Art of Hosting,[8] that maximize collective intelligence through participative methodologies. One of the best-known forms of co-creation in today's business is Design Thinking.

> **Design thinking** is a fundamental tool in today's process of innovation. It represents a creative way of building up ideas, and, as one of the leading areas for corporate innovation, integrates participation, collaboration and sharing as the core element to solve problems in the drive for innovation. Says Tim Brown, CEO of IDEO: "the consumer moves from being a passive receiver to an active participant."
>
> *Source*: Brown (2006).

- **Co-production:** These processes have also reached new ways of organizing production by sharing spaces and time. There are new co-production strategies where people with similar interests are banding together to share and exchange less tangible assets such time, space, skills and money (HUB culture, citizen spaces) task time and errands (Ithaca Hours, Dave Zillion). One of its most popular forms is co-working:

> **Co-working** is redefining the way we do work. The idea is simple: that independent professionals and those with workplace flexibility work better together than they do alone. Co-working answers the question that so many face when working from home: "Why isn't this as fun as I thought it would be?" Beyond just creating better places to work, co-working spaces are built around the idea of community-building and sustainability. Co-working spaces agree to uphold the values set forth by those who developed the concept in the first place: collaboration, community, sustainability, openness, and accessibility.
>
> *Source*: Co-working Wiki (2011).

- **Co-financing:** Network identities are also leading to new ways of organizing the financial flows into co-financing schemes, such as the communal lending experiences. Many internet users will consider taking a loan from their peers before they go to traditional lenders. In 2006 there were $269 million in peer-to-peer loans, and in 2007 a total of $647 million. Experts predict it will go up to $5.8 billion or 10 percent of the personal loan market, by the end of 2010 (Botsman and Rogers 2010, p. 163). Zopa for example, is a UK based network of borrowers and lenders where people with spare cash that they might otherwise put into their savings accounts or in the stock market, lend it to people that need to borrow. The lender gets higher rates on returns and the borrower lower interest rates.[9]

Co-finance schemes can also take other forms, whether it is time banks, local exchange trading systems (LETS) or the growing number of complementary currencies that are resulting in very useful tools for liquidity shortages, such as the one produced after the recent economic crisis (they are labeled complementary because most people agree that they should sit alongside national currencies and by no means replace them). Some complementary currencies are very recent, like Second Life's Linden dollars or the VEN of HUB culture.[10] These new forms of complementary currencies are inspired by older initiatives, some of them successful, such as the Palma currency in Brazil[11] or the WIR Bank in Switzerland:

Complementary currencies at WIR Bank

WIR is a "complementary currency." The term is understood to mean an agreement within a community to accept as a medium of exchange a currency different from the national currency. It does not replace the latter, but rather exercises a social function for which the national currency was not intended. Is considered important for the stability of the Swiss economic system and an efficient tool in recession times.

In the case of WIR, the members support each other mutually both by buying from one another and by gaining access to loans offered by the central office at more favorable rates than anywhere else. This access is especially valuable in times of economic recession or rising interest rates. The goal is to create prosperity and prevent unemployment. WIR Bank in Switzerland is currently used by more than 62,000 companies and generates transactions equivalent to SFr 1.6 billion and a monetary stock equivalent to SFr 800 million.

The WIR Cooperative has enjoyed the status of a bank and is subject to the controls of the Swiss Confederate Bank Commission. Banking law prescribes a certain obligatory relationship between a bank's assets [including outstanding loans] and its equity; thus the volume of available credit is limited. WIR-money is commodity-backed, in the sense that every transaction in WIR is backed by the exchange of concrete goods and services.

Source: Reinventing Money (2011).

Sharing new ways of production and consumption fundamentally requires trust among strangers, and this is where the identity of these new communities plays a crucial function. On the internet everything is transparent and everyone can participate. Free-riders or abusers can, of course, enter the system, but everyone will know of their existence after their first wrong, since the fast spread of reputation within the community will make these wrongdoings open to the public. The interconnectivity of many of these communities will make for a more efficient dissemination of bad credit ratings than any bank system. Since ancient times, community reputation has been a very efficient way of controlling behavior; losing face among your kin was the worst of all possible offences in tribal modes of living. This same losing face is now being reinforced by the new internet community. As a result, the credit defaults of these new lending companies turned out to be surprisingly low (at Zopa the default rate is at about 0.65 percent compared to the default rate on credit cards in mid 2009 of 10 percent; Bostman and Rogers 2010, p. 166).

Some of these new communities may be working to change the system; however, the majority does not see these new initiatives as something *instead of*, but rather as *complementary to* the system. These groups feel a shared identity in new modes of acting in the market as producers and as consumers. Having said that, it is likely that some of these new initiatives with time will consolidate into new ways of doing business in which costs are reduced and loyalty is increased.

5   Identity and the market

Identity in economics

George A. Akerlof, winner of the Nobel Prize in Economics, and Rachel E. Kranton have recently published a book *Identity Economics* which summarizes the results of their work on how identity affects economic behavior (Akerlof and Kranton 2010). This is work that they have been developing over the last ten years since publishing their first article "Economics and Identity" (Akerlof and Kranton 2000).

Their model is based on social identity theory, by which people are categorized into different groups each of which represents a certain behavior, and the persons belonging to that specific group then tend to interiorize this specific behavior. Following the line of social identity theory, the economic investigation they conducted is based on the careful observation of the minimal group paradigm, rather than on large statistics. Their experiments add the utility function to social identity theories: the idea that if a norm exists for a certain category, those belonging to that category will increase their utility function by adhering to it, or decrease their utility function by separating from it.

Utility function is an analysis often used in contemporary economics, by which people's decisions are described as maximizing their utility functions whether their choice is conscious or not. These authors assert that when it comes to utility function, the fact that people care about it, and how much they care about it, depends in part on their identity, and this has often been ignored.

Their model assumes three basic premises: first, that there are social categories; second, that there are norms for how someone in those social categories should or should not behave; and third, that norms affect behavior.

The utility function model is thus part of (Akerlof and Kranton 2010, p. 118):

- The social categories, and each individual's category assignment or identity.
- The norms and ideals for each category.
- The identity utility, which is the gain to be had when actions conform to norms and ideals, and the loss insofar as they do not.

Akerlof and Kranton have applied this model to a variety of contexts, including organizations, education, gender, work, minority status, and poverty.

As an example, they applied the model to organizations by addressing questions such as the ways to give workers appropriate incentives. Assuming the hypothesis that monetary incentives tend not to work too well in practice, an organization should not only rely on monetary incentives: adding the identity element, workers should be placed in jobs which they identify with, and firms should foster such an attachment (Akerlof and Kranton 2010, p. 41).

The model thus has two parts: the first is a boilerplate model – there is a firm owner and a worker, and the standard is that the owner will pay the worker more when revenue is high and less when revenue is low, linking revenues to the greater or lesser efforts of the worker. In the second part of the model, the authors added the three ingredients of their identity model:

- **Social categories**. Those who identify with the firm will be categorized as insiders, and those who do not as outsiders.

- **Norms and ideals.** Insiders think they should work on behalf of the firm; in contrast, outsiders think they should give only minimal effort and are often thinking about themselves and not about the organization.
- **Gain and losses.** In identity utility, an insider loses identity when he or she gives a lower effort rather than a higher one. An outsider loses identity when he or she gives a high effort to an organization which he or she does not feel a part of.

If the worker is an insider, identity utility will reduce the bonus needed to induce high effort; in other words, there will be less difference between the high-revenue wage and low-revenue wage. In contrast, an outsider loses identity utility by working hard. A higher wage differential is needed to induce him/her to work to compensate him/her for the loss in identity utility.

One addition to this model is the fact that studies have found that workers typically identify with their immediate workgroup rather than with the organization as a whole. A finer model is thus to appeal to loyalty towards a workgroup rather than to the firm as a whole.

Their findings show that the success of an organization depends on employees who share its goals; they are acting as part of a group, and this is what it means for workers to identify with their organizations. Therefore, if job-holders have only monetary rewards and only economic goals, they will game the system insofar as they can get away with it. But when workers are insiders, with the same goals as their organizations, such a conflict of interest disappears. Akerlof and Kranton conclude that, "worker identification may therefore be a major factor, perhaps even the dominant factor, in the success or failure of organizations." (Akerlof and Kranton 2010, p. 90)

The model was applied to other examples such as women at work. In this case, the findings conclude that if tasks are tagged as male or female, men and women will work in different occupations and women will have lower wages, because women will lose utility by working a man's job and men will lose utility by working a woman's job. Since men will lose utility when a woman works a man's job, they can actually sabotage the work of women; this sabotage increases the perpetrator's utility but leads to lower productivity for everyone. So the real problem, according to the authors, is the norms that stipulate that men and women should do particular jobs, irrespective of their individual tastes and abilities. According to that theory, society-wide changes are necessary to change gender norms: "the remedy for discrimination is to remove gender tags from jobs." (Akerlof and Kranton 2010, p. 90)

They conclude their study by suggesting that identities are not permanent: some are more fixed. like race or gender, some less so – they can be modified easily. Identity itself can be a choice. To a certain degree people can choose who they want to be.

Moving identities in a diverse world

Identities, as we saw in the studies of Akerlof and Kranton, are mobile and a question of choice. The choices people make as producers and as consumers in the market are linked to what they identify with and this identification is a product of two factors:

- **Personal identity.** Where we are as individuals, in our solitude, in the scale of self-development, described in previous sections and developed by psychologists and philosophers since the beginning of times.
- Consider *Maslow's pyramid of needs*: where we are in our path to self realization; whether all of our energies are dedicated to provide for our basic needs or part of this energy is spared for higher needs, and whether we are thus capable of dedicating our energy towards a common good once we are free from our ego claims. Or in *Arendt's terminology*: our activities as human beings are a combination of taking care of our biological life cycle (labor), our activity as fabricators of things (work), or once the lower necessities are covered, our capacity *to act* as free individuals with others for a common good (action).
- Castells also had a somewhat similar description regarding the emergence of the project identities of individuals that link their passions for personal projects together with others for a common purpose.
- **Communal identity:** Our personal identities will decide who we will choose to be with. Depending where each one of us is in each particular moment (since the scale of self-development can sometimes also move downwards), we will choose to act with others. Either we will share our necessity or act as free individuals, or a combination of the two. We can be in a job just to cover our necessities, without identifying with it (with lower rates of productivity as in the Akerlof model), and also act as free individuals in our chosen communities.

The movement on our self-development, as well as the communities in which we aspire to participate in, is affecting our behavior in the market as consumers as well as producers. The traditional divisions of owner, employee and client are getting blurred as consumers and producers join in collaborative networks, as described in the case that illustrates this chapter; the HUB.

This case illustrates the emerging paradigm in which the personal drive of individuals has pushed them to pursue in their professional lives activities they believe will help them as humans and also help society at the same time. In order to follow their dreams they have manage to co-create organizations, in which they can co-design, co-produce and share consumption. The new co-working modes of organization can assure a way of leaving although in the majority of cases is a trade off of less financial resources in exchange for time, and space to create.

6 Fourth movement: Identity and the market: Finding an equilibrium between labor, work, and action, in and outside the market

As we saw in the Akerlof's analysis, people tend to identify with smaller groups. However, larger identities, or identities of origin, mainly gender or race, still play a role in defining our choices as producers or consumers. In my personal experience, being from the Mediterranean has created in my pattern of behavior a taste for certain consumption habits; and so in my utility function for example, I am happier to spend some time and resources inviting my friends for some wine and tapas in an open terrace than I am to join a neighborhood's open garden.

Although some aspirational identities occupy our higher desires to be part of community, and thus lead to priorities as to where to work, and where and what to consume, the preferences embedded in our childhood and in our cultural habits will still be part of the universe we choose to live in; and how much room these old preferences occupy in our lives differs in each individual for a variety of reasons. A Brazilian friend told me once that when he arrived in Spain, he developed a taste for *sobrasada* (a very typical charcuterie from the Balearic islands). And so my friend would often buy *sobrasada* and bring it to the breakfast table every morning. Then one day his vegetarian roommate pleaded with him not to buy it any more since it reminded him too much of his grandmother's house in Mallorca where he spent his childhood summers. It was really too difficult for his roommate to overcome the impulse of his aspirational behavior, which was being part of the vegetarian community, and his childhood memories, the taste for *sobrasada* embedded in his childhood memories of warmth and love.

The illustration shows a reality, the fact that we can belong to many communities at the same time. This is what keeps us away from fundamentalism because our heart is shared with many different communities which many times behave differently. This was expressed in Obama's famous speech, "A More Perfect Union"[12] in which made the case for a better understanding of the issues of race. Belonging to many, often opposite worlds, of course raises our level of stress but it also keep us healthy – life is navigating on a sea of desires and compromises.

All of the communities we belong to, either by choice or by origin, have a role. Some are crucial in helping us make a living, others provide shelter for our emotional needs. However I have to follow Hannah Arendt's view that the highest aspiration of humans is to be free from necessity in order to be able to act. Sharing in labor or work is pleasant, yet the capacity to show our essence within a web of individuals and build a world made up of our differences – that is what we are here for. Hannah Arendt expressed, the hope of any newborn child is after all, the hope that he will make a difference.

But being able to show our true selves it is not a simple path, we first need to overcome the demands of the ego by fulfilling them or reducing them to a more manageable size, and after that we need solitude, time and space to be able to think and reflect, and we need a community of equals in which to act. It looks simple, but analyzing the world we live in, it seems that not too many have achieved this task, and if they have, there is no room for them since the public space is occupied by other matters.

Internet communities and collaborative consumption, as we saw in the previous section, are changing many of the market habits of people in our capitalist society, while tackling some of our most urgent problems of hyperconsumption and scarcity of resources. Reductions in consumption might also achieve other ends such as reducing the market to a more manageable size. If we consume a bit less and share a bit more we will have to produce a bit less to cover our needs, and thus time will be freed to act in our communities and in the new spaces provided by internet.

Having said that, it is a fact that there are millions who do not abide by these new communitarian practices, because they do not identify with – for a variety of reasons, none of which have anything to do with being more or less qualified as human beings. Many do not identify because they do not belong as much to capitalist society, or because they fit happily into capitalist patterns. It is just a question of identity and movement.

The new types of communities that emerged in the network society described by Castells are mostly populated by youngsters who grew up in capitalist patterns, whether in the west or in the east, and they represent new forms of tribalism, a tribalism resulting from a society that moved towards the furthest ends of individualism and now is swinging back. There is however, a crucial element in this swinging back and forth from community to individualism: the fact that in each move backwards and forwards there is the possibility of growing.

This new communitarianism is far apart from other forms of tribalism in primitive societies because now, unlike former practices, sharing is a product of individual decision, not an obligation imposed by the leader of a community we are forced to belong to. The fact is that this communitarianism is a product of decision and not of necessity is what makes it so rewarding to participate in. This is possible because we were individualized first, and in that individualization process, we gained, we learned how to use our minds as independent beings, we discovered that we could explore, create and design based on our own wishes and not from a community need. And all that freedom has lead to some of the greatest discoveries of humanity, but it has also caused us to lose some of the community bond, to the extent that we are close to destroying our very habitat. It is perhaps time to go back now to the community to share our individual minds with others. These communities of the network society are much more into sharing minds and ideas than into sharing feelings, unlike those of the 1960s; "feeling good" is desirable, but it's not the primary objective for joining.

However, communities that did not follow the capitalist path towards individualism do not have any need to go back to the community, quite the opposite. For them being, an individual is probably their aspiration, not to have to share would be for them an important gain. Communitarianism is a breath of fresh air in a world of excessive individualism, just as individualism is fresh air for excessive communitarianism.

The eras of individualism in history have proved to be crucial for the development of human beings in helping them find their creativity and their real self. And community shifts are crucial so that our real selves can be applied to our communities and help them grow. This happens in everyday life, we think in solitude and gain our essence, and together with others we show our essences in order to contribute to the common good. But it also happens on a larger scale, in shifts in history and civilization. Western civilization gained enormously from our individualistic period, but now is time to go back to the community, now globalized, and create together a better common world. Having said that, communitarian societies, without losing the freedom to bond with their community (as we probably did in the extremes of capitalist society), will gain enormously from a shift towards individual rights and freedoms, as the demands of the Arab revolution suggest.

Our movements are different, as individuals and as civilizations; however we will all meet once some of us harmonize our individualistic gains with our communitarian needs, and others harmonize their communitarian gains with their individual needs. This is true for individuals as well as for civilizations, as we will explore in the final chapter on identity and civilization.

I would like to end this chapter on the market with a phrase from Ana Maria Matutes, an 85-year-old Spanish writer who, in her speech receiving the Cervantes award in April 2011, stated "if we do not create we are not alive!" But to be able to create – a new artifact, a new poem or a new idea – we need time and space. We need time and some space to think and reflect in solitude, and we need a little bit of time and space to act, to share with others in our chosen communities, and together create something different by adding our differences, beyond private necessities, into the common human legacy, that is the purpose of individual lives, to bring our uniqueness to light with others and together build a world.

Case 4   The HUB: A collaborative network for an emerging world

Introduction

At the dawn of the twenty-first century, individuals from different backgrounds and interests gathered in different events and conferences with the purpose of shedding some light on the problems facing the world and finding imaginative ways to move forward. One of these encounters was held in Johannesburg in 2002 and focused on Sustainable Development. Many young people were present, some of them members of different youth movements such as AIESEC or Pioneers of Change, and, together with Nobel Prize winners such as Nelson Mandela, they actively shared their ideas on the changes that the world needed. Participants in the conference felt a special energy that made them believe that change was truly possible. The question at the time was how to maintain the energy generated by these types of gatherings? In other words, was it possible to create a "context of possibility" in which individual energies could be transformed into a much more powerful common energy that would empower people to undertake a significant change in their lives and the world as a whole?

To make the context of possibility a reality, two needs were identified:

• A living space in which this common energy could emerge and be maintained.
• Entrepreneurs (though it should be noted they would not self-identify with this term) working both individually and collectively as the engine of change.

With this in mind, some of the HUB[13] developers interviewed hundreds of entrepreneurs in an effort to understand their real needs; surprisingly they found out that more than resources and material goods, what entrepreneurs really needed was: "Not to feel alone, to travel with others in their journey." The HUB was created to attend these needs: a space in which a context of possibility is developed and people can imagine a different world as well as ways of building it together." This is how Max, co-founder of the Madrid HUB, explains the origins of the HUB.

As Pablo, co-founder of the São Paulo HUB, puts it: "The HUB is a vibrant platform of entrepreneurs that want to undertake their visions, co-creating a new world, accepting what is good to keep from the old ways while giving light to the new that is emerging."

Things have progressed a long way since the opening of the first HUB in Islington, London, in 2005. The HUB now unites a net of 33 HUBs and a community of nearly 5000 members in 21 countries and across five continents – and it is still growing.

The challenges ahead are important, among which is finding new structures of working and thinking together to be able to meet the new emerging realities of the global economy. The HUB is only one example, a pilot that illustrates some of the features of a new emerging paradigm; as Indy Johar from the London HUBs explains, "a shift to an "open social economy" in which deep transformations are on the way in what we do but also how we organize ourselves to do it."

The HUB structure: A global ownership

The HUB first opened its doors in 2005, in Islington, London. It was co-founded by a community of people: Jonathan Robinson (who continued on as leading director), Mark Hodges, Katy Marks, and Hetty Flanagan, among others. However, five years after and 33 HUBs larger, the organizational and ownership structure has moved into a horizontal mode, with a peer and membership logic focused on global access to shared support through the mutual leverage of trans-local synergies.

The HUB Company that coordinates and serves the different local HUBs is 100 percent owned by the HUB Association, both incorporated in Austria. At the General Assembly, the Governing Body of the HUB Association in which each HUB has a vote, the interest of the HUBs is coordinated and the budget and management team are formally approved.

The HUB Company provides support to the local HUBs, which includes the basics of branding and a platform for sharing best practices, as well as the maintenance of shared structures such as the virtual collaboration platforms. The Management Board in charge of these functions is the appointed management team of the HUB Company, currently comprising four people in an open structure where each is located in a different location and uses inputs from their network to inform their management activities.

Each HUB contributes with a one-time startup fee according to the economic reality and size of each HUB, and that can go from a maximum of €20,000 to a minimum of €10,000. In addition, each HUB contributes and "invests" with a yearly ongoing revenue share of 2.5 percent of core operations, starting after three months from the official launch.

The general structure of the HUB shows the basic features of the values of the network:

- Best and emerging next practices: a shared learning around a business model that brings opportunity for social businesses in the hands of passionate local entrepreneurs.
- Inspirational identity: an appealing branding possibility with great local impact that focuses on undertaking social change within a framework of shared values.
- Global Community: membership of a supportive community of entrepreneurs from around the world and across all sectors, with access to many different talents in a global learning environment.
- However, the most important of these values is becoming part of a trusted circle of innovative partners from all around the world who share the same vision and values, support each other in their mission and seek to materialize synergies and foster collaboration across multiple levels. The members agree that these days, it is fairly easy to create a global network with the help of virtual technologies; yet paradoxically, it is much more difficult to build trust within such a network, especially if it spans various cultures and local contexts.

At the local level, most HUBs found crowd funding to be the best way to finance the model. It enables them to put capital and resources into an idea they believe in, adopting in each HUB the legal form most suited for the context. In São Paulo, 50 original members gave an interest-free loan of 300,000 Reales that allowed for the opening of the São Paulo HUB in 2008, as a limited company with two owners. (However all the founders are still members and the last loan was paid back in 2011.) In Madrid the HUB is also organized as a limited company; however the founders also took out equity and so there are 30 shareholders (actually called care-holders to highlight their commitment beyond financial support). HUB Madrid has a total equity of €300,000 that together with another €160,000 in bank Loans makes their total capital €460,000. This amount is what allowed them to open in 2009. Therefore, HUBs have diverse models of funding and investment depending on their local conditions. At the same time, they all depend on a quality relationship with their investors.

A context for possibility

The first identified need that originated the HUB was to create a space of possibility in which things could happen, a space to host imaginative ideas to re-design the social fabric of the world.

Most entrepreneurs and other members of the HUB community see themselves as transformers. HUBs offer spaces and activities for debate about the problems of the world, as well as potential solutions. In those gatherings, new project ideas emerge and many find inspiration about what projects can be undertaken and how to develop them. People attending the different activities of the HUB tend to be people unsatisfied with the way things are and who want to make significant changes. They want to be part of these changes and they want to make a living out of it.

The HUB sees itself as an infrastructure to enable people to work on what they feel passionate about, and this can be a very diverse category; it is an illustration of a new emerging paradigm of networks moving into a common direction with a diversity of strategies in going about it.

A network of entrepreneurs

The HUB founders see entrepreneurs as the engine for economic change, and for that reason entrepreneurs and changemakers are supported at many different levels, from the bottom with their material needs to the more subtle supports of warmth, ideas and knowhow. The HUB also provides means to accelerate their endeavors through incubation programs such as HUB Venture Lab.

Most local HUBs have adapted urban spaces into a space for working and sharing, offering entrepreneurs flexible time-based membership and providing access to a space where they can work and meet. They include all an entrepreneur needs to run a project or a business: wireless internet connection and access to meeting and event spaces, printers, scanners, phones, fax, physical and virtual storage space, as well as administrative support according to the different tariffs. Membership also includes access to a community of like-minded professionals, as well as learning and social events and a small business support service.

However, the support for entrepreneurs goes beyond material goods, as Indy suggests: "It is more like a self selecting 'garden', a safe and connected environment where ideas at their pace and purpose." Indy affirms that there is enough capital in the world, and, due to the insecurity of the markets and the financial crisis, capital is seeking refuge either as storage in basic commodities, land, electricity etc., or is looking for equity, which in many cases means finding the right people to invest in. Therefore, this is one of the roles of the HUB, to identify who these people are and give them the knowledge that would transform them into the successful entrepreneurs that the new world needs.

Profile of entrepreneurs: Who goes to the HUB and what do they do?

The uniqueness of the HUB is that it was formed by a group of individuals who are seeking social change through economically viable innovation, and that it develops projects that tackle social problems while at the same time providing viable economic sustainability, for the project itself and for business aspects as well.

The community of the HUB is made up of people in their thirties (although it is common to see older and younger people participating) who share the vision of doing something different that is also economically sustainable. While members do change depending on the different cultural contexts where the HUB is located, they nevertheless share some common aspects.

The types of business encouraged by the HUB, have either one of these characteristics:

- **An Impact:** Businesses are developed because they offer innovation, such as the new marketing campaign they created for Obama, new technological solutions for providing healthcare services, or the example of Onzo in London, a company set up to help consumers become more energy-aware.

- **A Civic Target:** HUB members believe that while it is important to innovate, it is also necessary to look at how we organize the communities in our society to create mechanisms in which the private and public elements of a community can jointly invest in a business that has profound effects on their way of living. Examples can include investing capital resources into joint mechanisms of exploiting energy resources in a given community. The objective is to create a structure in which stakeholders are the owners of the business, and the emphasis is on organizing the communities we live in so as to effectively manage the existing resources and meet people's needs.

Businesses developed at the HUB tend to be services rather than products. Since HUBs are created in active urban spaces, they are good at developing rapid synthesis of the existing pieces in society. Occasionally, some entrepreneurs develop products, such as, for instance, one of the businesses in São Paulo which developed health products that are friendly to the environment, or a Madrid member who produces bags and other fashion products made from 100 percent organic cotton, using a sustainable supply chain connected to local communities in India. However, both examples base their production outside the city, and use the HUB as their office when they come into town and need to do administrative work or to develop different events.

According to the experience so far, the HUB tends to provide a good shelter for business of one to six members. For business that have from six to eighteen people, the HUB space is not very convenient, since it is not large enough, and in any case, during this stage of development businesses tend to be much more internally focused; therefore, a dominant group would significantly affect the culture of the HUB. In cases where a business has more than 18 people, the HUB again provides a good place where such a business can open up to new external possibilities. For instance, in São Paulo 20 out of the total of 180 members left the space after an initial period of growth to move into their own premises, although most continue their relationship with the HUB. In London, in the existing locations at King's Cross and Islington there is also a tendency either to find start-ups of less than six people, or large businesses, and this probably would be the same experience at the planned HUB at Westminster.

The membership profile also changes according to each city. São Paulo for example, is a very complex city with 20 million people and not very good local transportation, and thus to live near where you work is the key to quality of life. Therefore, a majority of members use the HUB as their permanent office space. According to Pablo, "Here in São Paulo it is either 8 percent or 80 percent. In other HUBs people can come from time to time, for lunch, to chat or to have some coffee; here this would not be possible because of the difficulty of moving around in the city. In Madrid, by contrast, out of their 400 members, half of them combine the HUB with other spaces, such as their home, regular office space or a café. They come to the HUB to connect with other entrepreneurs, contrast their ideas, gain new knowledge and accelerate their businesses."

The network of networks: Value creation and exchanges among members

Besides the traditional benefits of working in a network of entrepreneurs, the value of the HUB lies in the capacity for creation among the different members in each HUB, as well as throughout the network HUBs.

For that reason it is still a challenge to specify a measurement of how much interexchange is actually going on and what is its real value. Some HUBs, such as São Paulo, measure levels of interexchange among their members through annual surveys. HUB Madrid measures the level of connections between its members on three different levels: going from a personal connection ("...you should meet John who has a similar interest/project and could be of help..."); a collaboration between members (two or more members working jointly on a project which would have otherwise not occurred); and a formal partnership or company created as an outcome from two or more HUB members. In addition to measuring the quantity of exchanges, it is also necessary to measure the actual quality of business; in other words, to find new definitions for the success of a business.

São Paulo is one of several HUBs that have what are called Informal Centers of Excellence. They have recognition throughout the network, and as such, many newcomers demand their services. As an example, some of these centers produce good business plans and are in high demand for these services, others design websites, etc. In these cases, the type of payment among is decided on an individual basis, and can vary among several different methods, including an exchange for another service, money or any other form.

The HUB operates as a network of networks, and it has a pressing need to understand the real aggregated-value it has formed. For instance, in São Paulo they are particularly closely associated with the HUB of Amsterdam, and they share many practices, such as the idea of the Summer–Winter School. Other individual members also share with other HUBs. Another great way that networks are built is when sister HUBs give their support to the growth of new HUBs and help them in the early stages of development.

As Indy suggests, what HUBs can be good at is creating leading market entrepreneurs. For example, a new marketing innovation, regardless of where it emerged, can move to London to gain broader global appeal, since London is perceived as a leading HUB in that industry. Each place would contribute the best resources of its local community, and the flexibility of the HUB allows for a high mobility throughout the network.

Some HUBs are working on technical solutions to be able to implement innovative ways of exchange such as with complementary currencies. These will be tested first at local level in order to be able to gain a real measure of the value of these different exchanges. However, other HUBs as of yet do not see the need for some of these solutions because in their view, their task is to establish a link between society and innovation, and not so much to act as an internal community of exchange.

Practice at the core

While HUBs have unique, collaborative spaces and a diverse community, what further defines a HUB is the practice that supports the dynamic between the space and the people as well as that of the people with other people, both inside and outside the HUB. The practice of hosting, according to Tatiana Glad of HUB Amsterdam, is "to invite members to be at the heart of the HUB experience and to create the conditions for members to generate value for themselves and others." Each HUB has a hosting team that nurtures the physical and social infrastructure in support of its social innovators and to bring the values of the HUB into living practice. The team of hosts is there to connect members and catalyze new conversations, also listening to deeper patterns and needs emerging from within the community and being able to adapt resources and programming to meet those needs. Tatiana states, "Our aspiration is based on principles of hospitality: We welcome and stimulate a culture for people to be themselves, and offer their best. We create and nurture a platform (culture + infrastructure) that encourages people to contribute and collaborate." In addition to the core hosting practice of the HUB, many hosts draw from the Art of Hosting (www.artofhosting.org) to learn to work with diverse approaches to hosting groups and group dynamics; seeing a World Cafe, an Open Space and other collaborative social technologies is commonplace in a HUB and in their communities.

The business models

HUBs have a sustainable business model that relies on office and event space rental, as well as a co-working space. At the same time, higher-value revenue streams are being explored by different HUBs and shared through the network to be adapted to local realities or improved. These revenue streams include services offered to companies and entrepreneurs as well as trainings offered through summer schools and others.

"Today the transaction of the HUB is a space." However, as Pablo points out, the space as transaction is not longer innovative, "since there are increasingly numbers of co-working spaces being created every day. Therefore, if the HUB wants to survive it will have to reinvent periodically, always giving to its members the new possibilities that they need," or, in other words, as Max suggests, "The HUB should always be on 'beta,' fostering a culture of prototyping."

The constant beta phase is what makes the HUB a constantly moving process. As some of the new developments occurring after 2010 have illustrated, the majority of HUBs still find that their main source of revenue is in the use of the space; however, most have introduced important new ways to develop a more viable medium- to long-term strategy.

In São Paulo for instance, the revenues of the utilization of space come mainly from HUB Office, a work space in which entrepreneurs can find the basic structures needed for their business. The HUB also provides them with services such as coaching, mentoring or investor pitching. With HUB Events, HUBs rent their spaces for different activities, events or exhibitions, to different organizations and companies sharing the HUB spirit as well as their own members. Likewise in HUB Madrid, membership fees constitute 30 percent of their revenues while 50 percent comes from event hiring and the remaining 20 percent comes from services delivered to companies such as Philips and Telefónica, as well as to entrepreneurs. It is this last area of providing services for larger companies, which represents the highest value potential and which is currently being developed the most with prototype projects. The London model for revenues is at the moment very similar to Madrid since its main sources of revenue are also fees and renting out the spaces for different events.

However, all of the HUBs are also developing other mechanisms, including:

- **Knowledge-based mechanisms to spread knowledge among members.** For example, São Paulo has followed the Amsterdam model to develop a HUB Summer School. In it, around 350 members will assist special training events organized every six months and facilitated by HUB members and other outsider experts. In London they are also developing knowledge schools to help members spread strategic knowledge.
- **Services to companies.** Most HUBs help different company partners achieve higher levels of impact and develop a community-based organization in their existing business. In Madrid, these services to larger companies represent 20 percent of their revenue.
- Most HUBs are also developing **equity-based models**. Finding the right investors and the right investments is also a part of the HUB's identity. For example, HUB Parcerias in São Paulo has a business unit that creates partnerships with investors. During the last year, an investor wanted to finance a business with social impact in the field of healthcare. After a month of work, HUB managers found seven suitable businesses among their members. The HUB earns fees from the company and from the selected investor that can be part of equity in the business. Also, a new project is emerging being led by the London HUB, whose goal is to select and finance with already secured funds, the most innovative ideas among European HUB members.
- Therefore the business model will have different levels of revenue, from short-term revenues, (mostly defined by the space and some services to large companies) to short to medium-term revenues (through knowledge initiatives), and long-term revenues from equity participation in different businesses.

Each HUB can find within this range of possibilities their own particular approach that follows the needs of their members. As Indy suggests, "The HUB is just half of the business model. The members in each HUB have the other half of the business model. It is like an iPad: without applications it is useless. Thus, if the HUB is like an iPad, its members are like the applications that fit into it. The same way that Apple will be happy if the application producers are happy, the HUB will be happy if its members are happy."

To organize all activities, most HUBs have a small number of facilitators; however most work in specific business lines and many are paid by the investor of the particular business line they are involved in. In São

Paulo HUB there are a total of eight employees. They found there was dynamic growth without creating fixed structures: to incorporate new people only when a new business unit, normally developed in partnership with an investor, could afford to pay the salary of a new employee for that particular unit. The Madrid HUB has a team of seven full-time committed individuals, four of whom are employees, two freelancers and one intern. It is important to pay close attention to the fixed costs and building infrastructures of a start-up.

Community and identity at the HUB

The HUB is truly a participative society in which the members share the production and consumption processes, and also share in the generating of new ideas for social innovation. However, sharing can be as intense or as detached as people choose. Some of the processes involve an intense sharing experience, others a mere punctual collaboration. Whether strong emotional attachments or logic punctual collaborations, the HUB provides a common space for possibilities and is a real flexible model for work.

The HUB represents a step further in the co-working cultural movement since not only does it build a local network of entrepreneurs, but it also provides a space for a global network of entrepreneurs and innovators. Its potentiality lies in the fact that it taps into the technological virtues of today and brings them into an intense human experience. The HUB is an ultra-flexible format of weak links that can create both occasional and permanent projects, a new communitarian hardware that greatly enhances both creativity and innovation.

The challenges ahead are important, among them, how do we build an open system that can accept different realities, according to the diversity of the different HUBs, or how do we maintain and serve the important communities on the web. However members are well aware of the challenges ahead and the need to be in a constant innovative mindset to overcome the challenges and the changes of today's moving society.

New bottles for new ideas?

In his analysis of individualism during the era of industrialization Max Weber talked about the break-up of community support during the pre-industrialization period, which transformed workers into isolated and lonely beings and then into a mass used to fill the new factories. This process freed the efforts of making a living from the web of moral, emotional, family and neighborly bonds – but by the same token it also emptied such actions of all the meanings they used to carry before. The dignity attached to doing one's work well also disappeared. In order to fit into new clothes during the industrial revolution, the would-be laborers first had to be made into a mass, stripped naked of the old dress of communally supported habits. (Bauman 2008, p. 27)

In a way, the HUB can be seen as a twenty-first century return to the lost dignity of one's work, a return to the professional communal structures of pre-industrial Europe, with the medieval craft of guild-like communities of support that use new technology and the individual freedom and creativity of today. The long period of individualism that began in the nineteenth century and flourished in the twentieth is coming to an end in the twenty-first. Individuals are going back to communal structures, but with individual clothes and individual capacities being adapted into the communal life, as opposed to reverting back completely to our pre-industrial communal clothes.

The evolution of the HUB can be a significant pilot model on how to build new structures for new emerging realities, since our current structures are too old, or as Toynbee put it "new wine does not fit well in old bottles." The structures created by the HUB can result in the new support base for our society in transition. Some ideas on how the new model is going to be are becoming clearer, among them: a need for further participation of the stakeholders in any business, and a better distribution of financial resources. The HUB is tackling both and can help our society to transform into an open social economy that would offer more opportunities for all.

CHAPTER 5

Testimonies ... And who do you want to be?

1   Nisren Abasher Ahmed, Omdurman, Sudan

See http://video.dainutekstai.lt/w.php?a=uDxsthltB74

How would you describe yourself?
I am Sudanese woman, who chose the career of art; my specialty is sculpture. This choice in itself is a big challenge in a society where the representation of bodies or any kind of figure is against religious norms. I also make other, different kinds of art: drawing, painting, animation, performance and graphic design. I am a freelance artist.

Can you describe in one/two paragraphs your venture (activity in life)?
Beside the above-mentioned activities, I like manual work, which in my country is usually male-domain work. Due to my studies, I have to travel to different places in Sudan, so I am fond of visiting different regions in my country, and that helps me to get to know the ethnic, geographical, and cultural diversity in Sudan.

Does your activity relate to your personal goals in life?
Yes.

In what way?
All my professional activities have much to do with what I chose to be: a Sudanese woman artist. For instance I made postcards that aim to be part of a campaign to stop Female Genital Mutilation (FGM), which is one of the worst examples of gender-based violence (GBV) in my country. I am also working currently on a book of short stories for children, which is closely related to our cultural background, as story-telling in Sudan is being abandoned as an artistic expression.

Do you identify with it?
Working for causes such as both the women and the children issues is one of the achievements that I indeed indentify with.

What would you like to achieve?
Work more in the same line, plus use my art as a weapon to stop war and conflicts in my country, and disseminate a culture of peace and all that can lead to empowerment of women and the care of children, and end all kind of injustices in my community and the whole country.

What is missing?
One of the aspects that I believe is lacking is a fair level of attention at policy level in my country towards art; and how little it is valued, compared to other kind of career or business. I also find that art is little valued in the whole society, and for this reason art is having to overcome a lot of obstacles to achieve its goals in this society.

Is this activity your passion? What otherwise is your passion in life?
As mentioned before, this choice for me was not an easy one. Women usually get enrolled in other university careers, and it is a big challenge for any individual, especially women, to make this choice, where women are supposed to get other kinds of career and then their maximum aspiration is to get married and have children.

Are you active in developing your professional activities with a particular community? More than one?
I am quite active in my community with my professional activities, in spite of all kind of obstacles as a woman artist. I am working with some women's organizations in issues related to GBV and child protection. I work with other communities too, like the Egyptian, the Turkish, the German, and the Dutch, both in Sudan or in these countries while visiting for work: exhibitions, workshops, performance, etc.

Could you describe the community/ ies, you are part of in your professional activities?
As Sudanese, I am originally from the west of the country, which has a different culture from the capital, Khartoum, where I now live. In Khartoum, I am from Omdurman, which is the past capital of Sudan, and it is considered the most attractive city in the country. I got most of the inspiration for my artistic work from Omdurman.

Could you describe the community you would like to be part of in your professional activity?
I would love to continue to be inspired by my native culture, but I would also like to use my art as a bridge to other, different kinds of culture, as I have had the experience of working in different cultural contexts to my own and I can see the role of art in this perspective, especially for multiculturalism and cultural dialogue, and the culture of peace and tolerance.

2   Lotfi El-Ghandouri, Creative Society, Montreal, Canada

See www.creativesociety.org

Can you please describe yourself in one/ two paragraphs?
I like to call myself a twenty-first century nomad or a world citizen. My dad is from Morocco and my mom from Tunisia. We lived in France, and I decided to join the world during their vacation trip in Tunisia. When I was three years old, they decided to immigrate to Canada to provide us with a better future.

I studied International Marketing in Canada. Then, Conflict Resolution in Belgium, and I did a Masters in France. For decades, I have backpacked through many countries in Europe, Latin America, and Asia.

Can you describe in one/two paragraphs your venture (activity in life)?
I worked for many consulting firms before I decided to start my own. I needed to feel free to create and mostly to decide with whom to work and the kind of impact I wanted to have.

I founded Creative Society in Montreal and Madrid so we could work globally. I always thought that my work is ideal for the global community, with which I feel more identified.

Our philosophy is based on the firm belief that if each human being truly believes in his or her dreams and has the audacity to bring them to the world to contribute, to generate a better world, we will reach the true society: The Creative Society.

I have a natural talent for story-telling and managing groups: that is why I wanted to focus on that field by doing it in a meaningful way. I therefore facilitate dialogues and creative processes for social and corporate organizations. I am also a writer and public speaker.

Does your activity relate to your personal goals in life?
Yes.

In what way?
I work to provide new ways of thinking and supporting individuals, organizations and associations to accelerate their sustainable impact in a creative way. I am fortunate to see our direct impact on people and their projects. That (connects) brings me to life.

Do you identify with it?
Totally. I cannot do things that I do not identify myself with. It might be because of my parents, who always stood for their beliefs and their rights. My dad always told me: "They can take away your belongings, your house

even your family. But nobody can take away your dignity and your knowledge. Always be who you are and stand for what you believe in."

Doing something that I do not identify with is like walking towards the loss of my own self.

What is what you would like to achieve?

I want to make a difference and invite people to truly make a difference. As the Native American proverb says: "We are the ones we have been waiting for."

We are the ones who can change things. We are the ones who can bring social justice, sustainable wealth to all and bring true ethnics in organizations, and I feel part of the "we."

When I look deeper, I want my parents to be proud. That the sacrifice they made to provide us with a better future was a great investment because we did it. I did it. I want to honor my ancestors and my family for the journey they had and work so that I can generate a new cycle in our constellation.

What is missing?

My involvement in the Arab and Muslim community is missing. I contributed to many cultures, and I am just starting now with my own community. It might because I did not feel ready, or empowered, or that I was afraid of not being able to do it. Now I want and I am convinced that I can contribute within a greater team.

I am also missing my life balance. I am also working on this. Only by honoring oneself, can one honor and bring true value to society.

Is this activity your passion? What otherwise is your passion in life?

This is my passion. People are my passion. I get very emotional when I see anonymous individuals united to do extraordinary things. Because this is the greatness of humankind and this is when miracles are expressed. The humanity of each individual expressed in the collective action.

Are you active in developing your professional activities, with a particular community? More than one?
Could you describe the community/ies, you are part of in your professional activities?

I cannot belong to only one community. I belong to a variety of communities and I support a variety of communities that my purpose can nurture. I collaborate with education, civil society, organizations, governments, the arts. I belong to the youth, adult, Arabic, Latin, Muslim communities. I like to host in spiritual circles, human rights, social movements. I would say that my true community is the global community.

Could you describe the community you would like to be part of in your professional activity?
The Muslim community, and mostly women and youth, as well as (indigenous) native communities

Do you believe your activity will help your society?
Yes, but not enough.

In which ways is your society different than the civilization you are part of? Can you describe both?
It is different based on my origins. I work in a Judaeo-Christian, Anglo Saxon culture, based on individualism, while I am from a Muslim-Arabic-collective culture.

What are the main problems you believe your civilization has?
Trust and faith in themselves. Many people feel that answers or solutions must come from western civilization. So they are waiting. There is also a lack of belief in their capacity to provoke and create a new reality, new solutions.

Because of colonization, and lack of freedoms, and tough regimes, people distrusted their neighbors: an act of survival that makes it difficult to sustain communities or create together.

The Arab Spring was a collective healing of these situations. Pride is emerging, people are co-creating together a new reality and hope is filling their hearts.

How are you contributing in solving them?
Through Creative Society, we are dynamizing public conversation towards change, and we are providing tools so they can manage their own evolution. This is just a start. We hope to empower people, social organizations, and companies towards the creation of a new society.

3   Edgard Gouveia Júnior, The Global Game 2012, Brazil

Contact: edgardgouveiajr@gmail.com

How would you describe yourself (in one/two paragraphs)?
A Brazilian bio-architect, the only son of three kids raised by a lovely middle-class black couple that never disagreed aloud in front their children. An early lover of animals, waterfalls, forests, and long silent walks on the beach of Santos, my birth town.

I am a dreamer and a dream-realizer. A traveler who loves to meet, connect and learn with different cultures. A deep listener and an addicted searcher of strategies to avoid nature's collapse, to eliminate the humanity's pain and to increase our inner ability to connect out of love.

Can you describe in one/two paragraphs your venture (activity in life)?
To design tools and processes that will, out of joy, play and cooperation, unleash the human potential to build resilient communities and restore environments. Nowadays I, and a large international team, are focusing in developing the 2012 Global Game, that intends to enable children and youth to move 2 billion people in four years to restore social and natural environments in the whole planet.

Does your activity relate to your personal goals in life?
Totally!

In which way?
Stimulating more healthy and happier communities, restoring the environment, and promoting a better relationship between humankind and nature.

Do you identify with it?
Yes, totally. The things and places I work with are what I am in love with, and it is the path along which I can best challenge my personal skills and gifts.

What is would you like to achieve?
To awaken and activate everywhere a culture of confidence in abundance, generosity, and a deep sense of reverence and belonging to a community of life that includes all beings in the planet.

What is missing?
To articulate and disseminate a powerful global action based in generosity, pleasure, and efficiency to take care of the community of life in the planet.

Is this activity your passion? What otherwise is your passion in life?
Yes it is! To be in the presence of people bringing their excellence into action and to promote a deep, caring connection with nature.

Are you active in developing your professional activities, with a particular community? More than one?
Could you describe the community/ies, you are part of in your professional activities?
Several communities, such as Ashoka Fellows, Warriors Without Weapons, Oasis Mundi, The World Café; Art of Hosting, Berkana Community, 2012 the Global Game ...

Do you believe your activity will help your society? In what ways?
Is your society different than the civilization you are part of? Can you
describe both?

My society is a huge community of people all over the world who are focusing on finding, creating, adapting, and living more sustainably – better ways of living in relation to other communities and natural systems, in a particular way that promotes cooperation, lightness, peacefulness and playfulness.

The civilization I am part of emphasizes lucre, financial wealth, concentrated power, and unlimited exploitation of natural resources.

What is the main problem, in your opinion, that your society has?

The disseminated idea that the Earth was given, for God, to man to govern and explore, and the trance we are experiencing that make us believe in having more than being, in scarcity more than abundance, and seeing the different as enemies instead partners.

How are you contributing to solving it?

Creating and promoting methodologies, communities and movements to break the trance and to awake the human inner impulse of connecting, caring, and celebrating life together. Cooperative Games, Warriors Without Weapons Program, Oasis Game and recently 2012 the Global Game are some of these contributions.

4   Ayşegül Güzel, Zumbara, Istanbul, Turkey

See zumbara.com, facebook.com/zumbara, twitter.com/zumbaradan, zumbara.wordpress.com

How would you describe yourself (in one/ two paragraphs)?

I am a person living in this world. I am in love with the common assets of human beings: ability to care, communicate and love (as Edgar Cahn, founder of time banking, describes it) and maybe as being aware of these assets that we all have, I still have a strong belief in each of us, so I am an optimist. I am a self-analyzer: I am curious about what is happening deep inside me, so that I naturally track the path of my feelings and try to find out their reasons. When something is not "all right" I am brave enough to change instead of pressuring myself to live with it, thanks to believing that nothing is impossible!

I am an action-taker and sometimes anxious. So I need to be aware of the difference between to do and to be. Trying to remind myself to be open to what the universe is bringing to me, as I am worrying about not paying attention to these gifts or signals. Also, I am reminding myself to trust the process, to be patient and calm. I believe that we are all responsible for each and every choice that we make. So I am a person who is just trying to be a good person.

Can you describe in one/two paragraphs your venture (activity in life)?
I am trying to create an online sharing platform in which time is used instead of money. Basically it is Time Banking + Social Network = Time Banking 2.0. Time Banking is an alternative economic system where people help each other, and time is used as a currency for reciprocity. So I am creating an online platform which is using many functions of social technologies to serve as a tool for this alternative economic system to work more effectively and efficiently both in small and large scale.

We are working on contributing to a social change that makes possible more humanistic and participatory values, and fostering this change by reminding ourselves of the values that we forget:

- Everybody's time has the same value at the moment of necessity. It is an egalitarian system.
- In life there are things more important than money, and the only thing that we really own is our time.
- Our differences enrich us and we need each other.

Does your activity relate to your personal goals in life? In what way?
My personal goals in life are to be a good person and to live life as it deserves: with love, joy, and excitement. With Zumbara, every day is a new adventure in which I am learning a lot. I am discovering more about my areas of interests. I feel as though the Zumbara project is one of the milestones in my learning journey in life.

Do you identify with it?
Sometimes I feel that I am realizing this project because I am meant to do so. It is like all the dots are linking.

I have a big problem with the value we give to 'money'; the big prison that we have created for our imagination and creativity, which has made us forget that everything is possible. I have a deep belief in human beings' goodness of soul. I naturally see everybody's positive side, even though others have criticized me many times as being innocent, naive. Also I trust, love, care, and communicate easily in a society where we are generally advised to be careful about all these because of the fear we all have. Lastly, I believe that the fact we are all different to each other is not just a coincidence. It is because we need to carry each other.

What would you like to achieve?

I would like to create healthy communities inspired by 'campus life' in universities. I have studied in a university in Istanbul, where the campus was not just a physical space but also a culture and a community of sharing. I would like to create an 'open campus concept' for all neighborhoods. This campus idea has a circle of people with similar areas of interests at its core. Imagine I am checking zumbara.com where I can see the events happening that night. Near my home there is a 'Jazz Night' in which a jazz lover is simply sharing his best songs with five other people. The open campus idea also has its own library, stocked with books that people share, has its own kindergarten where mothers take care of the children of the neighborhood when needed. In this open campus, people from the same neighborhood create more bonds as they have much more opportunity to come together in a common space.

What is missing?

An efficient, effective, and user-friendly technological tool to reach the masses. Right now we are reprogramming our webpage with a more professional team. To reach the masses, participation of individuals in these masses in service exchange, and for the long term an offline system of time banking for non-internet users, are still missing. Even now, though we have financial investment in the project, a sustainable economic model in practice is still missing. We have many ideas and hopefully this year we will see which one will work.

Is this activity your passion? What otherwise is your passion in life?

For last two years, yes, this activity has been my passion. My job is my lifestyle. I live with it 24 hours a day. I never get tired of working any more, because it is not like working as we normally understand. I never realize when Monday starts and when Friday finishes. Yes, definitely it is my passion.

Are you active in developing your professional activities, with a particular community? More than one?
Could you describe the community/ ies, you are part off In your professional activities?

Right now we are more than 1300 people in Zumbara world. In order to enter this world you need an invitation, or you fill a form with some basic questions and we send you an invitation if we see that you are willing to share. This community is composed of first adapters. These people have something in common: they have some problems with the actual situation; they know that something is not going correctly. They are willing to share and meet with others. From these 1300 some are more active in that they have exchanged more than 100 hours of service with others. We meet with this community in our regular monthly meetings, which is like meeting with friends. It is great fun! Also when you make a service exchange with this community it is different than a professional service provider, it is much more real, humanistic, and friendly.

Could you describe the community you would like to be part of in your professional activity?

This year we are targeting young people, especially university students in Turkey. We are really excited with this adventure as generally it is older or middle aged people in other countries who participate in time banking. We want to track the behavior of young people and we are optimistic about the potential that they can provide for projecting time banking to the masses. This year, moreover, we have one foreign country (English-speaking) in our plans. As the Zumbara project has some innovative differences as a tool, we want to test the potential of time banking as an alternative economy all around the globe. We want to provide a tool both for local communities and also to global citizens. For the medium- and long-term we want to reach offline communities; such as prisons and neighborhoods with older people, or the countryside.

Do you believe your activity will help your society? In what way?
Is your society different than the civilization you are part of? Can you describe both?

I am not sure which civilization I am part of. Maybe I would have more relations with the civilizations that live with a gift culture and economy. The civilizations that were reached by giving more, where talent was a personal gift so could not be owned and the person with the gift was a channel to make this gift to reach others. I think once we become more civilized as a society we become more slaves of our possessions, and in seeking to possess we forget the assets of being human, and our gifts. Right now our economic system is making it almost impossible to remember that we can all care, love, and communicate, and the only thing we need to do is to create a sharing and supportive system in order to share the gifts that we all have differently.

What is the main problem, in your opinion, that your society has?

We are in our personal prisons that we have created in our own minds. We do not know the power of our choices, so maybe because of that we do not feel ourselves responsible and powerful. We need to remember our values, our responsibilities for communities, the environment and ourselves, and moreover that nothing is impossible.

The other problem that our society has is that value is totally given to money. All the tasks which do not relate to money become valueless. Taking care of children, old people, communities, or practicing personal responsibilities, are tasks that are mostly not related to money. So we are faced with the problem of describing as valueless the most valuable practices, which creates pressures for all the society.

How are you contributing in solving it?
Showing other alternatives. To start with, an alternative economic system, in which you have a marketplace for services based on people who are willing to share. People can begin to see that they do not need that much money to do what they really want to do.

Motivating people to think about and to do what they really like to do, and to make their own choices in this life. In our system, people are motivated only to provide services to others that they really like to do. Also, they have to ask themselves what they like to do and what they can do for others, these are the starting points.

Trying to create question marks for people about what is real value, and the demotion of money. Trying to create consciousness about the fact that value is related to what human beings really need, and the only thing we possess is our time – not money. Reminding people of their real values (the ability to communicate, care, and love) by practicing service exchange. In the medium term this service exchange can become a habit, so creating trust, relationships, and social capital.

5   Jay Standish, Symbionomics, Seattle, USA

See www.symbionomics.com

How would you describe yourself (in one/two paragraphs)?
I am a listener, a mystic, an artist, a big ideas person, an idealist, a writer, and an entrepreneur. I am an innovation junkie; I love to feel the pulse of the newest things happening to make the world better. I'm guided by a deep connection to the natural world and I try to listen to my intuition as well as my analytical mind. I believe everyone is a genius at something and I want to help as many people realize that full potential as possible.

Can you describe in one/two paragraphs your venture (activity in life)?
I do a lot of different things: HUB Seattle, BGI (MBA in Sustainable Systems), digital art, a bit of blogging, currency dreaming and Symbionomics. The Symbionomics Project is a web-based film project to

uncover new patterns of behavior that are changing the economy at a fundamental level. One major example is the Open Source movement. People are writing software code collaboratively with other enthusiasts and then giving away that software for free. Examples are Mozilla Firefox and the Linux operating system.

The Open Source movement is also beginning to extend into the physical realm, with people sharing their designs for anyone to "print" using a 3D printer. Wikipedia is an example of an open-source encyclopedia where thousands of people contribute their collective intelligence to build a vast and dynamic inventory of the world's knowledge. The rise of the digital commons means that there is a shared capital that can be leveraged by all to add new value, thereby reducing the barriers to entry.

Does your activity relate to your personal goals in life? In what way?
Yes. By helping people see how the world is changing, it makes it easier for people to use the full spectrum of tools, techniques and strategies at their disposal. This enables people to reach their full potential easier and follow their dreams.

Do you identify with it?
Yes because I am a co-founder.

What would you like to achieve?
I want to help people understand and cultivate their unique genius.

What is missing?
I would like to work more directly with people rather than just putting out a media product for people to watch. I would like to do stuff like facilitate conversations, consult, or do one-on-one sessions to help people understand where the world is heading and how they fit in.

Is this activity your passion? What otherwise is your passion in life?
It is one of my passions – the innovation junkie. I am also passionate about having deep connections with people. I am also passionate about enjoying life and inviting others to dance.

Are you active in developing your professional activities with a particular community? More than one?
Could you describe the community/ ies, you are part of in your professional activities?
The HUB Network – this is a global network of physical co-working spaces for social entrepreneurs. I'm a co-founder of the HUB in Seattle, and traveled in Europe visiting HUBs.

The Next Edge – this is an online community, curated by David Hodgson, of people looking at new solutions popping up around the "edges," i.e. not in mainstream thinking. We share articles and discuss system thinking, the role of the internal (consciousness), new forms of leadership, etc.

Could you describe the community you would like to be part of in your professional activity?
I want to be a part of a global community. I want to have a few deep collaborative relationships with people I am committed to, so that we are uncovering, discovering, and building together. I also want to be able to translate some of the new innovations from the edge so that business leaders in the mainstream can understand.

Do you believe your activity will help your society? In what ways?
The main reason it will help society is that I am doing something I am passionate about and that I believe in. We have gotten some good feedback that Symbionomics has been insightful and has helped people see the big picture and piece together ideas and make connections.

Is your society different than the civilization you are part of? Can you describe both?
It is not separate because my subculture is just one of many subcultures that makes up the whole of human civilization. But, yes, it is unique in the sense that some of the core underlying assumptions, beliefs, guiding philosophies, and ways of being are different than those of the so-called "dominant culture." I tend to operate well in a pro-bono or "gift economy," where people see the value of community and give openly and freely to one another because they see it supports the whole community of which they are a part and will therefore eventually fertilize the soil they stand on.

The dominant culture (economy really) tends to operate in a quid pro quo or individualistic way, and tries to hoard wealth and only let it go if someone offers something in exchange that appears more valuable. This view has little concern, and perhaps distrust, for the broader community and assumes that they must provide for their own needs without help from others, and that they are not strong enough to lend a hand to others.

What is the main problem, in your opinion, that your society has?
The main problem is that we are trying to live this gift economy inside a civilization that is pulling us to operate in a more individualistic manner. It is very difficult to truly live in full gift culture because we still have to have a life in "the real world." So the main problem is finding a way to continue developing the tools and strategy of an economy based on giving

our genius as a gift to the world while still keeping one foot in the world of taxes, health insurance, tuition and rent.

How are you contributing in solving it?
I am going to business school to study sustainable systems, and working on currency systems that can help us make a smooth transition into this gift economy. I'm also doing my best to uncover my own genius while also helping friends see theirs. I am trying to design a lifestyle and professional career that can pay the bills as I develop and live in this gift economy.

PART III

Civilization and identity

CHAPTER 6

Moving civilizations

Are maps real?
Fifth movement: Identity in civilization: Integrating unity and
diversity in a larger framework

1   Are maps real?

I consider myself an inquiring person with an average knowledge of human
sciences, including history. However, living and working in different cultural contexts has made me realize how subjective things are – even the
most objective facts can be perceived totally differently when using different cultural lenses.

A few anecdotes will help me explain what I mean:

I was really surprised when I first arrived to Boston and some
American colleagues at the university teased me over the defeat of the
Spaniards in the Spanish–American war. For weeks I really could not
figure out when we were ever at war with the United States! I was positively sure that I had never studied such a war in my life, until I realized
they were probably referring to what we studied in school as the "Loss
of Cuba and Puerto Rico" episode. We learned of it as a historical event
that traumatized the Spaniards. Somewhere in our textbook there probably was a word or two about the help provided by the North Americans
to the Cuban and Puerto Rican independence efforts, but it was so insig-
nificantly described that it never entered my consciousness that we in
fact had fought and lost a war against the United States. For the USA,
the war put it on the international spotlight as a rising military power,
and thus the episode was much more relevant and featured prominently
in their history textbooks.

History is also perceived differently by the Belgians, something I realized when I studied there during my last year of high school. I was expecting to shine in history class, particularly relating to the period that Belgium
was part of the Spanish Empire ... unfortunately the Belgians did not study
that episode with the same enthusiasm as we did in Spain; rather they had
a somewhat darker recollection of the same facts.

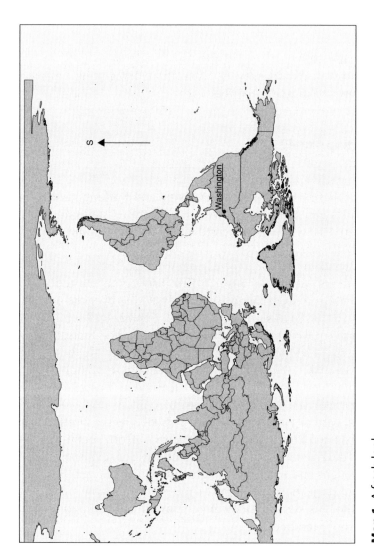

Map 1 A fresh look

An interesting moment also occurred when a Moroccan colleague was giving a joint conference with me regarding the mutual history of our countries. When we were preparing one particular slide, she labeled it "The loss of Granada" whereas I labeled it "The reconquest of Granada." We were just following what each one of us had studied at school, but as a compromise we finally opted to simply label the slide: "1492, Granada," and let everyone interpret the episode as they would.

I soon realized that it was not only we, the Spaniards, who saw history through our own unique lens, but that everyone else did the same. As an Iranian friend used to tell me, having been educated under the Shah, she saw the Iranians as being the inheritors of the greatest empire of all times. She was very shocked when she moved to the USA and found out that most people in the world ignored everything about the Persians, even their existence.

At the end, one realizes that universal history is in fact the remembrance of facts depending on whose eyes were used to remember them. Within Europe we have Asterix, who has allowed Europeans to see how our neighbors perceive us: this comic book has hilarious descriptions of the peculiarities of our European neighbors, although its descriptions are never too accurate when referring to our own country. I myself found all of the installments to be accurate, except for Asterix's visit to Spain, which I found to be quite insipid. On the other hand, my favorite episode is the one dealing with the UK, which my English friends in turn find rather unamusing.

And of course, all this historical subjectivity reflects in the way we draw our maps! Maps are intended to be a real scientific tool that represents real facts, a landscape with all its accidents and features, and yet even maps are full of misleading perceptions.

Growing up in Spain, I found it totally natural that all the maps with which we studied history had Spain at the very center, between Europe and Africa. It was of course natural to be at the centre of the world (as I always thought we were). It was then a bit of a surprise to arrive in Boston at the Fletcher School of Law and Diplomacy, and see at the Hall of the school a huge map that was wrong, since it had at the center the American continent; and thus Europe seemed to be much smaller when pushed over to the right side, and Spain in particular seemed to be especially small and cramped. They, too, wanted to feel that they were at the center of the world.

A popular map in the 1980s showed a version of the typical European map but upside down, so that the African continent was huge and right in the middle, and the legend said, "NO! The map is not backwards, it's just a different way to see the world."

Therefore not matter how much we try to be objective, we always see the world with the eyes of our culture: the legacy of our ancestors and their ancestors, and how all of them perceived the facts of history.

Our civilizational identity affects the way we see our culture and that of others, but as we have shown in our examination of the other identities analyzed in this book, civilizational identity is not single and fixed. Most of us are part of many civilizations, and many more cultures.

If I had to describe my identity in terms of civilizations, I would probably say I belonged to the following order of multiple identities: Christian, European, Spanish, Mediterranean, Madrileña, Latina. Other people coming from the same country could easily say: Catalan, European, Mediterranean; or Sevillano, Spanish, Latino, European, etc. Most people in my country share a number of civilizations that have marked us, but not in the same order and nor with the same relevance. Others may feel themselves exclusively as Spaniard, or from their hometown, but the majority of us live happily within multiple layers of cultural identities that make us share many traits with many different people. And as the world grows smaller, our local identities take on more importance. Thus, we are on the one hand more globalized and on the other more local at the same time, a condition which although paradoxical, does not have to be conflictive.

Cultural identities move with us. I feel more Spanish when I am abroad; I feel very European while in America, and very Mediterranean when travelling around the *Mare Nostrum*. All of my identities make me feel proud, because I feel that each one has contributed something valuable to our human civilization.

I would like to end this chapter with a homage to one of the most precious of my identities, the Mediterranean. Because, although it seems like the north and the south of the Mediterranean have been separated for centuries, I still believe that they are two sides of the same civilization; and in our movement towards a global world, I positively believe that the Mediterranean should come together again.

As I said, I grew up having the Mediterranean in the middle of my map of the world, and I still cannot help myself believing that it is still at the center. I am of course aware of the diminishing relevance of Europe and the Mediterranean in the world, aware of the rise of China and Brazil. But deep in my heart I feel the Mediterranean soul. And in this particular moment in history, I am convinced that all of us in the region need to work together, because that is the only way we will be able to face the important challenges of our times: desertification, the pollution in our sea, the challenge of growing more and healthier food, etc. Working together, north and south, we could resolve the crucial problems of economic development, immigration, human trafficking, poverty and human rights. But in order to be able to work together we need to be on equal terms; paraphrasing Hannah Arendt, only among equals can one be different.

With the rise of the Arab Spring in the south and the turmoil hitting the European cities of the Mediterranean, such as Athens, all of it while we try to navigate through the worst economic crisis in a hundred years, we need to take on these challenges while working together, north and south. We also have to look north of the Mediterranean towards the northern Europeans with whom we have shared most of our destiny. And we must include the south, the Arab countries plus the others who make up the Middle East, particularly Turkey. I do not believe that Islam is against Christianity, I believe in the Islamic civilization as well as in the Christian civilization, but I also believe in the Arab civilization, the Protestant civilization as well as the Turkish. All these civilizations have formed our past and made us what we are today. It is with the legacy of this past that we will be able to build the future.

But before getting into the Mediterranean, it is important to clarify what we understand as civilization, to understand the rhythm of history, the patterns that help to explain why some civilizations rise and others collapse; more importantly, we need to understand what we have gained in the process and how all of these civilizations are playing their role today in these confusing times.

2   The rhythm of history

Civilizations and cultures

Following the historian Marc Fumaroli (*El Atlas de las Civilizaciones* 2010, pp. 17–19), the first time the term civilization appeared was in Mirabeau's *Treatise on World Population* in 1756.[1] In that treatise, the term was almost equivalent to "courtesy" and "civility." It was used as opposed to the term "rusticus" (rustic), a term that defined a country-dweller.

The French philosophers of the time, in their effort to exalt the human spirit, attached to the term "civilization" the idea of progress, the will of people to move on and create institutions that helped them to further this goal. It was in this sense that Philippe Descola defined the term civilization in the nineteenth century, with a clear tendency to use it as nearly identical in meaning to the term "culture," and with the same meaning: the human capacity to collectively invent values and conventions (*El Atlas de las civilizaciones*, p. 22). This idea later led to the definition given by

Tylor in 1871 that considered the two terms interchangeably: "Culture, or civilization, taken in its broad, ethnographic sense, is that complex whole which includes knowledge, belief, art, morals, law, custom, and any other capabilities and habits acquired by man as a member of society..." (Tylor 1924, orig. 1871).

Descola describes how the somewhat theological orientation of the term civilization, as the quest for human spirit to progress, was overshadowed in the twentieth century by two academic trends: on the one hand *the concept of society* successfully introduced by Durkheim and his school into the French and British social sciences; and on the other, the idea of *culture* expounded by German intellectuals opposed against a too abstract and very French notion of the term civilization.

The German conception of culture was broadly based on the intellectual and material resources that define collectivities of people, resources inherited from their ancestors, ingrained in a language and a territory, all of which are ultimately responsible of the typical behavior of the members of the collectivity. This conception was adopted in the USA by the founders of the American school of anthropology at the end of the nineteenth century, which later came to influence the rest of the world, especially after the creation of the UNESCO in 1945 (*El Atlas de las Civilizaciones*, p. 23).[2]

Thus the original term "civilization" was increasingly relegated to the realms of historical studies. Further, the concept was assumed during the twentieth century by many to signify a certain type of civilization, western civilization as opposed to others, with a connotation of superiority; and thus "backward" people could achieve progress by assuming western ways, either voluntarily or by force. Progressively, the term began to have the same meaning as to civilize or colonize, losing its original meaning of a general human quest for progress.

Descola defends the term "civilization," in its actual use within anthropology, understood as the techniques that define a set of different modes of being and speaking, which link several geographical territories, which share the same mode of living because they the same main resource. According to the author, it is correct to use the term civilization in this way, since it does not try to define a shared essence but to put forward a crucial question for the social sciences: "Where does this apparent unity come from?" (*El Atlas de las Civilizaciones*, p. 23).

Because no matter what the terms and definitions tell us, we all can perceive unity in groups, sometimes on a small scale and sometimes in extensive territories. We are all aware of a unity amongst Latin Americans, or between Arabs or Europeans. Even so, it is not easy to define what unites a people, because if we try to do it by using ideas such as a unifying essence, an Arab soul or a European spirit, we will be accused of being idealists or spiritualists.

Yet no matter how difficult the task is, some outstanding scholars, in particular historians during the twentieth century, have tried to find a pattern to define that unity. Among them is a legendary teacher at Georgetown, Carroll Quigley, who has tried to find scientific patterns to help better understand civilizations. Distinguishing culture from civilization, he describes culture as "the consequence of persons seeking to realize their potentialities sufficiently to satisfy their inner drives" (Quigley 1961, p. 63). In this quest to realize their potentialities, human beings establish relationships with one another.

All these relationships as part of culture form groups of human beings, and there are many different kinds of these groups. We shall distinguish four types at this point: (1) social groups, (2) societies, (3) producing societies, and (4) civilizations. All are made up of aggregates of human beings with their personalities and external cultures (Quigley 1961, p. 65).

- He describes a *social group* as an aggregate of persons who have had relationships with one another long enough for these to have become customary, and for them to come to regard themselves as a unit with well-defined limits. The essential thing about a group is that its members can say who is in it and who is not.
- The next level is a *society*, a group whose members have more relationships with one another than they do with outsiders. As a result, a society forms an integrative unity and is comprehensible. A group does not have a culture of its own; the culture of a group is the culture of the society in which the group is.
- Societies are then divided into two kinds: *parasitic* (hunting or fishing) or *producing* societies (agriculture and pastoral).
- A *civilization* would be defined as a producing society that has writing and urban life.

In his analysis, Quigley states that the different levels of culture arise from men's efforts to satisfy human needs, and that each level has a purpose. For this purpose he defined six basic human needs: 1) the need for group security; 2) the need to organize interpersonal power relationship; 3) the need for material wealth; 4) the need for companionship; 5) the need for psychological certainty; and finally, 6) the need for understanding. To satisfy these needs different levels of social organizations come into existence. These instruments are normally called "institutions" (Quigley 1961, p. 101) (It is important to notice the resemblance of Quigley's collective needs to the Maslow pyramid of individual needs described in Section 1 of this book.)

For the purpose of this book and to facilitate matters for the reader (without claiming favor towards any academic definition), I will be using the term civilization to represent the larger societies of the past and cultures of those of the present.

Where do we come from?

Where do we come from? This is one of the fundamental questions than experts from many disciplines try to answer, anthropologists, archeologists, genetic scientists or linguists, each expert contributes in his or her field to reconstructing the history of humankind on earth. Their theories change after new discoveries emerge. Studies on genetics, and in particular on the Human genome, have accelerated tremendously our knowledge of what happened in a much more accurate and precise manner than ever before. All studies converge because one thing at least is clear to all: That the history of humankind is only one history (Cavalli-Sforza 1993, 1994, p. 146).

What we know

Although controversies still exist in many aspects, there are a handful of certainties on which most experts agree and that help to build the map of our past, to describe just a few:

- **We all belong to the same species: *"Homo sapiens sapiens."*** The external changes we perceive among different races are only superficial differences, genetically we cannot speak of races (Cavalli-Sforza 1993, 1994, p. 140). As humans migrated into new areas and continents, human groups separated from previous groups who in turn separated from their communities of origin and formed new aggregations, which in turn separated again and formed new groups. The further isolation of the different groups led to two inevitable phenomena: the appearance of genetic differentiation and the appearance of linguistic differences. History can be reconstructed via languages, as well as via genes, and both represent different parts of the same story.
- **Modern man first left Africa around 100,000 years ago.** The first traces of *Homo sapiens sapiens* found in South Africa and the Middle East can be dated 100,000 years back. Most experts thus believe that modern man must have left the African continent a little before 100,000 years ago. However, some experts disagree with that idea, believing that

Homo sapiens sapiens could have evolved from previous types of *Homo sapiens* in different places simultaneously, since traces of archaic forms of *Homo sapiens* have been found in different parts of the world dating back to around 300,000 years ago. Yet, since our ancestors *Homo habilis* and *Homo erectus* also left Africa (the first around 2½ million years ago, and the second around 1 million years ago), most experts believe that *Homo sapiens* followed the same path.

- **Modern man followed two main roads out of Africa.** According to the majority of experts and genetic discoveries, humans probably migrated from Africa in two main directions: the first was towards south India, southwest Asia and Australia. The second direction of movement was towards northern Asia with two ramifications, one towards the east from Siberia to America, and one towards the west to Europe and Central Asia. Genetic and archeological studies show that modern man was in Africa 100,000 years ago; in southwest Asia and Australia from 55,000 to 60,000 years ago, in Asia and Europe around 35,000 to 40,000 years ago, and in northeast Asia and America between 15,000 to 35,000 years ago (Cavalli-Sforza, 1993, 1994, p. 139).[3]

- **Agriculture was discovered around 10,000 years ago.** Agricultural discovery represents the first human revolution, due to which men were transformed from hunters and gatherers into settlers who worked in the fields with permanent settlements. One of the consequences of this change was a demographic explosion, since settlers started having more children because they were a great help in cultivating the fields in an agricultural society (nomadic populations tend to have fewer children since they will not survive the constant migrations). This demographic explosion also caused more migrations and as a consequence, the spread of the new inventions to most parts of the world.

- *Homo sapiens sapiens* **speaks 5000 different languages.** We can probably believe that at some point in the past, all humans spoke the same language, since there exist similar signs and structures for all current languages. Although not yet proven, this underlying unity is, following Cavalli-Sforza, one possible explanation for the fact that any human baby can easily learn any human language (Cavalli-Sforza 1993 and 1994, p. 184).

In the current era of globalization, when humanity is getting closer towards one global village, our technological discoveries are showing us that in fact, *we have always been just one human race clustered into different families.* We began our journey in the African continent, we colonized every single place on earth thanks to new adaptations facilitated by new inventions, and now these inventions are clarifying our common past. However, as we separated, each human family was also able to adapt to its different environment; and thus each human family made important discoveries that quickly spread to other human groups, at times naturally through imitation, at times through migrations or commerce, and also at times through wars and conquest. Each civilization has left behind a legacy and thus contributed to the constant advancement of humankind.

However, the road has not been easy and was certainly paved with cruelties and misunderstandings that, unfortunately, still are present today. In every big step forward it seems that we have moved a few steps back. Nevertheless, humanity up to now, no matter how hard the blow has been, has always recovered and continued, and the accumulated gains cannot be underestimated.

The rise and fall of civilizations

Accounts of the rise and fall of the Roman Empire, as well as the thousands of tales about the Egyptian Queen Cleopatra, and the other myths of ancient civilizations long ago, have flooded both Hollywood and our libraries. The question is always the same: why did some human groups suddenly form these very highly sophisticated societies we called civilizations? And if they were able to build such wonders how could they have collapsed? If one visits Petra in Jordan, or many other places in the world where mystery covers ancient stones, one is driven to ask, "What happened?" How did these humans manage to create that? And even more importantly, if they built it, why could they not manage to maintain their civilization? What causes civilizations to emerge and then to fall? Is this a natural consequence? Can it be prevented?

Some scholars have worked hard to find a pattern; they refuse to believe that history is a mere accumulation of facts, and do not want to accept that this constant repetition of rising and falling could be a matter of luck. These few scholars have been concerned with finding a rhythm in the pattern, and thus being able to learn from the riddle of history.

We can briefly review the three most prominent investigators of the rise and fall of civilizations, Quigley and Toynbee in the twentieth century, as well as Ibn Khaldun in the fourteenth. It is worthwhile reviewing their theories in some detail:

Quigley's Instrument of Expansion

Quigley saw the pattern of the rise and fall of civilizations as having an economic root, what he calls an *Instrument of Expansion*. In his view, the pattern of change in civilizations consists of seven stages, resulting from the fact that each civilization has an instrument of expansion that becomes an institution. Each civilization rises while its organization is an instrument of expansion and declines as its organization becomes an institution (Quigley 1961, p. 132).

The instrument of expansion is what helps society to accumulate surplus and to organize this surplus in such a way that it is used to finance new ways of doing things. For Quigley a civilization begins to decline when the social group controlling the surplus ceases to apply it to new ways of doing things because they have a vested interest in the old ways, since they are the supreme group and thus have no desire to change and risk their privileges. Moreover, by a natural and unconscious self-indulgence, they begin to apply the surplus they control to non-productive but ego-satisfying purposes, such as ostentatious display, competition for social honors, or prestigious constructions of elaborate residences or monuments and the like. By this process, the instrument of expansion becomes an institution and the tension increases, what Quigley calls the "tension of evolution" (Quigley 1961, p. 141).

The seven stages of civilization and the role of the instrument of expansion in them can be summarized as follows (Quigley 1961, p. 1):

- **Mixture:** civilization is always born from a period of mixture of cultures.
- **Gestation:** in their beginnings, expansions are characterized by four traits: increased production of goods; an increase in the population of the society (generally due to the declining death rate); an increase in the geographical extension of the civilization; and an increase in knowledge.
- **Expansion**: when expansion begins to decline as a result of the instrument of expansion becoming institutionalized, the core area becomes static and legalistic while the peripheral areas continue to expand. At the end of this third stage the peripheral areas are thus wealthier than the center.
- **Age of conflict:** as expansion begins to slow, this is a period of growing tension of evolution and increasing class conflicts, especially in the core area. It is a period of growing irrationality, pessimism, superstition and other-worldliness. As consequence, there are increasingly frequent and violent imperialist wars.
- **The stage of Universal Empire:** as a result of the wars of the former period, the number of political units is reduced and eventually one emerges triumphantly. With the universal state in place there is a period of a golden age, of peace and relative prosperity since there is

an absence of any competing political units within the area of the civilization itself; but this appearance of prosperity is deceptive. Little real economic expansion exists, new inventions are rare, and real economic investment is lacking.

- **Decay:** characterized by acute economic depression, declining standards of living, civil wars and growing illiteracy. The society grows weaker and weaker, decline continues, new religious movements emerge; it may last long but eventually the society will fail to defend itself.
- **Invasion**: the civilization cannot longer defend itself because it is no longer willing to do so. It lies open to barbarian invaders, and as a result of the invasions of outsiders the civilization ceases to exist. This stage of invasion also produces a mixture of different cultures and it may be, but does not necessarily lead to, a new first stage of a new civilization.

With this pattern in mind as the underlying scientific theory, Quigley analyzes different civilizations from the past to the present. For example, he defines the instruments of expansion of the Phoenician civilization as elements of *commercial capitalism. The priesthood* was the instrument of expansion that managed the surpluses coming out of agriculture in the Mesopotamian civilization; whereas in his analyis, the channeling of surplus into *inventions or slavery* was the instrument of expansion of Greek society.

Ibn Khaldun[4] – Asabiya *(group feeling)*

The first sociologist in history was Ibn Khaldun. Six hundred years before Quigley found a pattern in the rise and fall of civilization, he came to a surprisingly similar conclusion, particularly in identifying corruption and self-indulgence by the dominant rulers as the main reasons for the fall of civilizations.

In what was going to be the first volume of a universal history (*Al-Muqqadima*), Ibn Khaldun found a method to identify the general laws of history. His intention was to apply to history the development of a science of culture, defined as the study of the social interaction of men. This method would allow him to build a bridge between external events in history and internal determinants of those events. But also according to his understanding history, he believed he could bridge the commonly accepted opinions and the true nature of natural beings. For him, the key to the rise of a nation is the "*asabiya*" or "group feeling" that makes a group strong, with its members bound to each other and looking for the common good of the group and not of individuals. When a group is bound by a strong *asabiya* it takes over from the previous rulers and is run with justice. Members do not need much and thus they do not need to impose heavy taxes. Since the nation is secure and just, and taxes are low, new talented people can come to the city, new crafts begin bringing prosperity and the city expands. Specialization and the division of labor is made possible by the prosperity of the nation. Artisans know they will be paid, and traders know that their customers will meet their demands. Furthermore, with increasing prosperity, the price of luxury rises above the necessities such as basic foodstuffs, and this increasing price differential encourages further artistic efforts in the production of high-quality goods and even greater specialization.

Ibn Khaldun believed that civilized economic activities were conducted in the cities, where money is used for exchange and surpluses utilized to finance new arts and crafts, thus stimulating the development of new skills. The prosperity of the city is self-sustained as long as the ruler and those around him are not divided, and the bureaucracy remains free from corruption. However, in his analysis he identifies that after three generations the bonds of group feelings (*asabiya*) begin to weaken, rulers get used to luxury, and the desire for luxury grows among them. Soon the bureaucracy becomes corrupt and taxes rise, often in arbitrary manner, to finance the luxury consumption of the ruler and the courts, and as consequence security declines. With the tax increases and the rise in insecurity, most talented workers leave to work in other cities, and those who stay are no longer motivated by the common good. As a consequence, the city goes into decline and is overrun by invaders, either from the primitive countryside or from other, stronger, cities where the rulers have a stronger moral sense of purpose.

In his own words:

> Eventually, group feeling is altogether destroyed. They thus invite (their) own destruction. The greater their luxury and the easier the life they enjoy, the closer they are to extinction, not to mention (their lost chance of obtaining) royal authority. The things that go with luxury and submergence in a life of ease break the vigor of the group feeling, which alone produces superiority. When group feeling is destroyed, the tribe is no longer able to defend or protect itself, let alone press any claims. It will be swallowed up by other nations (Ibn Khaldun, chapter 17, p. 133).

The work of Ibn Khaldun has been appreciated by most modern sociologists and historians, and recognized by Arnold Toynbee as well (Toynbee, p. 172).

Arnold Toynbee's challenge and response theory

Carroll Quigley, as well as many other historians in the twentieth century, was deeply influenced by Arnold Toynbee, who was born 20 years before Quigley in 1889. Toynbee was Director of Studies at the Royal Institute of International Affairs and a professor of history in the University of London. Between 1934 and 1962 he wrote a grandiose work: *A Study of History*. Its ten volumes seek to find the pattern that explains the rhythm of history and the motive for the rise and fall of civilizations. Toynbee supports his views with a multitude of examples drawn from his impressive knowledge of history and all the civilizations from the past and present. Although his influence was clear on most of the historians of the twentieth century, including Quigley, he was later criticized for not being scientific enough. While his encyclopedic knowledge of history has been recognized by all, he has been criticized for his speculations on the patterns that make civilizations rise and fall. His work was considered idealist, since human spiritual evolution was part of his understanding of the rise and fall of civilizations, and thus for many this could not be accepted as a part of a scientific analysis of history.

Toynbee's purpose was to try to find the causes for decay, and then use this knowledge to reverse the course of a society in disintegration. In his work he identifies 21 civilizations in human history (plus a few more that aborted before becoming fully developed, or otherwise were arrested or stagnated) out of which only eight remained in his day, all but one already in the stage of breaking down, and the last one being western civilization, submerged in a process of decadence. As his colleague D. C. Somervell concluded in his abridgement of the ten volumes of *A Study of History*:

> the writer, born into the age of Late Victorian optimism, and encountering the First world War in early manhood, was struck by the parallels between the experience of his own society in his own time and those of the Hellenic society, a study of which had provided the staple of his education. This raised in his mind the questions: Why do civilizations die? Is the Hellenic civilization's fate in store for the modern west? Subsequently his inquiries were extended to include the breakdowns and disintegrations of the other human civilizations, as further evidence for throwing light into his questions. Finally, he proceeded to investigate the genesis and growth of civilizations, and so this study of History came to be written. (Toynbee, p. 393)

Toynbee saw the rise of civilizations as a process of challenges and the way that those challenges are met. Growth occurs when the response to a particular challenge is not only successful in itself, but also provokes a further challenge which again is met with a successful response. For him the successful response goes beyond the control over the human and physical environments. On the contrary, for him real progress consists of a process defined as "etherealization," an overcoming of material obstacles that releases the energies of the society to create responses to challenges that henceforth are internal rather than external, spiritual rather than material. (Toynbee 1957, p. 364)

For Toynbee the response is made by "creative individuals," since for him the "source of action" is in the individual. All growth is originated with creative individuals or small minorities of individuals, and their task is twofold: first the achievement of inspiration or discovery; second, the conversion of the society they belong to into new way of life. This conversion could in theory come about in two ways, either by the mass undergoing of the same experience of the creative impulse, or by the imitation of its externals or *mimesis,* which is what normally happens. The action of creative individuals may be described as a twofold motion of withdrawal and return. Withdrawal from a society that is in decay and in which the individual can no longer find a purpose. After the withdrawal some creative individuals can achieve the distance from the day-to-day that allows them a personal enlightenment, and at that point they may return to enlighten their fellow men.

As to the causes of the breakdown of civilizations, Toynbee identifies three main points:

- A failure of creative power in the creative minority, which henceforth becomes a merely "dominant" minority.
- A withdrawal of alliance from the majority.
- A consequent loss of social unity in the society as a whole.

As in his analysis of the cause for growth, Toynbee finds the causes for the decadence of society not in external factors but rather in internal sources, specifically in the lost capacity of leaders for creativity. Either because they ended up being infected by the mechanistic imitation of the followers, or begin to force the majority to follow them no longer by persuasion but rather by compulsion, the leadership becomes alienated and its leaders merely a dominant minority who are not respected by the majority.

But Toynbee also believes that the group that successfully responds to a challenge is rarely successful in responding to the next challenge: "those who have succeeded once are apt, on the next occasion, to be found 'resting on their oars'." (Toynbee, p. 369)

After social unity has been lost, society normally disintegrates into three fractions: dominant minority, internal proletariat and external proletariat.

The internal proletariat can be made up of the same society or brought into the dominant culture as slaves, as was the case in Hellenic society. As for the external proletariat, when a society begins to break it ceases to elicit admiration and fear from its neighbors, thus showing weakness and opening the door to invasions and turmoil. For him, a society in decay will establish a universal state to protect the old ways, which normally signifies the end. Since Toynbee believes that differentiation is the mark of growth, thus standardization is the mark of disintegration (Toynbee 1957, p. 377).

The causes of growth and development are thus found by these different authors in different circumstances. However, all of them agree on a few points: in the process of growth societies find ways to create and innovate, and this innovation brings prosperity. But they also agree on the causes for decadence, mostly coinciding that decadence is a result of a process of corruption and, or stagnation of leadership and its subsequent institutions. Perhaps we can draw some parallels to some of our own societies of today.

Past civilizations, present legacies

The ups and downs of civilizations make us what we are. Whatever form of classification we use today, every culture, civilization, or nation owes its legacy to a former civilization in the past. Every single civilization contributed to the progress of humankind. Whoever invented fire, the wheel, writing, or electricity, humanity as a whole benefitted from it. The further we go into the past, the more clearly we can see the different civilizations that emerged. The closer we come to our present day, the more difficult it is to describe a given civilization, since all are intermingled with each other and it is too complicated to clearly define the essences and the contours of any given one.

We now have a much clearer account of the emergence of the first civilizations on earth. As we said before, agriculture was first discovered around 10,000 years ago, and, around 5000 years afterwards, the first civilizations emerged in different parts of the world. These early civilizations have all the characterstics to be called such: they all developed a sophisticated urban life; they all had a form of writing; they all had an instrument of expansion; and they all had organized institutions that channeled the economic surplus into innovations that were then converted into new adaptations. Early civilizations appeared more or less simultaneously in five main geographical areas: America, China, the Middle East and the Indian subcontinent. Following this geographical classification we can see in the following boxes a summary of the main civilizations of the past and some of their influences and achievements.[5]

Civilizations that emerged in America

Two great civilizations emerged: the Andean civilization, which began around 1500 BC and culminated in the Inca Empire that ended about AD 1600 (a consequence of the Spanish arrival), and the Mesoamerican civilization that began about 1000 BC and culminate in the Aztec Empire and also died out as the sister civilization, and for the same reason, in AD 1550). Both civilizations probably derived out from a common culture probably located in some hilly area in the northern part of South America.

Civilizations that emerged in east Asia

The oldest civilization arose in the valley of the Yellow River after 2000 BC, and culminated in the Chin and Han Empires by 250 BC. This civilization was disrupted by the Ural–Altaic invaders around AD 400. From the debris of this civilization two others emerged: the Chinese that began about AD 400 and culminated in the Manchu Empire in AD 1644 (disrupted by Europeans from 1790 to 1930). And the Japanese civilization that began around the year AD 1 and culminated in the Tokugawa Empire after 1600, and was disrupted by Europeans in the nineteenth century.

We find the largest number of civilizations from this first period around the Mediterranean, in the Middle East, and the Indian subcontinent.

Civilizations that emerged in the Middle East

The Mesopotamian civilization

This began in the river valleys of the Tigris and Euphrates, with some early recorded discoveries around the end of the fifth millennium (normally called the Sumerian–Acadian civilization). They invented cuneiform writing around 3000 BC and remained together under different empires for more than 3000 years, including the Assyrian (between 900 and 600 BC) and the Persian, the last of its empires. The influence of this civilization lingers: we can find in the Old Testament numerous references that mention Ur, as the city of Sumer, where Abraham was born; and the story of the universal flood can be found in the Acadian *Epic of Gilgamesh*. Also, the Sumerian–Acadians counted with a base number of 60, which is the explanation of why for us an hour is 60 minutes each made up of 60 seconds. The empire was finally destroyed by Alexander the Great around 300 BC.

During its 3000 years the Mesopotamian civilizations strongly influenced other civilizations that emerged in the nearby territories, among which were:

The Minoan civilization in Crete

This flourished between 2100 and 1450 BC, and was destroyed by unknown causes, some suggest as result of the Santorini eruption. Its successor was the Mycenaean Empire on the European continent (Peloponnesus, Attica and Boecia (1600 to 1200 BC), also destroyed by unknown causes during the so-called "Dark Age" (traditionally from 1200 to 800 BC). Historians have tried to explain the recorded calamities of constant fires, other destructions, the loss of writing and other civilizational gains, perhaps due to earthquakes or climate change.

The Hittites in Anatolia

The Hittites had their beginnings after 2000 BC, and reached their widest expansion around 1300 BC. They were also destroyed in the Dark Age, some have suggested by a series of cataclysms or multiple earthquakes.

The Canaanite civilization

Emerging in the Levant during the same period and under Mesopotamian influence, it included two Semitic populations, the Phoenicians and the Hebrews; and one Indo-European, the Philistines. This mixed civilization rose around 2000 BC, and around 1200 BC it began its sea expansion towards the west, reaching its peak during the Carthaginian Empire in 900 BC and perishing under the Romans in 200 BC. They invented an alphabet that spread through the Mediterranean by the end of the second millennium BC and was adopted by the Greeks in 800 BC, with the important innovation of the use of vowels.

The Nile valley

Here emerged one of the civilizations that has most fascinated popular imagination for millenniums the Egyptian. First urban centers appeared around 3500 BC, and hieroglyphic writing originated around 3300 BC, reaching its peak in the Ancient Empire (2675–2200 BC). This civilization was destroyed by the Greeks around 330 BC.

Civilizations that emerged on the Indian subcontinent

The Indic civilization

Emerged in the Indus valley around 2600 to 1700 BC, culminating in the Harappa Empire. It was destroyed by Aryan invaders after 1700 BC. They had a pictographic writing that still has not been deciphered.

The Hindu civilization

Developed near the Indic territory, although affiliation has not been proved. The Hindu civilization reached its peak about 100 BC and culminated in a series of empires, with the strong influence of the Aryan population that conquered the territory and mixed with the population. Its last empire, the Mogul Empire of the sixteenth century, was destroyed by European invaders after 1700.

Using today's perspective, it seems logical that most of these agriculture-based civilizations emerged in fertile river valleys such as the Nile, the Tigris and Euphrates, the Yellow River and the Indus. However, as pointed out by Toynbee, these places were probably some of the most inhospitable places that humans could live in. What we do not realize is that thousands of years of labor upon the land has made the valleys the pleasant places to live in we see today. Toynbee suggests that primitive men went through the greatest difficulties to enter these jungles, and through great creativity managed to exploit them to make them inhabitable to humans. According to Toynbee, the creative response of a few courageous humans was provoked by a change in their habitat due to climate change or other external forces, such as the desiccation of the Afro-Asian grasslands, which affected Egyptians, Sumerians and even Minoans.

> When the grasslands overlooking the lower valley of the Nile turned into the Libyan desert and the grasslands overlooking the lower valley of the Euphrates and Tigris into the Rub' al Khali and the Dasht-i-Lut, these heroic pioneers – inspired by audacity or by desperation – plunged into the jungle swamps of the valley bottoms, never before penetrated by men, which their dynamic act was to turn into the land of Egypt and the land of Shinar... As it turned out, the venture succeeded beyond the most sanguine hopes in which the pioneers can ever have indulged. The wantonness of nature was subdued by the works of man; the formless jungle swamps made way for a pattern of ditches and embankments and fields; the lands of Egypt and Shinar were reclaimed from the wilderness and the Egyptian and Sumeric societies started on the great adventures. (Toynbee 1957, p. 70)

Either as Toynbee suggested, due to a change in the habitat conditions or some other unknown circumstances, the fact is that in the period 4000 years before our era, in many different parts of the world, great human inventions set the basis for most of the modern societies we have today; from these civilizations we have gained, among many other inventions: control of irrigation; commercial structures; measurement of time; alphabetic writing; and maritime navigation.

From these first civilizations and through their influence, emerged other civilizations that developed into the present ones. There have been several attempts to classify what civilizations gave rise to the rest; however, this is difficult since, as Quigley suggested, civilizations are like complex masses of quartz from which numerous crystals grow in various directions. The number of crystals in the mass might be disputed, and there would surely be disagreement about which atoms from the main mass of quartz should be attributed to each crystal. Just as it is possible for adjacent molecules of the quartz mass to be oriented in diverse directions, so they should perhaps be attributed to different crystals (Quigley 1961, p. 82).

For instance, it is clear that Greek civilization, which in turn became the Roman, which later transformed itself into the Christian, which ultimately became the modern western civilization, has its most direct origins in the Mycenaean Empire and thus in the earlier Minoan state; however, influences from the Mesopotamians or the Canaanites are more than evident, among other relevant facts being the adoption of the Phoenician alphabet.

Likewise the Islamic civilization had its origins in the peoples of the Arabian Peninsula; yet it also clearly has influences from the Canaanites, and also from the Greek and Mesopotamian civilizations of the time.

Many other civilizations derived directly or indirectly from previous ones that emerged in different parts of the world and greatly influenced the history of the world. Among them was the Ethiopian civilization of around 1000 BC, where legend locates the Queen of Sheba who, according to the Book of Kings in the Old Testament, visited King Salomon in Jerusalem; or the Altaic-speaking population of Turkic Moguls and Tungusics that led to great empires such as the Mongols, the Safavids in Persia, and the Ottoman Empire.

The analysis of past civilizations sheds light to some of our behavior today. Although races and languages tend to fragment and separate, by contrast, culture seems to have the tendency to unify. A good example is how the Indo-Europeans entered the Mesopotamian Empire and continued their influence under the Persians. Hindu civilization continued under the new race of Indo-European peoples. The Greeks continued, albeit with a different language, the earlier Minoan Empire. In many cases the previous culture manages to colonize the colonizers. Persian culture permeated Islamic civilization, the Greeks permeated the Romans, the Celtic civilization is still present underneath the surface of many European people, and influences from India can be seen in most of the world's literature.

All past civilizations have contributed to our present legacy, and it is the fascinating work of archeologists to trace their myriad of influences and how far they have reached. We divide our time in fractions of 60 because of the Sumerians; we write alphabetically because of the Phoenicians; we developed high mathematical operations thanks to the discovery of the zero by the Arabs; our intellectual way of thinking is much indebted to the Greeks; and most of our spiritual myths are tied to a handful of ancient animistic forms that later were absorbed into the great religions of today. It is entertaining to find the origin of our traits; but instead of separating us into who did invented what, this investigation should make us realize that all human inventions were made up of very small steps comprised of even earlier inventions. Each of these steps was part of a significant progress forward, and at the end, all contributions were useful to the human journey.

3   One world, many civilizations?

Moving civilizations, different paths with a common goal

As described in previous sections, human history is the history of the rise and fall of civilizations; and this movement has helped humanity advance through the methodology of trial and error.

What is the need to classify?

In the interesting work *An Intimate History of Humanity*, Theodore Zelding gave one of its chapters the suggestive title, "Why has there been more progress in cooking than in sex?" (Zelding 1994, p. v) Although the chapter refers more to the question of sensual attraction in different cultures, to me this idea also raises the question of how some areas of culture are easy to share, such as cooking or fashion; while others are very much embedded in our subconscious and thus are difficult to move, among them how we conceive time or relationships with others. Thus, we did not have difficulties in adopting potatoes from America or tea from China; however we are not at ease with some of the values and behaviors of cultures different from our own.

We tend to share certain things with our own group and not share them with other humans outside of it. To overcome this, we need to understand cultures and civilizations. It is not enough to formulate a desire for a global village; we need to understand as much as we can, including the families of our global villages and their differences, so that we can be part of a world of equals.

And although classification can lead to separation, it can also help us to understand this thing that has united us, giving us insight into our human journey, both together as human beings as well as within our communities and in the company of our kinship. We can then use different taxonomies to classify the nearly 7 billion people that today populate the planet.

If we define a civilization or a culture by language, we can divide humanity in 5000 groups. If we try to define civilization as a common *shared set of features*, including a mixture of language, religion, similar institutions, common history and shared intellectual legacy, the number of civilizations living today would be less than ten, depending the type of criteria used by the expert. For example, Toynbee in the 1940s defined eight main living civilizations: Western, Orthodox (and as an offspring of this, the Russian), Iranian and Arabic (together they formed Islamic society), Hindu, Far Eastern Societies (with Japanese as an offspring). Toynbee also named a few civilizations that lived in very small groups, almost as relics of past civilizations, including the Jewish, the Parsees and the Jains (Toynbee, pp. 13–34). In a similar approach, Huntington in the 1990s, in his famous book *The Clash of Civilizations and the Remaking of World Order*, described nine civilizations: Western, Orthodox, Latin American, Islamic, Hindu, Buddhist, Sinic, Japanese, and African (Huntington 1996, 2003, p. 26).

If for us civilization refers to *the main spiritual traditions* that have been embodied in different societies, we can then classify the existing world population into nine main religious families: Christians (33 percent of world population); Muslims (20 percent of world population); Jewish (0.2 percent of world population); Hindus (13,3 percent of world population), Buddhists (6 percent of world population); Confucians, Taoists, Shintoists and Animists make up 13 percent of world population; and the rest comprises atheists or agnostics.

Many other classification taxonomies can emerge in addition to these three. For example, the United Nations recognizes 193 independent countries in the world. Some writers argue that most of these nations were imagined and then built, adapted and transformed into a reality; but, nonetheless, the attachment of people to their different nations is real, to the extent that they are willing to die to defend them, as examined in the classic book *Nationalism* by Benedict Anderson (Anderson, 1983, 2006).

Furthermore, all of these classifications tend to be clustered into large families:

The 5000 human languages, some of which are only spoken in very small groups, can be grouped into 19 families, as shown by the work of Merit Ruhlen, who distributes them among the different continents (Cavalli Sforza, p. 192):

- Four in Africa and between Africa and Asia: Khoisan, Niger-Kordofan, Nilo-Saharian and Afro-Asiatic (formerly Hamito-Semitic).
- Seven in Asia and between Asia and Europe: Caucasian, Indo-European, Uralic, Altaic, Chukchi-Kamchadal, Dravidian, Sino-Tibetan,
- Three in America: Eskimo-Aleut, American Indian and Na-Dené
- Five in southeast Asia, Australia and New Guinea: Miao-Yao, Austro-Asiatic, Australian, Tai-Kadai and Papuan.

These 19 families can be further clustered into four super-families: Africans, Nostratic-Caucasians, Mongoloids, and Sino-Altaics and Amerindians.

The eight civilizations of Toynbee are often reduced to five main families: Western, Orthodox, Islamic, Hindu and Far Eastern.

Civilization defined by religion is often also separated into two main families, the Prophetic-Abrahamic (Jews, Christians, Muslims) and the Dharmic or Sapiential religions (Buddhism, Hinduism, Confucianism and Shintoism).

Most of the 193 countries recognized by the United Nations are further clustered in one of the seven main regional integration organizations, including: The African Union, The Arab League of States, The European Union, The Association of Southeast Asian Nations (ASEAN), South Asian Association for Regional Cooperation (SAARC), the Union of South

American Nations, The Pacific Union, and The Central Asian Union comprising five former Soviet, central-Asian republics.

We can thus see in the history of civilizations two clearly opposite tendencies, one towards diversity and the other towards unity. This movement between diversity and unity has been a constant in our human history; we diversify into smaller groups where we survive and grow, while in parallel we form larger unities.

Looking into our beginnings, we were once one family of people living in Africa. And if we look toward the future, it seems that sooner or later we will also be forming one humanity. *What is the purpose of this opposite movement towards diversity and unity?* History tells us that this movement is how we grow and develop. As we saw in previous chapters, individuals withdraw from their communities to develop in solitude and go back to their communities to act; likewise, in a civilization, humans form groups in order to survive. Inside their groups they find new inventions and adaptations that are then spread to other groups, sometimes peacefully and sometimes by force; in any case humanity learns from all of these potential inventions and continues to grow.

According to most experts, our maximum point of expansion was 15,000 years ago when we reached into all the corners of earth. It was probably at this very same moment that the movement towards unity began. However, origin and destiny are totally different; they are the *alpha* and *omega*, representing the start and end of the human journey. We may become again one family in the near future, but in the journey we will have transformed ourselves. Humanity has grown in every plane, physical, emotional, mental and spiritual. We have grown enormously in the physical control of our planet. No matter what cruelties still exist today, we have grown in our ability to love each other. We have grown in our mental capabilities and understanding. And we have grown in our spiritual consciousness of the ways we are bound together as one. In a very positive light, Paul Hawken analyzed the millions of people all over the world working to solve the main problems of the earth, including environmental issues or social injustices:

> Healing the wounds of the earth and its people does not require saintliness or a political party, only gumption and persistence. It is not a liberal or conservative activity; it is a sacred act. It is a massive enterprise undertaken by ordinary citizens everywhere, not by self-appointed governments or oligarchies (Hawken 2007, p. 5).

I for one believe that the human journey thus far, has been worth it.

Globalization vs. the westernization of the world

Most existing civilizations were seriously disrupted by the western civilization, starting during the eighteenth century (some point to earlier dates, pointing out the American civilizations). It was seen as being dominant to such an extent that for many historians of the twentieth century there was only one civilization left – the west. As Huntington described it,

> In the course of European expansion, the Andean and Mesopotamian civilizations were effectively eliminated, Indian and Islamic civilization along with Africa were subjugated, and China was penetrated and subordinated to the western influence. Only Russian, Japanese and Ethiopian civilizations, all three governed by highly centralized imperial authorities, were able to resist the onslaught of the west and maintain meaningful independent existence (Huntington, p. 51).

According to Huntington, Europeans or former Europeans in the American colonies controlled 35 percent of the earth's land surface in 1800, 67 percent in 1878 and 84 percent in 1914. By 1920 the percentage was still higher as the Ottoman Empire was divided among Britain, France, and Italy.

I have to clarify that I do not mean to imply that the other civilizations were peaceful and harmonious; all civilizations came to power after systematically conquering other populations: the Arab civilization conquered the Near East, North Africa, Spain and southeast Asia; the Turks conquered the Middle East and eastern Europe; the Incas came to be a great civilization after effectively eliminated existing rival cultures; the Japanese and Ethiopians invaded their neighbors, just to name a few.

Being of the same civilization did not give much comfort either, as we can see in the records of the Carthaginian rituals, the Mayan cruelties towards their own people, the European wars, or the famous Assyrian atrocities. We have to come to terms with the fact that *Homo sapiens sapiens*, without exception, has been aggressive, dominant and cruel – and still is. Yet we have a much higher consciousness of peace than ever before, which gives some hope for the future.

Having clarified the cruel nature of our human race, I do admit that Europeans have been particularly annoying to other civilizations in the last 400 years, and the fact that most of the world presents features of western civilization is the result of history. Evidently, it was not only through aggression that the west dominated the last four hundred years; the cultural penetration into other cultures was also the result of a European process of unification of its institutions, the rule of law, commerce, economic industrialization, the rise of the middle class, social welfare and political organizations, as well as an unprecedented rate of technological innovation. It was the cohesion of western states, despite their existing internal conflicts, together with the technological advances, which facilitated the spread of western ways to the rest of the world.

Particularly relevant has been the presence of western methods in the process of economic globalization. It is the through the influence of the western economy that the world has undergone the greatest degree of unification. The world financial markets are one of the best examples of globalization; in them everyone speaks the same language, uses the same technologies, and in just minutes news can reach the furthest corners of the world, resulting in global collapses such as we saw in 2008. Activists from different groups such as Attack, and other anti-system organizations fight against an economic globalization that they view as a form of western domination imposing a materialistic view of world relations. This opposition was demonstrated in the protests that took place on November 30, 1999 at the WTO's third ministerial meeting in Seattle, where 700 groups and around 50,000 individuals participated to protest against global capitalism (Hawken 2007, p. 117).

Nevertheless, the rise of material wellbeing for large numbers of the world population is also a fact, together with outrageous inequalities and patterns of domination. But at the same time, technology and the democratization of communication have allowed us to see the misery and atrocities happening in every corner of the world, leading to a growth of consciousness and effort to renounce and rebel against these injustices.

The process of globalization, in any case is not new. For most experts, the process we are immersed in today began after the Cold war in 1989, and is really the second wave of globalization. If we compare the volumes of trade and capital flows to the relative GNPs, and the flow of labor across borders relative to population during the period of globalization preceding the World War II, they are quite similar to the levels we are living today. According to many economic experts, the first globalization period began in 1800 and continued to expand until the second decade of the twentieth century, when different blows, including the Great Depression, World War I and the Russian Revolution, fractured the old world. The world emerged divided after World War II and remained divided during the years of the Cold War, exhausting both the Eastern Block and the United States, until in 1989 when the fall of the Berlin wall represented the beginning of globalization round two.

Friedman (1999, 2000) argues that this new version has a far more global reach in the number of peoples and countries involved, and that it is also different because technological innovations and the subsequent reduction of communication costs have brought many new actors into the global game. What is old are power politics, chaos, clashing civilizations and liberalism. And the drama of the post-cold-war world is the interaction between this new system and all these old passions and aspirations.

Friedman suggests that the real challenge is not so much the difference of cultural identities, but how nation states, communities, individuals and the environment interact with the system. This can be seen as the balance of three different powers:

- the balance between nation states;
- the balance between nation states and global markets;
- the balance between individuals and nation states.

The challenge in this era of globalization – both for countries and individuals – is to find a healthy balance that preserves a sense of identity, home and community, all while doing what it takes to survive within the globalization system (Friedman 2000, p. 42).

The sense of cultural identity, not only for Friedman but also for most experts, plays an important role in this new round of globalization. Cultures that were allegedly dead in the twentieth century have emerged from their ashes to have a say in the twenty-first century. Culture is relevant, among other reasons because it is the main source for social cohesion as well as for personal identity. Quoting Friedman:

> When you strip people's homes of their distinctiveness – either by homogenizing them or by destroying them environmentally – you undermine not only their culture but also their social cohesion. Culture at its best, can be one of the most powerful forms of voluntarily restraint in human behavior. It gives life structure and meaning. It sanctions a whole set of habits, behavioral restrains, expectations and traditions that pattern life and hold societies together at their core. When unrestricted globalization uproots cultures and environments, it destroys the necessary underlying fabric of communal life.
>
> And this brings us back to sustainable globalization. You cannot build an emerging society – which is so essential for dealing with the globalization system – if you are simultaneously destroying the cultural foundations that cement your society and give it the self-confidence and cohesion to interact properly with the world. (Friedman 2000, p. 302)

Today, most commercial global dealings are done in English. North Americans, identify with the maxims of Confucius, coaching programs are full of Indian metaphors and learning tools, and most humans use medical inventions to heal themselves. Therefore, we might have problems with power and domination, but we all tend to appreciate culture when it helps humans to grow, regardless of its origins. Politics divide, while culture integrates since we all learn from each other. Together we create a human legacy for all.

4   Civilization and identity

Huntington in the nineties saw the emergence of civilizational identity as one of the main potential conflicts for the world at the end of the twentieth century; in his view: "The 1990s have seen the eruption of a global identity crisis. Almost everywhere one looks, people have been asking, 'Who are we?', 'Where we do belong?' and 'Who is not us?' (Huntington 1996, 2003 p. 125). In coping with this identity crisis in his writing, he considered that what counted for people were the ties provided by family, faith and blood. For Huntington, the fear produced by a new and unknown world order in which the influence of the west was declining made identities which had previously been multiple and casual become focused and hardened. Communal conflicts were appropriately termed identity wars, and as the violence increased, the initial issues at stake tended to get redefined almost exclusively as "us" against "them." In this context, political leaders began to expand and deepen their appeals to ethnic and religious loyalties, and a consciousness of belonging to a civilization strengthened in relation to other identities.

Huntington stated that in the new cultural identity context, national politicians need to recognize the change and the emergence of different civilizational identities, while at the same time, each civilization should find its internal unity and cohesion that bind it together:

> The futures of both peace and civilization depend upon understanding and cooperation among political spiritual and intellectual leaders of the world's major civilizations ... In the emerging era, clashes of civilizations are the greatest threat to world peace, and an international order based on civilizations is the surest safeguard against world war. (Huntington 1996, 2003, p. 321)

Other experts believe that although the emergence of civilizational identity is a fact, it does not necessarily imply homogeneity within one civilization, since in today's world individual consciousness is as important as national or civilization consciousness. It is likely that we may find, for example, a young Egyptian who totally identifies with the west alongside another young Egyptian who totally identifies with his own traditions; moreover, many Egyptian youngsters will identify with both western ways and local traditions. They will love their Muslim traditions and love western technologies, read Arab poetry and American newspapers, and in their Facebook page we are likely to find twenty nationalities among their friends, and comments in at least three languages.

The real change in this new globalization period is that civilizational identity has to be dealt with not by national states but at the individual level most of all, in a complex framework in which individuals, communities, national states, and economic organizations need to be balanced amongst each other.

In Friedman's words:

> under the globalization system you will find both clashes of civilization and the homogenization of civilizations, both environmental disasters and amazing environmental rescues, both the triumph of liberal free-market capitalism and a backlash against it, both the durability of nation-states and the rise of enormously powerful non state actors. (Friedman 2000, p. xxi)

The key to survive in the new world we live in is to understand and act upon two opposite tendencies: one towards unity and homogenization, and in parallel, another towards diversity and fragmentation.

A few examples will help clarify both of these opposite tendencies:

- The global tendency to emphasize the environment, illustrated for example by the spread of global environmental organizations such as the WWF, runs in parallel with a very strong tendency to preserve local habitats, shown by the rise in local ecological groups. (Paul Hawken estimates there could easily be over one million organizations in the world working toward ecological sustainability and social justice: Hawken 2007, p. 2.)
- A tendency towards a global market allows every person living in Europe to consume any agricultural product produced elsewhere, regardless of the season. However, this tendency goes in parallel with a strong tendency to produce and consume locally and enhance local markets.
- The global financial markets allow any person in the Philippines to invest his or her savings in whatever American company they wish; but in parallel, there is an emergence of local complementary currencies

and alternative local financial lending practices that are meant to be used in closed communitarian markets.

- The global trend in music makes Shakira well-known in every corner of the world; but simultaneously, all over the world the old traditional rhythms are being modernized by youngsters eager to bring their contribution to global music, as we can see in the Sudanese modernization of Haqiba music, New Flamenco in Spain, or the renewal of Tango in Argentina.

- Nationalism within nation states is stronger than ever, as shown by the cases of Spain, Belgium, Turkey and many other places; however in parallel, there are global demonstrations asking for global action in favor of Iraqis and many other populations in turmoil (between six to ten million people took to the streets in 800 cities around the world to protest against the invasion of Iraq on February 15, 2003: Hawken 2007, p. 24).

- A global rise in spirituality has made the spiritual teachings from the most diverse traditions available to any person in the world. In this way many Spaniards have some knowledge of Islam, Qaballah, Hindu meditation, maxims from Confucius and Indian Shamanism, and in fact many use all of them in their everyday lives. Yet parallel to this, there runs a strong desire to explore one's own spiritual traditions, to understand oneself and the world, as illustrated by the new Christian mystic movements that follow the old Christian traditions of Saint John of the Cross or Saint Theresa of Avila.

We can go on, finding many examples in every aspect of our social, economical or spiritual lives of both of these parallel trends towards diversity and unity. It is not a paradox that one can identify with human civilization and at the same time identify with one's own particular group. One can feel proud of the achievements of the human race, and at the same time feel particularly close to one's own particular civilization. In fact, this should be considered healthy and normal, since it is easier to act within the culture we feel the closest to without closing the doors to external influences.

The case of SEKEM that illustrates this chapter is a good example of how to make use of both the unity and diversity of civilizational identity. The company took advantage of the global movement for sustainability as well as the existence of global markets for ecological agricultural products, while at the same time developing strong local markets, promoting producers as well as local consumers. The company harmonized both the spiritual western traditions exemplified by Rudolf Steiner or Goethe, while at the same time enhancing the knowledge of Islamic spiritual traditions and cultural legacies. The three regular working languages at SEKEM also reflect how a company can work in different languages without a need to homogenize. SEKEM tried to preserve the sense of identity of its workers while at the same time playing with the rules of globalization.

However true may be the two trends globally, an important fact to hold in consideration is the respect for the different rhythms in every civilization that illustrate the different path each civilization has followed to grow. There are two general trends throughout the world, one towards unity (globalization, etc.) and the other towards multiplicity, (cultural nationalism, etc.). Nevertheless, although this is a universal condition, each civilization still has a particular rhythm and a different path for its development, which means that these two trends will not necessarily be reflected in the same way within each civilization.

A few examples;

- For the last few centuries, the West has followed strong individualistic values. As consequence and in order to find a balance, new generations increasingly value community. However, in other areas of the world, such as Islamic countries, after a long history of community there is a trend towards promoting individual rights and values, without losing their community ties. Each civilization needs to identify what it is lacking most and, for each, finding this balance represents a movement forward.
- The west for decades has followed patterns of consumerism to their extreme. The result is that many people look to new ways of reducing consumerism and increase sharing. And yet, if we think for example of Africa, there is still a fundamental need to elevate the material level of wealth for most of its population in order to be able to secure their basic needs; thus, being able to consume more is not a defect but rather a positive move.
- For the west, the mind has been the most and sometimes the only appreciated quality of human beings. Since the nineteenth century, emotions have been increasingly repressed and, as a consequence, most new psychological tendencies strive to teach individuals to connect with their emotional side. For other civilizations, as for example the Arabs, the emotional side is well developed. Probably, for them a move to reduce the emotional component in their societies in favor of a more detached and rational behavior would be a move towards a more positive balance.
- Professional achievement has long been the most precious goal for many western individuals. Lately, thinking outside the goals of the professional life has become a positive trend for many Europeans, which is not the case for many Asians, for whom focusing on professional success is still a very positive trend in their society.

5 Fifth movement: Identity in civilization: Integrating unity and diversity in a larger framework

Civilization represents the legacy of our elders, an immanent force that hold us together regardless of our different personal and communitarian identities. Yet in spite of this, the immanent is not static, the legacy of our elders is with us as a force that helps us move forward; and as the individual members of a civilization move and grow, so grows the civilization that one is a member of. Respect for the past does not mean we have to re-live the past – it is past. What our legacy allows us to do is to have the necessary self-confidence to move forward using, in our own way, whatever innovation we can find wherever we can find it.

We will all meet at the end, since humanity is going inevitably towards unity. The movement towards unity that began 15,000 years ago is now accelerating at an enormous speed. However, the way we have innovated and grown has been kept under the umbrella of our own civilizations, making each civilization move at its own speed and choosing its own path; thus each civilization will find its way to connect with others when the time comes.

In the introduction to this book there was a diagram showing the necessity of harmonizing, in individuals as well as in civilizations, physical, emotional and mental elements. It is my belief that we are getting closer to fulfilling all parts of this schema. Individuals have developed at great length their physical, emotional and mental capabilities, each of us in uniquely different proportions. Therefore, the individual task for most of us is to harmonize. For some, this means an increase of the emotional over the mental, for others action over the reflection – each one will have to find their own way. Cultures and civilization also have to harmonize these three levels, freedom of action with physical security, emotional cohesion of its members with their mental fulfillment. At the moment, each civilization is trying to balance these elements to achieve harmony. To explain the current state of international chaos, we must understand that we are immersed in globalization, and yet at the same time, each culture is finding its own development and internal balance; therefore, we are living in a great confusion that is the consequence of a unifying process occurring simultaneously with the efforts of a great number of cultures in search for their own balance.

The evolution of human kind is not only an evolution at the material level and of mental capabilities, but also and foremost, the rise of our common consciousness. The journey has also been very painful where the gains of some have often resulted in the suffering of many. Today's human miseries are still countless; nevertheless, for the first time in human history there are global efforts to stop these sufferings, global demonstrations against war, and global organizations to protect human rights for all. These are the most recent human creations, and although still in their infancy, they signify that humanity is not only developing its material control over natural resources, but also developing a human consciousness and a human soul.

Case 5   SEKEM, Egypt: Unity in diversity for global business competitiveness

Introduction

It is past 7 p.m. on February 1, 2011, the eighth day of the Egyptian revolution. Curfew, set this week at 3 p.m., has long passed, but still some workers stayed voluntarily at the premises to protect the companies which are providing their livelihood against looters. Maximilian Boes from Germany feels really proud of being part of such a community: the community spirit and loyalty of SEKEM employees has been particularly high during the weeks of Egyptian revolution. SEKEM employees are coming to work and are doing night shifts to protect the firms from potential "attacks" despite the fact that they have stayed awake for days to protect their own families and property. This was not the case with other firms in Egypt. "This is a very strong symbol of sustainability and underlines the value of a strong community and belonging," says Maximilian, who certainly expresses also the feelings of his Egyptian and international colleagues.

Maximilian arrived a year ago, after finalizing his Masters Degree at the Grenoble Graduated Business School in France; he decided to move to Egypt to quit his "comfort zone" in Europe and to pursue his interest in things related to sustainable development. He finally found SEKEM through one of his old friends who already worked in this organization, well known in Germany for its organic products, produced along the guidelines of Rudolf Steiner's biodynamic agricultural principles. Maximilian wanted to study and work in this unique combination of European and Arabian culture, where both are working together, harmonizing the best of each world.

In Goethe's words, "Those who know themselves and others will recognize here too that the Orient and the Occident cannot longer be separated." (As quoted in the SEKEM *Report on Sustainable Development* 2009, p. 60.)

Dr. Ibrahim Abouleish established SEKEM in 1977 in Egypt. The overarching goal of the initiative is sustainable development, which is achieved through a unique integration of economic, social, cultural and ecological aspects. The principal SEKEM business activities are land reclamation, organic farming, food, phytopharmaceutical, and textile production. SEKEM companies include the largest packer of organic tea and the leading producer of herbs in the Middle East. In 2010, the SEKEM Companies and its Foundation employed 1856 people and its total net sales were 224 million EGP and the net profit 18 million EGP. Fixed assets (property, plant and equipment, and biological assets) reached 392 million EGP during 2010. The group is owned by the Abouleish Family, and since 2007, the GLS Bank and the Triodos Bank, each hold shares of 2.5 million EUR, representing each approximately 11.9 percent of total capitalization.

The foundation: A vision of a garden in the desert

The history of SEKEM is closely related to the life and dreams of Dr. Ibrahim Abouleish. He described how the idea of SEKEM came into being in his book *SEKEM: A Sustainable Community in the Egyptian Desert.*[6]

Ibrahim Abouleish was born in 1937 in Egypt. His father ran various industries, including a soap business and a confectionery factory. At the age of 18 Ibrahim Abouleish decided to go to Austria, where he studied first technical chemistry, and later pharmacological studies. He then worked as pharmacologist in different medical companies

In Austria, he became familiar with the writings of Rudolf Steiner, and became friends with some of the members of his anthroposophy movement, one of them Martha Werth. In 1975 she proposed a trip to Egypt that left a deep impression in Dr. Abouleish. Deeply moved by the conditions he found in his country, such as the poor state of the economy, a devastated agricultural sector, poor health-care for the people, and a poor quality of education, he decided back in Austria to return to Egypt with his family to help improve the situation of the country and to develop the land and the people.

As he explains himself, he had a vision of a garden in the desert:

> I carry a vision deep within myself: in the midst of sand and desert I see myself standing at a well drawing water. Carefully I plant trees herbs and flowers and wet their roots with the precious drops. The cool

well water attracts human beings and animals to refresh and quicken themselves. Trees give shade, the land turns green, fragrant flowers bloom, insects, birds and butterflies show their devotion to God the creator, as if they were citing the first Sura of the Koran. The humans, perceiving the hidden praise of God, care for and see all that is created as a reflection of paradise on earth.

For me the idea of an oasis in the middle of a hostile environment is like an image of the resurrection at down after a long journey through the nightly desert. I saw it in front of me a model before the actual work in Egypt started. And yet in reality I desire even more: I wanted the whole world to develop.

I thought long and hard about what to call this project which a wanted to implement following this vision. Because of my interest in ancient Egypt I knew that at the time of the pharaohs there were two different words for the light and the warm of the sun. And the sun had a third element attributed to it: SEKEM, the life-giving force of the sun, with which she enlivens and permeates the earth's entire being. I choose this name for the initiative I planned to start at the edge of the desert. (*A Sustainable Community in the Egyptian Desert*. Foreword.)

He was convinced that part of the agricultural problems of Egypt were caused by the excessive use of artificial fertilizers and pesticides and the resulting over-salting of the earth. He wanted to created his initiative based on the principles of the biodynamic agriculture following the ideas of Rudolf Steiner. For that reason he studied Steiner's teachings and went to visit some biodynamic farms in Italy, he then realized that marketing and distribution were the weakest part of the Biodynamic movement.

Biodynamic agriculture is an advanced organic farming system that is gaining increased attention for its emphasis on food quality and soil health.

Biodynamic agriculture developed out of eight lectures on agriculture given in 1924 by Rudolf Steiner (1861–1925), an Austrian scientist and philosopher, to a group of farmers near Breslau (which was then in the eastern part of Germany and is now Wroclaw in Poland). These lectures, as well as four supplemental lessons, are published in a book titled *Spiritual Foundations for the Renewal of Agriculture*, originally published in English as *An Agricultural Course* www.attra.ncat.org.

A basic ecological principle of biodynamic farming is to conceive the farm as a self-contained and self-sustaining organism. Emphasis is placed on the integration of crops and livestock, recycling of nutrients, maintenance of soil, and the health and wellbeing of crops and animals; the farmer too is part of the whole. In an effort to keep the farm, the farmer, the consumer, and the earth healthy, farmers avoid chemical pesticides and fertilizers, utilize compost and cover crops, and set aside acreage for biodiversity. It times all operations to coincide with cosmic rhythms, particularly lunar cycles.

Demeter Certification is the main body that certifies biodynamic farming in the world. http://www.demeter.net.

Ibrahim Abouleish launched SEKEM in 1977 to become an all-inclusive development initiative. The SEKEM "Mother Farm" was founded in the region of Sharkia, situated at the border of desert land in the Nile Valley near the town of Belbeis, 60 km northeast of Cairo, and consisted of 70 hectares of desert land. The first large economic venture of SEKEM was the production of the medicinal compound ammoidin (a plant extract) to export to an American company. Soon it also began to manufacture of herbal teas for domestic sale and export to Europe, mainly Germany.

As he reflected on his experience, Abouleish recognized that one of the greatest opportunities for poverty reduction could be found in labor-intensive agricultural-based production. In view of this, he ultimately developed three fields of value-added agriculture-based manufacturing: natural medicines (phytopharmaceuticals), organic foodstuffs, and naturally grown fabric products. Right from the start he had a view that the commercial business had to go along with cultural and the social development. Over the years, projects in health, education, and research have been established and today the Heliopolis Academy for Sustainable Development advances applied research in these fields.

The SEKEM business model[7]

Ibrahim Abouleish's holistic model is based on the integration of different areas into one common organism, inspired on the Rudolf Steiner vision of the social question.[8] The different spheres of the social organism can be regarded as the organs in the human body. Each one has its own functions and specifications, but only when the parts work together in the form of an organism is the single organ able to fulfill its functions in the entity of the organism.

SEKEM's idea of a four-dimensional model illustrates the dynamic relation of cultural life (education, arts, belief systems), social life (civil society, human rights, legal systems, politics), economic life (all aspects of fair trade, business interactions), and ecology. All four dimensions (economical, social, ecological, cultural) stand equally on the same level and all embrace each other.

The organizations that channel the different dimensions can be described as (i)The coordinator of the economic life, *SEKEM Holding*; (ii) the Coordinator of the cultural life; the *SEKEM Development Foundation* (SDF), accountable for the entire cultural aspect of the group; (iii), *the Cooperative of SEKEM Employees* (CSE), accountable for human rights within the group and the relations between the people.;(IV) the fourth dimension, the ecological, embraces aspects of air, energy, water, soil, plants and animals.

Economic life

The SEKEM Holding embraces several companies which represent the integration of production and commercialization of food, medicine and clothes. "My vision always encompassed covering the basic needs of the people by producing food, medicine and clothes and with these products working in a healing way."[9]

The eight main companies and its functions are distributed as follows:

- **Lotus:** was the first company of SEKEM founded in 1977. It produces natural and chemical free herbs, spices, seeds and cereals. Half of its production is sold to Isis and Atos.
- **Lotus Upper Egypt:** was founded in 2007 and is mainly concerned with drying herbs and spices.
- **Atos:** founded in 1986, produces and markets Pharma products.
- **Libra:** founded in 1988, supplies biodynamical raw materials to other SEKEM companies. For the last three years has also produced and sold compost to other SEKEM companies as well as to other companies and/or governmental organizations.
- **Isis:** founded in 1997, together with Hator (specialized in international markets) packs and distributes foods and beverages to local and international markets.
- **Naturtext**: founded in 1998, manufactures and exports cotton and textiles with a total of 35 different products.
- **Mizan:** founded in 2006 as a 50/50 joint venture between Grow Group Holland and SEKEM Group Egypt, offers grafting and plant cultivation services for fruit and vegetable plants.

- **SEKEM for land reclamation:** established in 2008, is planned to reclaim and plant 2000 feddan (840 hectares) in north Sinai, 2000 feddan at the Bahareya Oasis and 2000 in Minia governorate.

Net sales reached 224 million Egyptian pounds in 2010: 43 percent of the net sales were achieved in fast moving consumer goods, 29 percent in farming, 15 percent in textiles and 13 percent in pharmaceuticals. In the same year the company made a net profit of 18 million EGP. The group uses most of the gross profit to pay for recent investments made for the acquisitions of three new farmland. Companies donate at least 10 percent of their profits to the SEKEM Development Foundation.

Societal life

The societal sphere of SEKEM is coordinated by the Cooperative of SEKEM Employees (CSE), accountable for human relations development and human rights. It ensures the healthy relations among all employees by watching over the equality of its rights in their diversity of needs and beings and dignity.

The 1856 people employed at SEKEM Companies and Foundation are distributed geographically as follows; three employees in Germany at SEKEM Europe, 15 in Assiut in Isis, 27 at the Delta (Isis), 35 in Alexandria (Isis), 470 at Salam City in Cairo Headquarters, 974 on the Mother Farm near Bilbeis and 242 under the umbrella of the SEKEM Development Foundation.

The minimum entry level salary in SEKEM in 2010 is established at 600 EGP. In addition there are over 28,000 seasonal workers employed by the suppliers of SEKEM.

In SEKEM, employee diversity is very present in everyday life, in gender and religion but also in profiles and various backgrounds. In management meetings English and Arabic are both frequently used. English is widely spread in the company and the employees are also offered German lessons. This comes from a small German, Austrian and Swiss community that helped to build up SEKEM from the beginning and who are still living on the SEKEM Mother Farm.

The company manages differences by making each employee feel unique, and also making everyone feel part of the community. That is the reason why employees gather in circles from the daily start of work to the end of week assembly. In the morning the employees of each company meet in a circle for a communal start, where each person briefly reports its intentions for the coming day. At the end of the week all SEKEM employees gather together in an end of the week circle. At the weekly Monday Forum, scientific lectures and arts performances are held at the Heliopolis Academy. During regular meetings Dr. Ibrahim Abouleish discusses aspects of the daily work with all employees and opens their mind to new perspectives on their work, especially spiritual and ethical issues.

The circle is perceived by Abouleish as the symbol of social equality. "Standing in a circle shows all participants are equal, an equality which springs from the dignity of the human being. The individual person experiences himself as part of a community of individuals who are equals, and through this becomes aware of the other members of the community when he acts for the good of the whole. In doing so he takes responsibility for his fellow people. At the same time every person as an equal has to represent himself to the others, that is, he has the right to be taken into the consciousness of his fellow people."[10]

Cultural and spiritual life

"The SEKEM Development Foundation (SDF) is the organism in charge of improving the quality of human life amongst SEKEM employees and Egyptian citizens and to be a sound continuation of the SEKEM vision for comprehensive sustainable development."[11]

The cultural and spiritual life ensures an understanding of what sustainable development means at its core. Arts open up the soul and allow the soul to experience and embrace its environment. By grasping, experiencing, the world in this way, people are able to grasp the holistic unity of it: and this is what sustainability is all about. Without the arts there is no sustainability and thus no future competitiveness.

The SEKEM Development Foundation, (SDF), accountable for the entire cultural aspect of the group, represents the integration of the natural, physical and spiritual aptitudes of each individual in their diversity.[12] All SEKEM companies donate 10 percent of their yearly profit to the foundation to finance community projects which serve educational, health and cultural development purposes. In addition, donations from other associations, boards and national and international funds for research, training and social development projects are generated.

The cultural and spiritual dimension of the SEKEM organism is a cross-dimensional driver by which the individual is empowered by an immersion in the higher works of human civilization, from the Occidental and Oriental world. Integrating the diversity of human arts has been also one of the main principles in Ibrahim Abouleish's strategy:

> During my studies in Graz I noticed other inner changes taking place. I became thoroughly involved with European culture, getting to know its music, studying its poetry and philosophy. Somebody looking into my soul would not have seen anything "Egyptian" left, so completely had I absorbed everything new. Despite this I still felt grounded in the Egyptian culture because of my upbringing during childhood and adolescence. I existed in two worlds, both of which I felt were completely different from each other: the oriental spiritual stream I was born into and the European, which I felt was my chosen course. But during this time I also started experiencing moments with these two streams met in my soul. This occurred particularly when I was experiencing art. For example, I started hearing Handel's Messiah or Mozart's Requiem with Muslim ears as praise to Allah. The two completely different worlds within me began to dissolve and merged into a third entity, so I was neither completely the one nor the other – I could live in both worlds think both ways. But what I experienced was not not cheap compromise, nor just tolerance but a synthesis even an elevation in the Goethian sense, a real uniting of the two cultures within me. These experiences give me a wonderful sense of freedom and these months were filled with greatest happiness and joy.[13]

Ecological life

The ecological dimension at SEKEM consists of all components of the ecosystem: energy, soil, air, water, plants, and animals need to be sustainably developed for general improvement and for the improvement of men's consciousness in the process. In 2010, SEKEM cultivated more than 782 hectares of fertile soils, of which 86 percent were newly reclaimed farmland. Thirty percent of the raw materials used in processing come from SEKEM firms. To secure supplies for a growing demand especially for herbal and medicine plants SEKEM also contracts other farmers and thus helps them to convert to biodynamic production methods: 175 associated small-scale farmers from the Egyptian Biodynamic Association (EBDA) cultivate more than 8000 acres in total.

Organic farming in Egypt

The Nile Valley is home to 98 percent of the Egyptian population and divides Egypt into two desert areas: western Egypt and eastern Egypt. Two percent of the population lives in oasis or reclaimed irrigated desert land. Depending on soil and water conditions, three types of farming can be found in Egypt, farming in the oases, farming in the Nile Valley, and recently also farming in desert lands. Farms in the reclaimed desert land tend to be more intensive due to political and economic incentives to promote foreign investment and lower prices of land.

In 2007 in Egypt there were approximately 460 organic farms, covering an area of 14,165 hectares. Most of them are concentrated in the Middle Nile in the region of El Fayoum, 100 km south of Cairo. Most organic farms are small, from 4.5 to 20 hectares; only a few are larger than 400 hectares, most of which will be located in reclaimed desert land, in the Nile Delta, and in the Upper Nile.

Exports to Europe drive organic production in Egypt. The major crops exported are herbs, vegetables and fruits. The most important herbs are camomile, dill, lemongrass, hibiscus, marjoram, parsley, peppermint, and spearmint. For vegetables, the most important crops are potatoes, onions, garlic, green beans, peppers, and peas. As for fruits the major exports are mangos, grapes and olives. Egyptian organic exports benefit from off-season supply to the European market, and potatoes and onions have found a niche due to storage and preservation problems of these products in cold and humid climates.

raises the costs of putting in place additional measures for control and supervision for producers and consumers.

Domestic sales of organic products are concentrated around the urban areas of Cairo and Alexandria. Outlets in high-income areas with a presence of affluent foreigners account for much of the market. Shopkeepers estimated that 60 to 70 percent of consumers are foreigners. Increasingly organic products are not only sold in special outlets but also in supermarkets like Carrefour, Metro Alfa and Spinneys.

SEKEM approach to ecology: Composting

SEKEM is perceived as a living organism following ecological principles of systemic interdependencies, in that respect the use of crop residues and cow dung as natural fertilizers is one of the key components of the concept. Therefore, since its foundation, composting has been one of the keys to SEKEM's success.

Soil fertility in desert lands such as the one in which SEKEM is located can be enhanced naturally by increasing organic matter levels in the soil, for instance by the application of compost. Although compost can hardly be seen as an innovation, it is the application of compost in the desert that SEKEM has introduced that has proven truly innovative. The compost is produced by combining organic material in windrows and by inoculating special microorganisms. During composting the material is regularly turned, in order to avoid an anaerobic milieu. Under anaerobic conditions methane accrues, which is 21 times as climate-active as CO_2.[14]

The development of compost facilities, in addition to having beneficial consequences on soil fertility and reduced irrigation-water-use, has had other benefits, like rcingedu emission of nitrous oxide due to chemical fertilizer production, and carbon sequestration in the soil. Composting is approved by the UNFCCC for emission-reduction projects as part of the Clean Development Mechanism. This means that the innovative techniques of composting are acknowledged as a method of reducing methane emissions from landfills and mitigating climate change.[15] Composting one tonne of Egyptian organic waste mitigates the greenhouse effect of 0.44 tonnes of CO_2 equivalent.

SEKEM has been producing compost for fertilizing the soil since its beginning. In 2007, due to the increase in demand, SEKEM Company Libra began a cooperation with Soil and More, Egypt, to produce their own compost at one of SEKEM's farms in Adleia and at another site near Alexandria. Each year, 120,000 tonnes of organic material are converted into 60,000 tonnes of high-quality compost. The organic material consists of chicken and cow manure, rice straw and green waste originating from SEKEM's own farms and, neighboring farms, as well as from river plants from irrigation canals.

SEKEM innovation through managing diversity

Innovation in SEKEM comes from its uniqueness in managing a large diversity of businesses peoples and skills into a unity of objectives. SEKEM was especially skillful in integrating all areas of its businesses, including marketing and distribution of its products, and closely related in obtaining successful partnerships with key global players in the field.

Part of the success of its marketing and distribution has been the skill in combining resources and partnerships with local and international organizations since the very start. Among the different partnership in SEKEM development the following are particularly relevant:

- The first shipment abroad was to an American company, providing extracts of amminoi in 1981.
- In 1985, *Isis* brand herbal tea was launched, both in the domestic market with the support of a strong advertising campaign, and in the international market through business relations with companies in Europe among them; Lebensbaum in Germany, Eosta in Holland, and later Organic farm foods in the UK and Alnatura foodchain in Germany
- In collaboration with the German Development Company (DEG) in Germany, SEKEM launched the first phytopharmaceutical business in Egypt in 1986.
- Mizan was founded in 2006 as a 50/50 joint venture between Grow Group Holland 2007, the GLS Bank and the Triodos Bank, each holding shares of 2.5 million EUR.
- SEKEM's involvement with the International Association of Partnerships, which is a forum established amongst organizations from different countries that are interested in organic agriculture, has helped SEKEM market its products internationally.

SEKEM is also active in a variety of organizations that help in the recognition of its activities globally, among which are the Social Entrepreneur Council (Schwab Foundation), the World Economic Forum (WEF), the World Future Council, and the IFC of the World Bank.

In the age of diversity, integrating the multiplicity of beings and resources into a common goal becomes crucial for business sustainability and competitiveness. SEKEM Egypt represents a unique combination that in turn constitutes its real competitive advantage. The integration of the multiplicity if activities in all areas of life into a unity of a living community, in which its members live both their individual dimensions as well as their communal life.

Annex: A Mediterranean tale

Having a coffee in a terrace anywhere in front of the Mediterranean I feel at home, whether in my ancestors' town Salobreña (Spain), Sidi Bou Said (Tunisia), or Marseille (France). I feel I belong there and that the Mediterranean identity is one of my most precious ones.

A few years ago, Spanish National TV organized a contest entitled "The Most Popular Song of Our Lives" to choose a song that best represented the symphony of our lives. Over six months, thousands of Spaniards voted, ultimately selecting *Mediterranean* by Juan Manuel Serrat[16] as the winner. This was a surprising result, since the singer Juan Manuel Serrat represents Catalan nationalism. However, for most Spaniards, regardless of their political ideology, this song evokes a Mediterranean air that is in the collective subconscious of Spaniards.

This special ethos has been rationalized by many intellectuals who have identified with it, such as Albert Camus, who used to say that rather than European he felt Mediterranean (Ives Lacoste 2010, pp. 100–102). Reputedly, over the years these intellectuals from the north and south of the Mediterranean have worked to provide an integrated Mediterranean framework that could help to build a common future together, reframing the past and moving away from stereotypes and endless grievances. Fernand Braudel stands out among these scholars, with his production of works of high poetic value and historical rigor, in which he transmits a deep love for his Mediterranean identity, for the sea and its people that had such an important influence on the history of humanity. Braudel states that only by questioning the past can we give some answers to our present, since, paraphrasing his words, to have been is a condition of being (Braudel 1989, p. 9).

We can also find outstanding scholars on the southern shore, among them the renowned Algerian philosopher Mohammed Arkoun,[17] who with an enthusiasm equal to Braudel's, attempted to reframe the past in order to build a better future together that would integrate both shores. Arkoun stresses the importance of rethinking the local to help rebuild the global. He points out that against the present global modernity that tends to unify and exclude, it is necessary to look back at the Mediterranean identity and overcome its present conflicts to build a stronger future together. This future will in turn contribute to a stronger global world. The present trend of globalization is deprived of a clear humanistic project, and according to Arkoun, if we look at Mediterranean history we can perhaps find in its thinkers, spiritual visions, creative works and heroes, the inspiration we need to give light to the fights of humanity for emancipation in the twenty-first century – all without having to fall into idealistic speculations or nostalgic evocations (Arkoun, 1990).

In order to build an integrated space, Arkoun has put forward a new cognitive strategy (Arkoun 2010). In this strategy it is of paramount importance to set the basis for a fundamental equality among the Mediterranean peoples. For that purpose, we have the common task on the north and south shores of revisiting with critical eyes and courage the role of each in the creation of the recurrent violence in our past. But we also need to look back in search of our common space. In addition to this endless violence, we can also find some of the greatest achievements of the human mind, among which are three major religions and a philosophical and scientific thinking that has crossed all linguistic, ethnographic, cultural and social frontiers.

Braudel and Arkoun, together with other intellectuals from France, Spain, Algeria, Morocco, Italy, Tunisia, Egypt and Turkey, have been instrumental in influencing governments and policymakers to include Mediterranean relations in the political agenda of the European Union.

Not only have European scholars felt a fascination for Mediterranean history, renowned American scholars have also dedicated part of their work to trying to understand the complexity of the Mediterranean, among whom Professor Andrew Hess deserves a special mention. In 1978 he wrote *The Forgotten Frontier*, a book essential to the understanding of the history of the Mediterranean (Hess, 1978). Hess, just like many other thinkers from the Mediterranean, highlights the relevance of the sea as an element for the union of cultures.

The following text from Quigley is a good example of the contributions of American scholars:

> The geographical significance of the Mediterranean Sea of course is that it divides Europe from Africa, but its cultural significance is distinctly different because it has served to link its shores together rather than divide them. This binding influence of the Mediterranean in the cultural sphere lasted for 4000 years, from the first establishment of distinct maritime travel at about 3500 BC, to the Arab conquest of North Africa around AD 700. During all this time, the cultural division was not along the Mediterranean Sea but on the mountain barrier running parallel to the north. During that time, maritime transportation was more efficient than land transportation; but for periods from 700 to 1700, the superior influence of maritime transportation was counterweighed by the cultural division between Moslem and Christian.

Then after 1750, the technologies of rail and land became superior to that of the seas.

Classical civilization was the culmination of Mediterranean influence. This was reflected in the Roman Empire in the name of *Mare Nostrum* given to the Mediterranean sea ("our sea"), while peoples of the north of the mountains (who were biologically closer relatives but culturally remote) were called "Barbarian" for most of the classical period (Quigley 1961 p. 170).

But the sea can also change, as observed by Hess and others, from a vehicle of union into a vehicle of separation. Union and diversity are the two fundamental factors to understand the history of the Mediterranean; its history is of peoples who, although they shared a common history and many similarities in their way of life, also represented very different civilizations that often ignored their mutual fertilization. As Roque points out, "The Mediterranean represents a mosaic of diversity but also the space of numberless cultural fusions and mixtures in which each culture practices a selective memory by which its own contribution to civilization emerges, ignoring systematically the contribution of others (Roque 2005)."

The reconstruction today of a common past is a difficult task full of complexities. First is the fact that the selective memory of each culture tries to elevate their own over others; but there is also the problem posed by the recent history of colonization, and the way that, as pointed out by Arkoun, after independence it forced the cultures of the south to develop a new identity in opposition to the colonizers. Therefore, the discourse over later decades has denied common history and instead stressed the differences with the north (Arkoun 1996).

We will first analyze in further detail some of the elements that unify Mediterranean history, and later we shall discuss the details of its diversity.

Unity in the Mediterranean

Take a trip in the Mediterranean, anywhere from Andalusia to Izmir, no matter where you stop, whether it is Tunis, Oran, Messina, Santorini, or Marseille, you will notice a "common air," as Pitt Rivers puts it, "a certain *air de famille*" (Pitt Rivers 2000). It is something to do with the the way that the towns are built, the way of life of their populations, what they eat, their sense of humor – in a word, the Mediterranean ethos is what the traveler exierices. It is defined by Roque as a system of thought and action that provides a coherence for local ideas, such as the idea of family and society, the behavior of children, work and leisure, and the concept of honor (Roque 2005, p. 21).[18]

The question arising here is: Where did these similarities in people's behavior come from? Is it history? A Mediterranean race? The climate?

Braudel suggests that the basic unity of the Mediterranean is based on the land and its characteristics, among which he highlights: the climate, that has imposed a way of life that impregnates the personality of its inhabitants; a particular diet a consequence of the specific climatic conditions; and the sea, the conquest of which is marked by the courage of millions of humans since the dawn of humanity. (Braudel 1985–86),

Let us now look at these elements in more detail:

The Mediterranean climate: The tourist paradise

The climate of the Mediterranean is a product of two main external elements: the Atlantic Ocean in the east and the Sahara in the south. The Sahara dominates for six months during the summer, making the Mediterranean the only area in the world in which the rain rarely falls during the summer months. This influence is replaced in October by the oceanic depressions that sweep the region from west to east, bringing the anxiously expected rain. Its dry summers make the region the paradise of tourists; however, they also make it the nightmare for farmers always waiting for the rain (Braudel 1985–86, p. 21).

Water has always been one of the fundamental elements of Mediterranean life, and its scarcity helps to explain some of the communitarian practices of its peoples: the sanctification of the wells; the strict policies regarding irrigation; the discipline in communities; as well as some of the most magnificent constructions to improve water efficiency, from Roman aqueducts to Arab cisterns (Ives Lacoste 2010, pp. 100–102).

As Roque mentions, the sanctification of water is visible in a number of primitive religious images both north and south of the Mediterranean, as well as in a number of cultural tales in which water is perceived as the guarantor of life, possessing purifying as well as regenerating virtues (Roque 2005, p. 71).

The Mediterranean diet

The Mediterranean littoral it is not an easy place to make a living. The permanent dryness adds to the constant danger of flooding on its plains,

compounded by a permanent risk of conquerors arriving from the sea. It
is therefore logical, as Braudel remarks, that settlements were established
in the mountains, where people were protected from the constant invasions and unexpected floods. Mountains are safe places to live; however,
agriculture there is difficult. The scarcity of farming land and the rigorous
climate greatly reduced the products that the Mediterranean populations
were able to develop, since they could only farm on artificial terraces stolen from the mountains. Therefore, the basic products of the Mediterranean
diet have been traditionally reduced to three: olives, grapes, and wheat.
Livestock has also been an important part of the Mediterranean diet; sheep
were domesticated as early as 9000 years before our era, followed by pigs
and finally cattle around the year 5000 BC (Braudel 1989, p. 260).

While the sea provided many resources, the Mediterranean suffers
from chronic biological deficit, perhaps due to its age and also to the fact
that its deep waters lack the superficial platforms necessary to facilitate
reproduction. Its scarcity can also be caused by the lack of nutrients as
well as lack of streams to move them; unlike oceans, this condition makes
Mediterranean waters scarce in plankton which is necessary to maintain
a rich sea life. Thus fisheries are to be found only in small numbers and
sizes, except for the tuna that has been one of the fundamental ingredients
of the Mediterranean diet since the earliest times. On the positive side,
the lack of quantity is balanced somewhat by a rich variety of species and
consequently, a high level of biodiversity (Braudel 1989, p. 39).

Navigation and the conquest of the sea

Navigation in its most primitive form began 2500 years before our era
with the first Egyptian boats going to Byblos. These primitive boats are
the ones we can see in the Egyptian papyrus scrolls. Theywere made of
reeds and had remarkably shallow draught, in order to not get trapped in
the wetlands. These first boats were then superseded by simple wooden
vessels with a sail that allowed them to sail upstream with the wind and
return by following the flow of the Nile's stream. These boats were probably financed by Egyptians and piloted by Canaanites. Perhaps as early as
2000 BC, if not earlier, another type of ship was already being built on the
northern shore of the Mediterranean, and this would be the instrument that
facilitated the Aegean civilization. These boats had sails and oars, with a
keel and a hull, both of enable boats to float with a deeper draught, resulting in a greater stability and stronger resistance to the winds.

Therefore, by the year 2000 BC, two strong centers existed in the north
and south of the Mediterranean where boats were built and sailors were

to be found. At this time, according to Braudel, we can already talk about proto-Phoenicians and proto-Greeks, the two most distinctive navigating civilizations of ancient Mediterranean history. We can, therefore, already discuss a Mediterranean way of life that built great cities and developed an urban culture thanks to highly intense commerce. Today, archeologists can explore these ruins and find that the contributions of many civilizations are intermixed (Braudel 1989, pp. 65–66).

Then after years of splendor, and for unknown causes, from 1200 to 800 BC the Mediterranean sank into a period of darkness, during which the active cultural exchange and Mediterranean commerce and splendor ceased to exist. Only the Canaanites seem to have taken advantage of these dark times: although Ugarit disappeared and Byblos was in decay, these centers were soon replaced by Sidon and Tyre, which by the year 1000 BC had become the dominant trading centers of the region. Small states emerged at that time, among them the Jewish state, which in the year 950 BC was divided into two: Judea in the south and Israel in the north.

During this dark period, the Canaanites made good use of two important revolutions that changed the history of mankind: iron metallurgy, which had been a Hittite monopoly, was extended to all areas; and the invention of alphabetic writing, which would become crucial for the structuring and recording of commercial exchanges.

After the dark ages, around the eighth century BC, the Mediterranean resumed its important role and the region entered into a new period of prosperity in which the sea and its exchanges returned to life, with the ports of Phoenicia in the south and the Greek cities in the north. Both centers would then begin the conquest of the west following three main shipping routes (Braudel, p. 75):

- **The northern route**: This followed the Greek Islands, going to Corfu and then to the Coast of Otranto, then along the eastern coast of Italy and finally reaching the Straits of Messina. This has been the route of the Greeks since Mycenaean times.
- **The southern route**: Running along the north coast of Africa from Egypt to Libya, ending at the Straits of Gibraltar.
- **The middle route:** through the middle of the sea and supported by a chain of islands, Cyprus, Crete, Malta, Sardinia, and the Balearic Islands. Although this was the most dangerous, since it forced sailors to challenge the sea, the Phoenicians used it as much as their southern route.

From that time until today, the heirs of these earlier empires of the north and south of the Mediterranean have fought to dominate these routes.

History shows us that both northern and southern cultures have had subsequent periods of domination, as can be appreciated in the following brief historical timeline:

Canaanite Civilization: from 2100 to 146 BC (the date that marks the Destruction of Carthage by the Romans).

Greek Civilization: from 800 to 146 BC (the date of the Battle of Corinth, the beginning of Roman domination).

Roman Empire: from 146 BC (after conquering Greece, although from the year 335 BC it had already taken control of the Italian Peninsula) to the fall of Rome in AD 476 to the Barbarian invasions.

Byzantine Empire: From AD 479 to 1453, the date that marked the taking of Constantinople by the Turks.

Islamic Empire: from AD 632 to 1258

First period, from 632 to 661 (Khulafa Aarrashidun, Mecca)

Second period, from 661 to 750 (Umayyad Caliphate, Damascus)

Third period, from 750 to 1258 (Abbasid Caliphate, Baghdad) 1258 marked the taking of Baghdad by the Mongols.

Ottoman Empire: 1453 to 1924, the date on which Ataturk abolished the Islamic Caliphate (although the empire had been in decay since 1683).

Western civilization:

First expansion, 970 to 1270 Feudal kingdoms

Second expansion, 1440 to 1800 Renaissance

Third Expansion: 1770 to 1914 Industrial Revolution

Colonial period 1800–1945

Independence of the southern Mediterranean Countries: 1945 to 1962

Islamic first reform movements: Efforts to return to Islamic principles to overcome decadence, Abd l Wahhab Saudi Arabia (1703–92), Sanussi Libya (1787–1859) Mahdi in Sudan (1848–1885)

Arab Nahda: Arab Renaissance (illustrated in artistic creations of painters and writers as Taha Hussein 1889–1973 and politicians of pan-Arab nationalism such as Nasser (1918–1970) (inspired by the earlier reform movement of the eighteenth and nineteenth centuries as (Muhammed Abdu (1849–1905)

Cold War: USA and Soviet hegemony 1945 to 1989 (Fall of the Berlin Wall)

1979 Iranian Revolution: Third wave of reformist movements in Islamic Countries

2011 Arab Spring

The struggle to dominate the sea marked the conflicts between Christians and Muslims but also led to internal fights such as the ones between Genoa and Venice, and also Barcelona, etc. Several sea battles entered into history, such as the famous Battle of Lepanto in 1571, in which more than 100,000 people participated to determine the primacy of the Spanish Mediterranean Empire over the Ottomans. Soon afterwards, the leadership of the region was turned over to France and England in 1648.

At the end of the sixteenth century, exchanges between northern and southern shores began to slow down, marking the beginning of the long period of decay in Mediterranean history that has lasted until today. Hess stressed that this decadence began with the change of focus in the Mediterranean after the discovery of America in 1492. Spain's shift towards the Atlantic and the eternal fights in the east with the Habsburgs, pushed the Ottoman Empire into a near-east economy, rejecting naval adventures and opting for a more continental expansion. The consequent reduction in commerce, marked the separation of these two powerful civilizations in the Mediterranean into distinct cultural spheres and thus marks the decline of the Mediterranean as the light of western civilization. According to Hess:

> After 1580, the Habsburg and Ottoman Empires participated much less in the unified maritime culture that the sea encouraged. Rather, the history of their common frontier showed how each imperial center contributed to the formalization of a border structure that inhibited cultural diffusion. By the first decade of the seventeenth century, the two empires entered an era in which Mediterranean civilizations drifted apart under the influence of social and cultural forces. For the Ibero-African border, this separation further reduced the level of exchange and conflict between the two opposing societies, permitting the frontier to be "forgotten." (Hess 1978, p. 211)

Braudel suggests that the final blow was given once the Mediterranean was conquered by northern European countries, mainly the English and Dutch, around the end of the sixteenth century. Trade began to be conducted from east to west without the Mediterranean passage, and the Mediterranean forever lost its grandeur. The northern Europeans became the masters of the sea, their ships resisted better and were better equipped and better armed. So little by little, the northerners conquered the most important traffic routes. For example, Dutch vessels transported bales of wool from Spain to Livorno, and these would then go by land to Venice. By 1620, spices did not arrive in the Mediterranean through the old routes up the Red Sea, but by the Atlantic and Gibraltar via Dutch vessels (Braudel

p. 128). The British conquered Gibraltar in 1704 and thus became the guardians of the western exit of the Mediterranean; soon after, Britain also established bases on the eastern Mediterranean border in order to secure its commercial routes to India which they were establishing as early as 1757. Thereafter, Britain secured its commercial shipping by conquering different important spots all over the Mediterranean, such as Malta in 1800, Cyprus in 1878 and Egypt 1882. In summary and in agreement with Braudel, after the sixteenth century the Mediterranean was taken over by foreigners and would never again be returned to its coastal inhabitants (Braudel 1989, p. 129).

Diversity in the Mediterranean

In the Mediterranean, unity is illustrated by the circumstances of its climate, diet, and the common development of navigation. However, the Mediterranean is also the story of divisions and fragmentation.

Arkoun relates how the fragmentations and disputes that began in ancient times are still present in our day, among which we can mention a few (Arkoun 1999):

- Religious and cultural disputes between Christian Europe, and then secular Europe together with the Jewish world, against the Arabic–Turkish–Iranian world.
- Collective memories created by the long disputes between Europe and the Ottoman world in their effort to dominate the Mediterranean.
- Internal conflicts: in the Christian world between Catholics; Protestants and Orthodox. In the Islamic world among Sunnis, Shi'ites and Khariyies; and in the Jewish world the clear difference between southern Sephardics against the northern Ashkenazy. And on top of all this, disputes between religious and secular factions in all the three universes.
- Nationalistic conflicts: Basques in Spain, Corsicans in France, Hungarians in Romania, Flemish and Walloons in Belgium, and Kurds in Turkey – to name just a few.
- Conflicts between reflexive philosophy and technoscientific reason.
- Conflicts between tradition and modernity, between scientific progress and the belief in magic spirits.
- Disputes between closed societies and open, dynamic societies.
- Disputes between agricultural worlds and urban–industrial worlds.

Having a common narrative of the past that is shared between north and south can help to resolve present disputes in a more integrated Mediterranean framework in which all options and peoples have a role to play and all could feel relevant.

North–south, east–west

In addition to the number of existing conflicts, there is a more fundamental division in the Mediterranean in which a broad diversity of cultures is divided along the lines of two main civilizations.

The first obvious division is between north and south, which generally means between Christianity and Islam. The north has been made up of various civilizations – Greek, Roman, Medieval Christian, western – which, despite the incursions of Islamic periods, for the majority of its history has remained Christian. The south has also has counted a large number of civilizations, such as Canaanite, Islamic, Ottoman, and, despite important Christian periods and the fact that Christianity began in its lands (and therefore important Christian minorities have lived there since the times of Christ), the majority of its population is Islamic. The third civilization is semitic Jewish, which although born in the south, has spent most of its history in the north where it has remained intellectually, constituting an important element in western civilization.

Religion is not the only factor that has constituted a civilization. Although it is unquestionably an important element, religions tend to settle in homogenous cultural worlds that are then transformed by the new spiritual learning, but without losing their cultural distinctiveness. According to Braudel, it is not a coincidence that when protestant reform came about in the sixteenth century, it settled the division between the Catholic and Protestant worlds along almost the exact location of the double frontier of the Roman Empire – the Rhine and Danube. Likewise, although Roman civilization conquered the Greek city-states and islands, these never assimilated the language as did the rest of the empire; therefore, it is not a matter of chance that after the Roman Empire collapsed, the Orthodox world continued under the Byzantine Empire for another thousand years in a territory demarcated by the original language distinction within the Roman Empire.

Religion was thus a movement into a higher consciousness that occurred in already-united populations, who shared other distinctive features in addition to religion.

Therefore, the north is a Christian world, separated into three distinctive cultural areas, each of which has had a fundamental imprint in what is today the western world. Highly summarized, we can described the three as follows:

- **Greek (later Orthodox)**: they provided the western world with the most sophisticated rational concepts of its thought, many of which are still valid today, such as the works of Plato, Socrates or Aristotle.
- **The Roman (later Catholic)**: contributed a distinct way of life, an emotional understanding of life, urban sophistication and a way of being able to absorb anything from anywhere and then transmit it to others. It is probably its capacity to connect in all planes but mostly emotionally, the legacy of the "Latinos" to western civilization.
- **Northern Barbarians (later Protestant)**: provided a common love for nature and simplicity. Since the seventeenth century, the Protestant world has shown the most admirable capacity for action, giving western civilization unprecedented scientific discoveries.

The three formed western civilization by balancing each other. If we follow the schema we have used throughout this book, that of harmony between mind, emotion and actions, we can project these elements on to a map of these different civilizations. This would result in the Protestant world representing the physical world and thus action; Roman Catholics, the emotional side of things; and the Orthodox world as the basis for our primary mental concepts.

Table 6.1 shows the three northern civilizations in further detail.

The Islamic civilization tends to consider its origin in the seventh century, specifically in the year 622, which marks the migration of the Islamic prophet Muhammad and his followers from Mecca to Medina. However, as in the case of the northern civilization, Islamic religion settled in a specific cultural universe. The strong reception of this religion and its adaptation to the ethos of a particular culture have left a strong mark on the three main cultural bodies of southern civilization.

Toynbee argues that Islam fertilized a land that had previously had a common history, and that after one thousand years of Hellenic influence, the region accommodated its original ethos into the Islamic expansion.

> Behind the Abbasid Caliphate of Bagdad we find the Ummayad Caliphate of Damascus, and behind that a thousand years of Hellenic intrusion, beginning with the career of Alexander of Macedon in the

Table 6.1 The three northern civilizations

	Language	Context: neighbors/enemies	Sociopolitical structure	Civilization	Splendor	Causes for decay	Contributions	What can they bring in the future?
Orthodox	Greek or Cyrillic	Turks, to whom they feel they have lost their historical role	Strong national identification inherited from the patriarchal state	Orthodox later western	Greek VIII to II BC Byzantine AD V to XI	Excessive dogmatism Corruption Decomposition into nations under a weak patriarch pitted against strong empires	Spiritual contribution Not too strong in the material or emotional sides	Management of a large world made up of small nationalities
Roman	Latin	German protestants, whom they admire and follow Levantines in the south, against whom they feel strongly and tend to ignore	Transcendental unity in the Catholic doctrine, while having cultural and political diversity	Roman, then Medieval Christian, now western	Roman Empire II BC To AD V	Due to its dogmatism in the face of Nordic liberties after XVI	Emotional predominance	Family values Artistic creativity A way of enjoying life
Protestant	Germanic languages (Including Anglo-Saxon)	Latin, to whom they feel less emotional and more rational	Empires built on strong identity nation-state expansive and economically effective	Leaders in western civilization	Germanic X–XII Reformation XVI Industrialization XVII–XX Modernism Positivism XX	Strong emphasis on individual freedoms that can also lead to strong individual selfishness and capitalist selfishness which results in a crisis during the postmodern period	Practical predominance Material effectiveness Simplicity Tendency to evade emotional matters Spiritual difficulties	The language of globalization XX–XXI Efficient scientific-economic patterns

latter half of the fourth century BC, followed by the Greek Seleucid monarchy in Syria, Pompey's campaigns and Roman conquest, and only ending with the Oriental "revanche" of the warriors of early Islam in the seventh century after Christ. (Toynbee 1946, p. 17)

Toynbee describes how the ethos of a given civilization always finds its way back and while adapting to foreign influences still has a latent soul that fights to emerge. In his words:

The cataclysmic conquests by the primitive Muslim Arabs seem to respond antistrophically, in the rhythm of history, to the cataclysmic conquests by Alexander. Like these they changed the face of the world in half a dozen years; but instead of changing it out of recognition, "more Macedonico," they changed it back to a recognizable likeness of what it had been once before. As the Macedonian conquest, by breaking up the Achaemenian Empire (i.e. the Persian Empire of Cyrus and its successors), prepared the soil for the seed of Hellenism, so the Arab conquest opened the way for the Ummayyads, and after them the Abbasids, to reconstruct a universal state which was the equivalent of the Achaemenian Empire. If we superimpose the map of either empire upon the other we shall be struck by the closeness with which the outlines correspond; and we shall find that the correspondence is not simply geographical, but extends to methods of administration and even to the more intimate phenomena of social and spiritual life. We may express the historical function of the Abbasid Caliphate by describing it as reintegration and resumption of the Achaemenian Empire, a reintegration of a political structure which had been broken up by the impact of an external force and the resumption of a phase of social life which have been interrupted by an alien intrusion (Toynbee 1946, p. 18).

Thus, Toynbee described the three main components of the southern Mediterranean shore: first, it was an *eastern* culture, represented by the Indo-Europeans that constituted the Persian empires, the first of which was the Achameanian that took over the former neo-Babylonian empires and the lands of the Mesopotamian civilization; second, came the *Semitic* cultures of the sophisticated centers that flourished for almost two thousand years in the Levant; and third, the cultures of the Semitic *nomadic* peoples of the Arabian Peninsula, which came back after thousand years to once more unite the territory, in which, very distinctive cultures have coexist, later replaced by the nomadic populations of Central Asia, the Turks.

So as with the cultures of the north, the cultures of the south can be devided into three classes:

- **Levantines:** made up of the historical cities of the region known as the Fertile Crescent:[19] Damascus, Baghdad, Byblos and more. Most of its populations, the majority of them of Semitic origin, accepted Islam and soon also the Arab language, while at the same time always preserving a way of being very different from the conquering Arab Bedouins. Culturally close to the Latin civilization of the north, Levantines have been the "connectors" for the south; they have been the fundamental instrument for the exchanges from east to west and north to south, absorbing all and exchanging all. Their way of living, very similar to that of northern Latinos, illustrates the "*joi de vivre*" that makes most visitors from the Arab Gulf dream of spending a part of their year in the Levantine regions of Lebanon, Syria, or Egypt, enjoying their cuisine, urban sophistication, social happiness, and summer climate – very much like the fascination that Spain or Italy produces on the rigorous Dutch or Germans.
- **Persians:** Based in the east, this civilization was crucial to help build some of the rational pillars of civilization, not only during the old Achaemenian Empire, but also during the splendor of Islamic civilization. During that period, intellectuals of Persian origin such as Ibn Sina and Al Ghazali, constituted some of the highest mental and spiritual achievements of humanity. Iranian Sufi Mysticism, through the work of figures such as Sohravardi, or al Rumi[20] has also been particularly relevant to the spiritual history of humanity.
- **Nomads (Bedouins, Berbers and Turks):** Islam emerged in the desert, among the Semitic populations with nomadic traditions. Islam brought these populations together and soon extended its influence over the Semitic populations of the Levant as well. Interestingly enough, it quickly became fascinated by them, to the extent that only 30 years after the death of the Prophet, the capital of the Empire moved first to Damascus in 661 under the Ummayads and then in 750 to Bagdhad with the Abbasids. Islam also extended into the nomadic populations of North Africa, including Berbers, which later had a great influence upon Islamic civilization in North Africa. Both nomadic populations, Berbers and Arab Bedouins, shared some of the same characteristics: shaped by the hardships of the desert and nomadic life; a strict moral honor code; and an emphasis on respect. In many ways, nomadic tribes share some of the values of the northern Europeans; they are pious; and strict, they reject luxury and waste, and have a strong love of nature. In addition to the nomads of the southern deserts, the nomads of Central Asia were particularly relevant for the Islamic world, specially the Mongols and Turks of the Altaic linguistic family. Those populations, although sharing some characteristics with the nomads from

the southern deserts, had specific traits as a result of coming from the colder deserts of the north.

In any case, if we follow the same analysis as we did with the north, Levantines represent the emotional contribution, the Persians the mental, while the nomads (Arab Bedouins, Berbers and Turks) represent action and domination over the physical world. We can see this relationship in further detail in Table 6.2.

Therefore, it is not a coincidence that upon closer inspection, we will find that the matching cultures in the north and south to observe good relations among each other; for example, the Levantine and Latin, as we can see in the many initiatives bringing together the Spanish and Italians with Tunisians or Egyptians. Likewise, it often noted that the Texans and the Saudis have strong ties of familiarity. When Texans started to work in the oil wells of Saudi Arabia, although there were obviously visible differences, they also found many striking similarities, such as the value placed on nature, a straightforward attitude, and love of the land. Likewise, if we analyze the biggest historical confrontations between north and south, although it has been true that everyone fought against everyone, of particular relevance are the eternal rivalries between the three components of each civilization against their equivalent on the other shore: Byzantines against Persians (formerly Greeks and Persians) both representing the eastern side of civilization; Phoenicians against Romans, (as well as Romans against the Levantine cities, Israel, Egypt, Syria), both representing the connectors of both shores.

The three main civilizations and cultural modes of the north have balanced each other to form western civilization; likewise, the three main components of the southern Mediterranean have balanced each other to form Islamic civilization. Both sides need to find a better harmony between them by using the potential of all their components. Harmonizing the north and south can help bring back a stronger civilization more capable of facing the challenges that lie ahead for both sides. The Arab Spring and the turmoil in the southern Mediterranean might provide a new framework for mutual understanding, leading to a stronger and lasting connection between both civilizations.

Commerce is in the blood of Mediterranean peoples

Commerce has been the main economic activity for Mediterranean peoples, and, in fact, is the reason for the emergence of its first civilizations, the Mesopotamians and Egyptians. Although the first Neolithic

Table 6.2 The three southern civilizations

	Language	Context: neighbors, friends / enemies	Sociopolitical structure	Splendor	Causes for decay	Contributions	What can they bring in the future?
Levantines	Semitic languages: Canaanite, Aramaic, Arab	Orthodox, against whom they identify as Muslims Arab Bedouins with whom they will assimilate	Self-managed ethnic communities Arab mercantilism	VIII–II BC Canaanite and Babylonian Empire in VI BC Afterwards dominated by the Hellenistic world, then the Arabs and Turks	High diversification caused difficulties for internal unity without an external authority	Material and commercial efficiency High emotional intensity (poetic, animist)	Creativity, community and *eudaimonia*
Nomads	Semitic (Arabic) Berber (family of nomadic zenetes, shanhaya) Altaic (Turks)	Intermediaries between black Africa, Indo-Asia and the Mediterranean Ottoman, Greco-orthodox from whom they receive a political and commercial structure	Islamic Caliphate 632–1258 Ottoman XVI–XIX inherited from the Byzantine and improved upon thanks to Arab mercantilism	Strengthened the imperial model of the Sasanide-Abasid Persian from XIII onwards VIII–XII political and commercial expansion	After XIII fragmentation began The imperial model became old after XIX Admiration towards and subjugation by western science.	Spiritual order and political discipline Commercial discipline and respect for rituals If the soul is conquered, the spirit can open and expand	A clear and straightforward religion with physical-emotional harmony (poetry)
Persians	Indo-European	Nomads of Central Asia, and the Orthodox world	Achaemenian From Parthos, Sassanid, Seldyucids to Persian.	Early heritage from Babylonian civilization was maintained for a longer period: longest surviving civilization in the world	Older civilization, submerged into Arab-Islamic	Physical, mental, and spiritual harmony that in general is less efficient than specialization	Spiritual passion

centers can be traced back to 9000 BC and are found in the mountains of Anatolia (Çatal Hüyük) at 600 to 900 meters elevation, it is in the valleys of the Nile and the Tigris and Euphrates rivers where the populations began to exchange their products using the rivers to move the goods from one place to the other. Once these primitive riverboats became sophisticated enough to venture into the sea, a fundamental step in civilization occurred, and exchanges began to flourish: goods, techniques, ideas, diplomatic correspondence, and movement of people (Braudel, p. 63). In fact, the actual landscape of the Mediterranean is full of traces of its history of exchange: orange trees from China, eggplant from India, tomatoes from America and peppers from the Guiana Islands (Braudel, p. 11).

If the causes of the emergence of civilizations in the Mediterranean can be traced back to commerce, the causes for their decline can be traced back to a decline in commerce. During the sixteenth century, northern Europeans replaced the old Mediterranean masters in the art of commerce, and this tendency was further intensified and consolidated with the Industrial Revolution during the eighteenth and nineteenth centuries.

Industrialization opened the way to a new form of enterprise far removed from the traditional family-based Mediterranean enterprise. The Industrial revolution involved heavy capital investments that needed to be financed either by governments or by an incipient capitalism. At the end of the nineteenth century and in beginning of the twentieth, the new private Anglo-Saxon corporations were financed by small capital savers who bought shares in the financial markets, and this in turn led the way to an increasing separation between owners and managers of companies. As a consequence, this new form of enterprise adopted procedures and processes that were independent of the owner's personality and easily replicated in mass, thereby facilitating the expansion of corporations and soon resulting in the giant multinationals of our era.

This type of company differed greatly from the older modes and organisations of making a living based on traditional means of production and finance supported by the old infrastructures of family and extended local relations. The traditional family business that dominated the landscape of Italy, Spain or Egypt, became obsolete as the new multinationals competed and thrived in an increasingly global economy.

The colonization of the south during the twentieth century was marked by the influence of the Anglo-Saxons and their new economic strategies; and although Italy had Libya as a colony and Spain the northern part of

Morocco, and there was also a large presence of France as a colonial power in the Maghreb and in the Near East, the influence of the Anglo-Saxon mindset (the UK and soon after their American relatives) on the economy and business management practices, has until recently remained as the "way of doing business."

Therefore, as Bouchara suggests, industrialization and the consumer society we have today, were late arrivals to the Mediterranean. Modern consumer society penetrated into the Mediterranean during the 1960s and transformed the behaviors of its people, first along the northern shores and later penetrating into the southern lands; and thus the Mediterranean ethos began to fade away. The previous way of life, based on the Mediterranean tradition, was considered up to the 1980s to be a primitive behavior in contrast to the modern way of life of industrialized northern Europe.

However, the crisis of the 1980s and the changes occurring at the end of that decade have led to a new type of entrepreneur, particularly in the southern Mediterranean. These entrepreneurs support their economic activities using both the new form of individualism and modern global finance, but are also capable of tapping into the mobilization of traditional groups of support, such as the family, the clan or local communities (Bouchara, 1997).

These new entrepreneurs understand management techniques very well, and the processes and efficiencies of business; they have inherited the individual drive of the Anglo-Saxon entrepreneurs but in addition, they have combined it with their group identity to create a new ethno-entrepreneurship. These new forms are leading the way to a new manner of business in the Mediterranean.

Mediterranean letters

As a final illustration, I end this chapter with samples of different commercial letters. These letters are fictional: they were not written in the time period they are set in, but are creative works of writing. Nevertheless, they provide us with a realistic portrayal of these bygone eras, capturing a sense of time and place, political trends and the types of trades and traders that lived and worked during certain periods in time. Particular attention has been given to the religion and cultural traditions of the characters involved.

Each letter is accompanied by a short explanation of its historical context, and together, they illustrate four crucial moments in Mediterranean history, as well as the history of its main players.

First letter

From Balhurran, who lived in Ugarit, to Bitrutt, son of Mattawii, living in Hatissas, capital of the Hittite Empire. Set during the height of the Hittite Empire in Anatolia around 1300 BC, the letter concerns iron trading, probably in exchange for gold and burial pottery.

Ugarit in the year 1300 BC was the main port on the oriental Mediterranean coast, the place through which flowed most of the trade between Mycenaean Crete and Babylonia.

It is in Ugarit where the first alphabet was developed, distinct from the hieroglyphic writing of the neighboring empires. Also, the first musical score in history was found in Ugarit, in a magnificent palace library dedicated to the lord of the city.

At this moment, two powers were fighting for domination, Egypt in the south and the Anatolian Hittite Empire, in which area of influence Ugarit found itself at the time of this letter. Ugarit had to pay tributes to the Hittite Empire, however it was free to develop its commercial life with the empire, as illustrated by the letter, but also outside the empire.

About a hundred years after this letter, prosperity in the Mediterranean disappeared as a consequence of the expansion of tribes probably from the north called "the people from the sea," which destabilized traditions of peaceful trade and provoked invasions of immigrants seeking the wealth and luxury of southeastern civilizations. This deep instability contributed to the fall of Mycenae, Egypt, Babylonia and the Hittite Empire, but at the same time, it contributed at the to the development of the Levantine coasts; and in this manner the Ugarit culture spread south, creating the cluster of Phoenician cities along the Mediterranean coast all the way to Egypt (Byblos, Tyre, etc.).

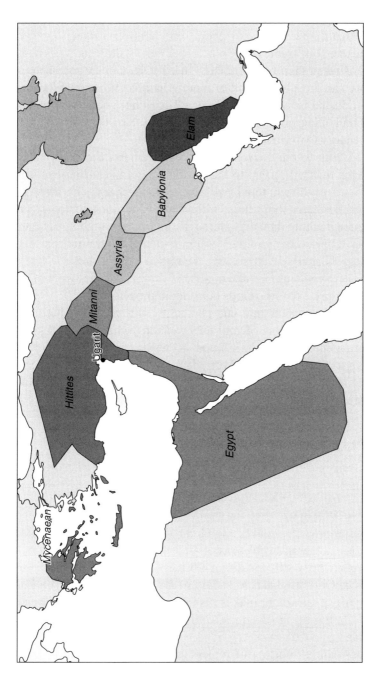

Map 2 Mediterranean, c. 1300 BC

Dear Brother Bitrutt,

I hope that the Gods of your people will continue protecting us, our families and our trade.

It was more than two years ago that I visited, with your help and support, the prosperous land of inner Anatolia, close to the heavens. The products I brought back to warm Ugarit have been distributed to Crete, and today, our brothers and customers from the holy island ask us for more of your iron.

According to our agreement and engagement, I'm going to hire a caravan that will go up to the northern land in four moons in the next month of the sun top. I will send to you a charge of crafted gold and burial pottery that I hope will satisfy your Gods and ours. I can guarantee you that they will please the guardians of the death gate in our city. They come from the best craftsmen of Crete and Ugarit, and will pass through Ebla to receive the blessing of its lords.

Please pay attention to the quality of the product and we will both accept the price that the Gods consider appropriate.

My family expects that you personally will come to Ugarit with the iron and some more of your holy weapons, where we shall receive you as a member of our own blood. As we have discussed before, we are like a tribe of traders. We traders are brothers in our souls; we irrigate and feed our cities with the pleasure of the Gods who bless our transactions. We are united in by the power of the Gods of our cities.

Hoping for your prosperity as I do for my own.

Balhurran

Dear brother in the land of the Great Shore, may Aserdus, Goddess of all things that grow, bless you,

Your memory still remains with me and with my people here in Hattusas. Our agreement is sacred to my family and me. You know the saying: a fair trader makes his father ten times happier, while the word of a liar brings disgrace to his father, his sons and the sons of his sons.

This year, our northern frontiers have been at peace and our dear Maryannu rested at home instead of going to war. Soon, a caravan will arrive from Merzamor from the sons of Hasammelilive, bringing to me the fruit of their sweat. I expect the most finely crafted double axes, the sharpest swords and the most useful tools for the renowned shipyards of your land. In addition, from the mountains of the east, the most beautiful of lapis lazuli stones are soon to arrive.

One of my messengers will wait for your caravan in Ebla. He will be loaded with my presents to your family and you can accept his word as my own in order to price your goods. Next season, when the waters of the Hattussa River are growing, two of my beloved sons and I will take the road to Ugarit. As you know, our King and master has said to us "during the good season, the traders – sons of Ura – will trade in Ugarit, but in the winter, they are not allowed to stay and they will return to their country."

My prayers will be with you. I hope that the sea respects your ships, the sand your caravans and death your family.

Bitrutt, son of Mattawii

Second letter

Mecca, AD 566, correspondence between two Arab cousins, one living in Alexandria and the other in Medina, who are trading with Constantinople in the Byzantine Empire.

Ten years after this letter the Prophet Muhammad was born, leading to the rise of Islam. Our fictitious character is addressing this letter to his Christian cousin in Alexandria, where a community of Arabs is prospering and incrementing their position as traders.

At this moment the Arabian Peninsula is under the influence of the emerging Persian Sassanid Empire, which is also extending its influence over all the fertile crescent. The Byzantine Empire is the other major power of the era, although at this time its influence is somewhat in decline, since the Byzantines have been immersed in heavy internal fighting with Phocas, the murderer of Emperor Maurice who has become a tyrant. These circumstances have facilitated the rise in power of the Sassanid Persians, as demonstrated by the fact that during this time, King Koshrau of Persia conquered most of Mesopotamia.

The former trading villages of Palmira and Petra have been destroyed and only Arab caravans move along the coastline villages of the Mediterranean and the Indian Ocean south of the Euphrates.

In this period, the Arabs were a "neutral" people spread across the borders of both empires. In fact, the huge deserts between both regions were

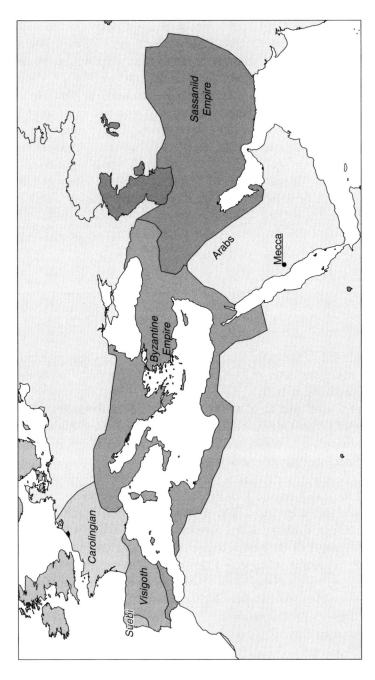

Map 3 Mediterranean, c. 566 AD

under the control of different Arabian clans that fought against one another and were unable to build a confederation. The Arabian people lived and traded in both empires; they moved freely without being disturbed by either of the opposing factions.

As described in case study 3 on the Dana bank, the most praised woman in Islam is Muhammad's first wife Khadijah, like Muhammad a member of the Arab tribe of Quraish, who, at the time of our letter, was around 11 years of age. Khadijah successfully managed her father's inheritance and became the owner of some of the largest caravans in her region. After hearing the reputation of Muhammad as a reputable merchant, she hired him as her agent to take care of her caravans to Syria and other regions. Soon afterwards they were married. Khadijah was the mother of all of the prophet's children except one, and was his only wife until her death.

After that period of huge diversity at end of the sixth century, AD 610 brought about important changes when simultaneously the Byzantine Empire was renewed and more importantly, the Arabic uprising came to be following Muhammad's revelation, and quickly conquered all of the eastern world, becoming a hugely influential center for a re-invigorated Mediterranean.

The letter mentions the famous Ukaz fair of Mecca, where traders often met and recited poetry. It was something similar to Olympia or Delphos where Greeks often enemies came together peacefully from different cities, to play sports or show their devotion to the god Apollo.

Dear Brother[21] Hassan,

May the Gods and Djins[22] of the sandy mountain bless our friendship through our holy and poetic language. Even if we have settled on the opposite sides of our sacred desert home, and even if your Gods and my Gods are different, our Arabic language is our common home. I know that you and your family have converted to Christianity. Your one human God is far from our Djins, but thanks to you, He is closer.

A huge caravan from Oman and India has just arrived in our city of Mecca, and I have been allowed by my uncle to participate in the spread of this wealth. The greater part will leave early for Alexandria through Aqaba and from there on to Constantinople. The current route will enrich the coffers of the Byzantine traders that you know so well. I hope that you will be interested in taking part of this venture and that you will participate in future caravans with my family.

Your family and mine are small buyers, but if you are able to reach an agreement with the Jewish family of Aaron, we can probably get our goods directly from India to Constantinople without any mediate. I hope that the profit and the dignity in our business will be according with the honor of our tribes.

This past moon I visited Ukaz and participated in the great meetings of traders and poets from all over the desert; all the clans came together to exchange good words and wishes. We believe in our poetry over our different Gods, and gather around the kaaba to show our gratitude for our honor and power.

The word and the holy art of trade, this is the splendor of our tribes and of no other people, even the beyond glory of the emperors of Byzantium or the Sassanid Persians. Yes, I am proud of our language, our poetry and culture; and it is my desire, dear brother, to work to increase the power of our tribes.

God bless us both

Dear Brother,

All blessings are needed in these times of change and confusion. God, kings and people are moving like the sands in the desert of our ancestors. Only the wisdom of our Lord remains, God above all Gods.

Your good fortune fills me with happiness. When the gifts from the east arrive, it is said that they are like water raining from the Kingdom of Himyar. I am interested in allowing our hopes and fears to be carried by future caravans.

As you know, the Aaron family is closely related to us. In the times of the Emperor Justin, when the Sassanids took Dura, two members of Aaron were forced to run away. My father took them behind the walls of our home, and brotherhood was established between our families. They will be happy to open the doors of Constantinople for us.

By the way, news from Constantinople is like stormy clouds. On earth, while the Emperor is facing the Persians in the east, new Slavic tribes are crossing the border in the north. And in Heaven, the old Patriarch Eutychius has confused the people with his beliefs that the body will not return as such after the resurrection.

Fortunately for us, humble traders sons of the desert, Constantinople is and always will be like a fanciful woman, hungry for luxuries and novelties. I have no doubts that gifts from India and Oman will be welcomed and appreciated even beyond our expectations.

Receive my desires of prosperity, abundance and health. Djins and Saints bless both our hearts.

Third letter

Venice, 1495. A letter between Joseph from Sevilla and a Venetian merchant, Michelle de Cretona.

The following letters are an exchange between Michelle de Cretona, a Venetian trader trying to break into the Castilian luxury market, and Joseph from Sevilla, a Jewish convert. Three years earlier, Castilian kings Isabel and Fernando expelled the Jews from their Spanish kingdoms, except for those who converted to Christianity, which is the situation Joseph is in.

Some time later, personal correspondence such as this will be used as a justification to accuse converts with the serious charge of apostasy, punishable with death by the Inquisition. Taking account of this risk, the response letter has tone that combines the sincerity of the memory of his Jewish friends with an attempt, not without difficulty, to demonstrate a new faith in Christianity on an equal level to his Spanish neighbors and trading partners.

The two correspondents came in contact thanks to a mutual acquaintance Benjamin della Umbria, a Jew living in Italy. At the time, Venice was probably the principal Jewish community in the Catholic world. The Venetian government was the only one which dared to disobey the Roman Pope on this critical point.

The strategic reason for this letter is the wish of a Venetian trader to open commercial links between Venice and emerging Kingdom of Castile, thus defeating the mortal enemy of the Venetians, the Genoese.

However, Genoese traders had begun to establish trade links with the Castilians in order to wage a commercial war with the other main Iberian power, the Catalans. The Castilians had made an alliance with Genoese against Catalonia for the control of the western Mediterranean

The underlying idea in the letter is that the Venetians want to use the antagonism felt by newly converted Jews against the Castilian authorities, and on the other hand, the fact that a converted Jew from Seville would prefer to trade with more tolerant people (the Venetians) rather than the Genoese, or even the Castilians or Catalans.

The Sevillian Jew is not sure about the most convenient nation for the shipment, because he knows he is under suspicion of having relations with non-Catholics. Joseph hopes that trading with a Venetian will not attract any suspicion. In any case, he feels that Venice has a better position, as well as a healthier disposition, to trade with the emerging power of the Ottomans.

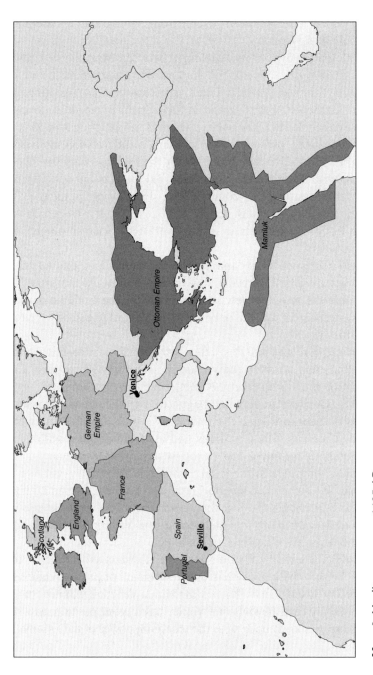

Map 4 Mediterranean, c. 1495 AD

My Highly Esteemed Joseph,

Thanks to the good offices of our friend and brother in the arts of trade, Benjamin della Umbria, I am pleased to share with you some news that may lead to our mutual benefit and that of our homelands.

As Benjamin has shared with you, I come from the well-known family of Cretonna. For eight generations the Cretonna have lived in the Serenissima Republica de Venezia, trading with Greeks and Turks and even the peoples of the Levant as far away as the Armenians and Iberians of the Caucasus.

Generation after generation, we have managed to gain and maintain the confidence of our trading brothers in Istanbul, Smyrna, Algiers and Cairo. From perfumes to spices and sugar, the objects of our trade have proven to be desired and appreciated around the Mare Nostrum.

However, like your family in Seville, we also suffer damage from the Genoese. Just as a land suffers from a plague of rats that eats what others produce, our trade is threatened by the Genoese who reduce our profit and close our markets.

Nevertheless, Divine Providence has given us a way for justice to prevail. I have heard of the great need in Seville for perfumes and dyes for its leather industry, so famous in the Courts of Christendom. My family has accumulated knowledge as well as stocks of these goods, and with your help, it would be a great business if we were to supply the Castilian markets with them, avoiding the Genoese greed.

As you know, the Almighty has given Venice the most difficult mission among all nations, to bring infidel souls to the Lord through trade, since each good is a reflection of His wisdom and kindness, no matter how His holy name is pronounced. Proof of His will is our permanence within the Second Rome. Therefore, our agreement is not only profitable, but also good for our souls.

Receive from me the highest consideration of you as a partner in the brotherhood of trade.

Michelle de Cretonna

Greatly Respected Michelle de Cretonna,

The memory of Benjamin is held high in my soul, and I open my heart to your proposal. Nevertheless, you must know that I have become an honest Christian. For me, the holy Talmud has been changed to the Gospels, which for me represent a great and wonderful discovery and to whose study I dedicate my highest aspirations.

Yes I am interested, and I really appreciate your invitation, even if the conditions do not make it easy to trade with you because of the prevalence of Genoese in this town and the trust they have gained in this kingdom. I am preparing to make delicately contact with the authorities to prepare for the arrival of your valuable goods. But of course, in this case we will need a ship to return with an exchange of goods. Have you a craft available for this transport in the next three months? To me it is critical that you manage the ship, because here all of the boats headed to the east are linked to Genoese interests.

The price of the perfumes you mention is increasing due to the prestige they are gaining in the Amsterdam markets. But I promise to set a good price for you as soon as you confirm the quantity and the availability of this first pioneer boat. Remember that Turkish or Greek vessels will suppose an inconvenience for me.

May the glory of our Lord Jesus Christ and the former prophets help us,

Joseph de la Santa Cruz, known as Spinoza

Fourth letter

Messina, September 5, 2011. A letter from a consultant to a technical officer of the EU located in Brussels.

This fictitious letter tries to show the relevance of the European Commission in fostering exchanges between Mediterranean countries. As result of the influence of politicians and intellectuals, the EU has been intensifying its relationships with southern countries. These policies reached a high point in the 1995 Barcelona process, intended to establish a European free-trade area by 2010. Relations with neighbors to the south have thus been one of the key areas in the external relations strategy of the European Union as it moves towards a greater integration of both sides. We can see this happening over the recent historical development of EU policies towards Mediterranean countries:

- **Cooperation Agreements:** In 1967 the CAP (Common Agricultural Policy) was established. Soon after, the six countries that at the time constituted the European Union signed special agreements with the countries of the south in a country-by-country strategy. The agreements assured agricultural imports for Europe and industrial EU products to the southern countries.
- **From 1972 to 1992, Global Mediterranean Policy:** after the extension of the union with new countries in 1972, the Paris European Council of that year established a Global Mediterranean Policy that guaranteed the preferential entrance into Europe of certain agricultural products, but also introduced some technical guidelines and gave financial grants following specific protocols.
- **From 1992 to 1996, Renewed Mediterranean Policy:** A new formula of cooperation was drafted into an agreement based on past preferential commercial policies, while at the same time introducing financial and political cooperation.
- **The Euro-Mediterranean Partnership (the Barcelona Process):** In 1995, the Euro-Mediterranean conference of Ministers of foreign affairs was held in Barcelona, establishing a Euro-Mediterranean partnership with 15 European and 12 Mediterranean countries. The conference established the goal of a free trade area between north and south by 2010. Discussion focused on three main areas:
  Politics and security, establishing a common area of peace and security; Economic and financial partnership, creating an area of shared prosperity; Partnership in social, cultural and human affairs, developing human resources and promoting understanding among cultures and exchange between civil societies.
- **The European Neighborhood Policy, (ENP) 2007:**[23] The countries that took part in the Barcelona process became partners in the European Neighborhood Policy, developed in 2004 following the enlargement of the EU to include eastern countries. The ENP complements and reinforces the Barcelona Process on a bilateral basis, through action plans agreed upon by the partner countries and taking into account their specific needs and characteristics.

The members of the ENP are the 27 EU member states and nine Mediterranean partners (Algeria, Egypt, Israel, Jordan, Lebanon, Morocco, Palestinian territories, Syria and Tunisia), while Cyprus, Malta and Turkey are three countries that were part of the Barcelona process at its launch. However, Cyprus and Malta joined the EU in 2004, while in December

1999 at the Helsinki European Council, Turkey became a candidate country for EU accession and is currently seeking accession talks.

This policy has enhanced trade in both regions and has made the EU the main trading partner of the Mediterranean countries in both goods and services. More than 50 percent of the trade in the region is with the EU, and for some countries the EU is the destination for 70 percent of their exports. The EU is also the largest direct foreign investor in the region, the first source of tourists, and the biggest aid donor. Total trade with the EU was worth € 127 billion in 2007 – some 5 percent of total EU external trade.

However, and beyond just trade, EU policies are also trying to enhance relationships between civil societies on both shores. Different European budget lines under MEDA and now under ENP policies, have fostered knowledge and exchange between NGOs and organization across both northern and southern banks. The level of commitment is shown in the amounts spent on different programs, including MEDA and the ENP instruments.

The European Neighborhood and Partnership Instruments (ENPI) allotted for the budgetary period of 2007–2013 total approximately € 12 billion in funding, available to support reforms in its partners. In the previous period, through MEDA I (1995–1999) and MEDA II (2000–2006), the EU supported the Barcelona process with € 16 billion from the community budget, plus loans from the European Investment Bank that amounted to approximately € 2 billion per year. In addition, special initiatives have independent budgets, such as the Initiative for Democracy and Human Rights (EIDHR), Humanitarian aid, (ECHO), educational programs such as TEMPUS and ERASMUS, as well as environmental projects, healthcare and research.

However, and despite indisputable progress in north–south relations, the following letter implies an increasing bureaucratization of EU officials and excessive procedural requirements, both of which are often criticized as marking an impediment to the prosperous future of this relationship.

To Mr. Pierre Clayessens, European Aid Technical Bureau
EU Commission, Place Schuman 1040
Brussels, Belgium

Messina, September 5, 2011

Dear Sir,

I hope you remember me, we met last December at the congress "The Barcelona Process 15 years Later," organized by the research center E-Med.

At that conference you gave an interesting speech regarding the support from the Commission for ecological agriculture in the Mediterranean. In that respect, I would very much appreciate your views on a project I am working on. My organization is Eco-Agro Consulting, a leader in the field, and we are developing a project that will hopefully be approved in the next meeting of the "ENPI CBC Mediterranean Sea Basin Program 2007/2013," which is a multilateral cross-border cooperation program co-financed by the European Union under the European Neighborhood and Partnership Instrument (ENPI).

My group is seeking to form a consortium in which we already have four partners: Ecologistas en Movimiento; the city of Granada, Spain; Eco-Med Egypt; and one of the main producers of olives in Lebanon.

The general objective of the project is to improve the capacity for producing and exporting organic agriculture (fruits and grains), fostering cooperation among territories as well as building a culture of cooperation inside local territories themselves.

The objective of the project is to build up together in cooperation agricultural local clusters in order to spread the benefits of organic agriculture, which are in fact less energy dependent, a smaller carbon footprint, and the adoption of best practice in order to increase fertility of land through long-term agriculture and water management.

We are convinced that this project can jumpstart a movement towards sustainability and cooperation in ecobusiness in the Mediterranean area. I have gone through the application forms and honestly, I find them confusing. Therefore, I would appreciate your valuable advice and, if possible, I would like to hold a phone conversation with you in the near future.

With my best regards,
Franco Pinya

Brussels, September 6, 2011.
Mr. Pinya,

Please ask, in writing, specific questions that you might have regarding the proposal. The questions would be answered through our regular procedure and published publicly in our web page within a maximum time of one week.

We recommend that you consult the application forms on our website:

http://www.enpi-info.eu/index.php?lang_id=450

Regards
Pierre Clayessens, Europ Aid Technical Bureau. EU Commission, Place Schuman 1040

Epilogue: Managing identities within Organizations

1   Movements in identity: Practical recommendations for organizations

The previous chapters have described an emerging paradigm that can be summarized as an increase in the level of consciousness about what we want to do and with whom we want to do it. This change has led to a new way of being together, resulting in new schemes for working and consuming. Many organizations, aware of these changes, are facing the challenge and adapting to it, and in the process they are identifying new practices in the management of their human resources as well as in the products and services that they are offering to their clients.

In this last section we will briefly analyze a few examples of each of the five movements in identity and their effects for organizations, as well as a few recommendations on how organizations can react to gain the greatest advantage from this new paradigm.

First movement: Identity and the self, a continuous process of development from the ego to the self

In Chapter 1 the movement within the self was described as a tendency in all of us to move away from our strictly physical needs in an attempt to find a balance for our emotional and mental needs. This is part of a constant process of self-development that moves us away from the needs of our ego and helps us to increase our consciousness of our relationship as individuals to our societies.

Successfully covering our physical needs does not mean that we are balanced. The only things some people think about all day long; are eating and sex: in their case, intellectual activity will do them good. Other people live in a perpetual emotional race, always looking for the next rush of emotion: for them, focused physical action is good and necessary. Still others live inside an ivory tower, detached from the world and dedicating their lives exclusively to thinking; they will benefit from some healthy emotional experiences. In summary, most of us need to cover our basic needs but in parallel, we also need to work on balancing our actions with our emotions and our mind.

The harmonization of our physical, emotional and mental needs and capabilities will make us more self-fulfilled individuals. Instead of spending most of our time satisfying desires, we can contribute more to the external world beyond the needs of our ego.

As mentioned in Chapter 1, positive psychology has recently emerged as an important tool helping individuals to grow and pursue more fulfilling lives. The growth of public interest in this field is illustrated by recent Harvard University initiatives detailed in the following box.

Positive Psychology at Harvard

The course PSY 1504 – Positive Psychology – taught at Harvard University by Professor Tal Ben-Shahar, has become one of the most popular courses at Harvard with more than 1400 students having taken it since its inception.

When asked in interviews why more people sign for his class than for introductory economics, Prof. Tal Ben-Shahar answers, "More people want to be happy than want to be rich."

This course on positive psychology help students to focus on what works, while at the same time helping them to face the most difficult challenges in life. It has been described as follows: "The course focuses on the psychological aspects of a fulfilling and flourishing life. Topics include happiness, self-esteem, empathy, friendship, love, achievement, creativity, music, spirituality, and humor."

Another interesting element in the area of positive psychology, is the *Coaching and Positive Psychology Initiative*, developed at the Institute of Coaching at McLean Hospital, a Harvard medical school affiliate, which aims to advance the field of positive psychology through its application in clinical interventions and in life. The center's activities include the development of scientific research in the area of positive psychology, and "educating coaches, executives, managers, therapists, educators and others on how to use positive psychology theory and methods to help individuals and organizations to flourish."

Sources:
http://wn.com/Psychology_of_Happiness,
http://www.instituteofcoaching.org/index.cfm, http://isites.harvard.edu/icb/icb.do?keyword=k29664.
(All websites accessed December 13, 2011.)

Personal Development can be pursued through self-initiative, by taking specialized courses and/or coaching programs, but it also can be attained when an organization uses these programs as tools to enhance its human resources and build a more developed workforce. Several corporations offer self-development courses as well as personal coaches to help the individual development of their employees; PWC assigns each employee a coach to guide them in the areas where they can continue to grow and develop,[1] and Kaiser Permanente offers mentoring programs to help its employees reach their professional and personal goals.[2]

However, it is important to take note of certain recommendations in order to effectively use personal development training for corporate development:

- **Personal development should not be imposed.** Each person has his or her own rhythm and a different path. Many women for example, have a very good natural connection with their emotional side, and thus a course on emotional intelligence is not going to be as useful as a course on collective intelligence. Having said that, I do not mean to suggest that all women have an emotional surplus and therefore are not fit for emotional intelligence courses; what I am saying is that each person should decide what it is that they need, and the company should offer a variety of different courses for their employees accordingly.
- **Personal development does not have standard outcomes.** Executives should not be evaluated by their results in self-development courses, as is sometimes the current practice. Participants under the pressure of being evaluated tend to act upon what they perceive as the conventionally expected outcomes, without really benefiting from the training in a deeper way. It is a good idea if a company wants to offer personal development courses; however, the capacity and willingness of any employee to develop is something that the company does not have the ability to influence.
- **Personal development should not be focused on any particular group of origin.** When a particular course on self-development is organized targeting a specific group, members of the group might react badly and feel stigmatized. For example, if the company offers assertiveness courses in their women's strategy, many women can feel offended, thinking that the company is showing a prejudice against their assertiveness and promoting stereotyped views of women for the rest of the company. However, this same course can be offered by the women's network at the company, since networks are private and do not represent all women in the company nor the company's opinions.

Second movement: Identity and community, from communities of origin to communities of aspiration

Most people aspire to be included in the organizations in which they work and to be treated as equals to everyone else; at the same time, most individuals, regardless of their origins, would rather chose the community where they can actively perform their special professional talents without being perceived as members of a particular minority community and linked to a specific background. As we saw in Chapter Two, people reflect in solitude and act in community, and today there is a hunger for developing one's ideas in the company of the community one wishes to belong to.

Today, a common issue for large companies is the large amounts of their free time that employees will spend happily working to further initiatives with their internet communities. These are efforts happening outside the company, which they really feel a passion for, with the result that employees give only the minimum amount of energy to their regular jobs. The question is thus: how do you capture this enthusiasm and energy so that it also benefits the company?

An interesting effort to capture the passions of employees and their drive to work in what they really love inside the community of their choice, is an initiative developed by everis that won the seventh Human Resources Innovation award. This award was developed with the Spanish economic newspaper *Expansión y Empleo* together with the academic support of IE Business School.[3]

everis is a multinational consultant company that offers consulting, IT, and professional services. The company offers solutions for the following sectors: telecommunications, utilities and energy, banking and insurance, public administration, media, and health. everis began its business in Madrid in 1996, and currently operates in various European and Latin American Countries as well as in the United States. It has among its investment partners the investment fund 3i, the Landon Group and the UK investment fund Hutton Collins, in addition to a minority group of small shareholders. In 2010, total sales in declared income amounted to €506 million.

In 2010, everis received the seventh annual Expansion and Employment Award for Innovation in Human Resources, recognizing their company project everis Initiatives (eI). eI aims to incentivize the entrepreneurial spirit and internal talent of the company.

Thank to this initiative, the 7300 employees of Everis can develop their business ideas without having to leave the organization. Every employee, regardless of his position in the company, can become an entrepreneur and help in the creation of new businesses inside the company.

The initiative works as follows: Every employee can send his or her idea to the everis Initiatives team via an intranet portal called Emprendebox where potential entrepreneurs fill out a form explaining their initiative. The form is then evaluated by the team, consisting of eight partners and eight managers. If the idea is approved, the potential entrepreneurs will be granted the necessary time to develop their business plan and the company will offer coaching sessions to help them in the development process. The company will also facilitate the presentation of their idea to expert committees and investors' panels. everis will also facilitate the capital needed to launch the project, and the financial needs of the new business will be covered by everis for a period of five years, to allow the new company to gain a position in the market and became independent. The business plan is jointly developed with the entrepreneurs working with a group of specialized consultants, holding periodic meetings and following a well-defined work methodology. eI is also open for any SMEs that want to develop new ideas, and for investors who are looking for new projects.

As of 2010, 60 business ideas have been evaluated, and four ideas have already become independent businesses, such as:

exerelia, a company specializing in the design, implementation and management of integral and technological solutions in the field of energy efficiency. http://www.exeleria.com/
i-deals, which selects technological innovations and helps them to enter the market. http://www.i-deals.es/index.html

Sources:
http://www.expansion.com/especiales/empleo/premios_eye_10/everis.html   http://www.everis.com/spain/es-ES/inicio/Paginas/inicio.aspx
(All websites accessed December 13, 2011.)

Traditional network groups based on primary identities (race, gender, culture, etc.) can still be useful for companies, not so much to integrate the group but to establish a dialogue with members to find out what barriers may still exist for individuals coming from a particular group. Companies can include this knowledge in their general development programs, taking into account that the network may not represent the view of all the members of that particular group. Moreover, for some people it is important to engage and be active in their group of origin; therefore, since the 1970s, networks groups of origin exist in most organizations. For example, the Wells Fargo Company has 52 active groups, such as: Amigos (Hispanic), Asian Connection, CheckPoint (African-American), disabled employees, Veterans, Parents, Indigenous populations, PRIDE (LGBT), among others.[4]

Also, companies tend to engage in dialogues with the networks of external groups to better understand their reality of minorities and thus be able to adapt inclusion programs to their needs. IBM is a good example because they engage actively with many external partners among which are: the American Association for the Advancement of Science, American-Indian Science and Engineering Society, Asian-American Engineer of the Year, National Society of Black Engineers, National Society of Hispanic MBAs, Out for Work (LGBT focused), Society of Women Engineers, and many others. IBM obtains crucial information that helps it to attract new talent from those groups and design new strategies for their effective inclusion into the company.[5]

An increasing tendency in corporations is to support external communities that are not included in traditional minority identities. Young networks, Facebook communities, or some of the other employee external networks built around many different passions, are useful ways to engage with communities and discover the latest tendencies. For instance, Nike got into the community trend by financing social hubs such as NikePlus,[6] created together with Apple, where runners across the world communicate in a community of runners to exchange exploits, objectives or music. As Nike president Charly Denson said, "Consumers want to be part of a community, whether it is a digital community or a virtual community, or whether it is a physical community. They want to feel like they are part of something. They want to be engaged."[7] (Botsman and Rogers 2010, p. 201)

Some practical recommendations, could be useful for organizations:

- Individuals like to choose affiliation within their multiple identities, and tend to reject imposed identities from the outside. Therefore, networks aiming to serve minority groups should originate bottom-up and with limited interference by the company management. For many, participating in networks originated by the company management can be perceived as an obligation, and even, for some, as a stigmatization of their identity because they feel that the company holds a stereotyped vision of them instead of considering them as independent individuals.

- Companies should be careful when supporting some internal networks over others. Although for the public image of the company it may be good to have a certain networks, such as a women's network, giving more resources to one particular network over others will produce resentment and can end up in conflict and rivalry inside the company.
- Networks of aspiration, in contrast to networks of origin, can be developed either by members or by the company management, since these are based on professional capacities or particular interests, and membership is open and free to whoever wants to join regardless of their background.

Third movement: Identity and gender, resolving gender archetypes: rediscovering the meaning of giving by learning how to receive

Values that were traditionally perceived as feminine are increasingly appreciated in business organizations. Proof of this is the large number of documents, articles, books and research that emphasize the emergence into the business world of values that used to be considered feminine, which, alongside masculine values, have led to a broader range of competencies and abilities for companies.

The feminine archetype at work in a modern business environment normally includes a few of the following features:

- **Corporate identity**: Traditional masculine values, such as maximizing the financial value of the company, are today appreciated alongside feminine values related to characteristics such as empathy and caring. This is illustrated by a new interest in engaging with stakeholders and the community in which the company operates.
- **Training and talent development:** In the area of training, some of the new values include a concern for the self-development of company employees, in addition to improving their technical knowledge.
- **Daily life in the organization**: New values have also emerged alongside traditional ones, particularly in the interest in finding a balance between work and private life, as well as in a concern for the inclusion of all members of the organization.

- **Communication skills:** Communication is one of the values highlighted in the feminine archetype, and it can be perceived within many companies by a new emphasis on internal and external communication.
- **New abilities in management skills and competencies:** These are also considered to be more feminine, and include negotiation skills, teamwork, and emotional intelligence. In this respect we should point out a few differences in styles, mainly transactional (driven by objectives) vs. transformational, (including more participation from the group). More intuitive styles alongside the rational traditional of male archetype, and a more holistic style, not only concern with objectives but also in the general wellbeing of the members of the organization.

All of these new company values are considered to be feminine since they are all related to the traditional feminine archetype – empathy, sensibility, emotional intelligence, communication and multitasking. These qualities are expected to coexist alongside more traditional masculine ones – rationality, directness, detachment, and competitiveness.

In the interest of enhancing their relationship with these formerly ignored qualities, most companies include in their training courses several new values: emotional intelligence, intuition, empathy towards colleagues during teamwork, etc.

In addition, most companies have strategies to improve the numbers of women in their companies in all positions, helping them move forward with their career path, which they recognize to be more difficult to develop due to the challenge of balancing work and private life.

Some companies link both strategies: they work to promote a higher number of women to the higher ranks and at the same time try to enhance feminine values and management styles in their daily operations, as in the following example:

> Deloitte LLP won the 2010 Catalyst Award with a program entitled, "Women's Initiative: Living the Lattice." The award recognizes the success of the initiative in the retention and advancement of women.
>
> The initiative was launched in 1993, addressing two issues: a high rate of female attrition and the under-representation of women in leadership positions. After seven years the initiative has shown important results for the company, including the fact that women's representation as partners, principals, and directors has risen from 6 percent in 1995 to 22 percent in 2009; and the representation of women at senior manager level has increased from 23 percent to 36 percent in the same timeframe.

"Unique components include a broad range of leadership and development programs. Nationally led Women As Buyers workshops *address the distinctive communication and decision-making styles of women,* while regional career development programs prepare Deloitte's women for advancement at all levels."

To enhance opportunities for women, the company also promotes local, community-based, virtual learning and networking events. The company promotes an inclusive and flexible culture and has opted to adopt a customized model of career growth, development, and advancement that guarantees a sustainable balance of career and personal life without sacrificing a high level of performance.

Source: http://www.catalyst.org/page/69/catalyst-award-winners (Accessed December 13, 2011.)

In the business world, this increase in the appreciation of values that were formerly relegated to the household, will certainly contribute to the growth of companies and to their ability to face current challenges; however a few recommendations should be taken into consideration:

- Although emotional intelligence, communication and transformational decision-making styles are labeled as feminine, Chapter 3 demonstrates that it is a fact that *feminine qualities are not exclusively held by individual females and are not nonexistent in individual males.* Many men have strains of feminine qualities such as emotional intelligence or intuition, and conversely, there are also many women that lack them. For this reason, companies should be careful not to equate feminine characteristics with individual women, since this might very well produce a backlash from many men, as well as many women, who happen not to have those traits in their personalities.
- A healthy human being, as shown by Jung in his work with archetypes, should have high levels of balance between masculine and feminine qualities. Training programs and coaches should emphasize an awareness of what characteristics each individual has, while also focus on the other aspects that they might lack. A person who is good at multitasking should be aware of this characteristic and use it to his or her benefit, while at the same time, learning more abilities by trying to see the positive attributes of monotasking. Trainers and coaches must identify the specific needs of their trainees rather than adopting a course of action determined only by their interpretations of the communities of origin of their participants.

Fourth movement: Identity and the market. Finding an equilibrium between labor, work, and actions, in and outside the market

We can observe today how many executives, as well as employees in many organizations, have a passion and talent for art and crafts. Many happen to have a talent for painting, others enjoy music and take piano classes at night, while still others may invent new objects. The fact is that people, in addition to their regular jobs and regardless if they like them or not, also want to produce things that have value to them.

In addition to fabricating things outside their regular work, many executives and employees also spend hours contributing altruistically to their internet communities. Many hours are spent at night on internet forums or adding tweets in their chosen communities, bird watchers, nature buffs, pipe smokers, fans of medieval history and many other passionate interests of their choosing. And of course, both men and women are increasingly appreciating the value of spending more time with their families. In short, everyone needs more free time!

The fact is that people, in addition to making a living, want to do other things – basically, produce creative objects and act altruistically in the communities they are passionate for. There is a clear paradigm shift from the workaholics of the previous generation, which I happen to belong to. A feature of my generation and the one before it, was to work as hard as possible. After focusing in on their jobs as their only priority in life, once the routine was over, either because of retirement or because of a lay-off in times of financial cuts, many of these hard-working individuals fell into deep depressions, and a substantial number ended up with serious health problems. Many of my generation found it extremely difficult to figure out what to do with their time once the daily life of the office was no longer there. Today's generation is different, and it is also influencing these older generations into having a more balanced life. People think that work is fine, and can even be passionate about it; but nonetheless other facets of life are also important, such as a healthy family life and a passion for doing other activities.

Companies have realized that being flexible with time allows people to develop themselves further, more fully, leading to more fulfilling family lives and also the possibility of developing other talents. However, everyone needs to admit that all choices have drawbacks, and thus, more free time does necessarily imply a lower salary. One can choose to pursue a passion, or train in a sport, or spend more time with one's children. One is choosing free time in exchange for a salary reduction. This is a difficult choice, since a salary reduction necessarily implies a reduction in consumption that many cannot afford, but then again, there are many that can and indeed do. In any case, difficult times are ahead and the reduction in salaries along with the practice of sharing jobs, seem to be a likely condition for the future. Some companies are introducing sharing schemes by which people close to retirement work less and share with newcomers whom they also train. Older workers are happy to maintain their job in spite of working fewer hours, and even at the cost of a reduction in salary, and the young newcomer is happy to find a job, even if it is part time. Both parties can use their extra time to pursue their other passions in life, whether or not these are remunerated.

Having more flexibility with time does not have to imply moving away from the promotion ladder or from the possibility of participating in the strategic decisions of a company. Having more time and space for oneself does not mean a lack of commitment, rather the opposite. This person can see things with detachment, can grow and find new angles and perspectives, a better understanding of what is going on outside, refresh themselves by breathing new air and then going back to focus on their job with new ideas. Companies have increasingly realized that working many hours does not necessarily mean being more productive, and that people who are more fulfilled and happy perform better, even with reduced work hours.

Flexible time is one of the best achievements of recent business history. Starting as early as the 1970s, with efforts to help women in their maternity leave, it is now increasingly perceived as a right. All members of a company, from the secretary to the CEO, deserve to develop themselves as individuals, to focus on being good parents or with achieving other objectives.

Hewlett-Packard is considered to be the first US Company to institute flexible work arrangements, as early as 1973. Soon afterwards most large companies followed, including IBM,[8] JP Morgan Chase[9] and Ford[10], among others. According to Patricia Schaefer, data released by the Bureau of Labor Statistics in July 2005 showed that in 2004, 27.5 percent of all full-time workers in the US had flexible work schedules.[11] Flexible times include different schemes: part time, adjusting start and departure times to accommodate personal schedules and needs, telework or flex work that implies occasional work from home, and many more. Global companies soon extended these practices to different countries, and their influence was also important in the development of many different local initiatives across the world.

A good example is the *Premio Empresa Flexible* (Corporate Flexibility Award), which is very much sought after by companies in Spain.[12]

The *Premio Empresa Flexible* (Corporate Flexibility Award), is an initiative campaigning for the balance between work and personal life. It was launched in 2001 by the Spanish communication agency CVA (*Comunicación de Valor Añadido*), and since then the campaign has spread throughout most of Spanish corporate culture and is actively supported by national and regional governments, as well as other governmental bodies, in addition to the academic and scientific support of business schools like ESADE and the IE Business School. From an initial 150 companies that participated in 2001, the 9th campaign in 2010 had 1850 participating companies divided into three categories: large, medium and small.

A good example is the 2010 winner in the category of medium-size company, **Kellogg España S.L.,** recognized for its total work flexibility. The company is based on a model of management by objectives, and thus the only requirement for all employees is to be available either by phone, email or in the offices, between 10:00 and 17:00. Kellog provides its full-time employees with ADSL internet, Blackberry telephone and portable computers, and covers all related costs. Space flexibility is also an important feature of the company: no one has assigned seats or offices, including the CEO. They all share a common space, though all employees have a personal locker where they can deposit their personal effects every day, thus freeing up as much space as possible. For special privacy or meetings, the company has 16 small meeting rooms, two big meeting rooms with ten individual seats, and other informal spaces, all equipped with internet connections and the technology necessary to work.

Vacations and special leaves are also organized in a flexible mode, since the company believes that flexibility is not a privilege but a right.

Sources: http://www.kelloggs.es/, http://www.cvalora.com/empresa-flexible/historico-de-los-premios.html (Accessed December 13, 2011.)

To work with flexible times and in different work arrangements will continue in the years to come because new technologies allow for easier connections amongst employees; thus, having everyone physically present in the same space is becoming increasingly less relevant. In addition, people are taking more time off for personal needs, and therefore, one can frequently see that both professional men and women are developing discontinued professional tracks.

Perhaps the only recommendation for companies is to be careful *not to limit flexible arrangements only to women and maternity*. If flexible time arrangements are perceived by the company staff as being exclusively for working mothers, these will be stigmatized in the company and perceived either as a group that has unfair privileges or as workers that do not contribute with the same effort as the others. Extending flexible arrangements for all individuals would facilitate for more fathers to take parental leave to balance out the number of women who do so. Other employees, regardless of their family status, would also be able to pursue whatever needs or aspirations they might have.

Fifth movement: Identity in civilization. Integrating unity and diversity

It is an enormous effort to integrate into a larger framework two opposite tendencies in the context of civilization, one towards unity and homogenization and the other towards diversity and fragmentation, while holding in consideration the different rhythms of every civilization.

"Think global, act local" was the motto of the 1980s, and companies such as Coca-Cola mastered these ideas with beautiful global campaigns and logos that made us all part of a global community, while at the same time developing very specific campaigns for local markets, such as the one developed in the 1990s in Algeria depicting local people dressed in local attire, sharing Coca-Cola during Ramadan.

Towards the end of the 1990s the motto of "think global, act local" gradually changed to *Think and act Glocal*, meaning to act global and local at the same time.

If there is a new motto emerging for the current times, it would probably be something along the lines of *Co-create in local networks with global results, and, in parallel, co-create globally with local results.*

Communities create together with companies, jointly defining the goods and services they want and how they want them. Participatory techniques have proven to be very powerful tools to help companies engage with communities either locally or globally. Many of these techniques are enclosed in what is called "the art of hosting."[13] A good example is the process of engagement facilitated by *open space technologies*,[14] by which the management of Wal–Mart, the largest US retailer, initiated a process of dialogue with different community groups of detractors as well as supporters, and as a result, jointly designed a leading environmental initiative. Wal-Mart announced an effort to cut some 20 million metric tons of greenhouse gas emissions from its supply chain by the end of 2015 – the equivalent of removing more than 3.8 million cars from the road for a year.[15] These participatory dialogues in which supporters as well as detractors of the firm took part, helped to focus together on what good could be done instead of focusing on the different grievances the different interest groups had against each other; and thus the process managed to engage and build together a join initiative of corporate responsibility that is a great success.

The first experiences with the art of hosting techniques were in local communities, and afterwards they spread globally through networks created both in local and global communities. For example, the signs and symbols of civil movement Madrid 15 M can be traced back to the art of hosting techniques. And although most members of the 15 M movement probably ignore the meaning of the art of hosting or open space technologies, the practices and symbols they use to organize their assemblies and make decisions are originated in these types of participatory techniques.

Sometimes, communities co-create globally and then act locally, as in the case of Edgard Gouvia and his initiative (see Testimonies, Chapter 5). Others in contrast, co-create in local communities and then share the practices globally. The example of the HUB described in Chapter 4 is a good illustration of co-creating locally and globally at the same time, leading to a global spread of ideas and practices while maintaining a local approach in each HUB.

Companies are rapidly learning to engage with communities, whether local or global, and co-create with them new services or products. Engaging with local or communities helps companies understand what is on people's minds and what the real needs of the communities are, and companies can then apply technological solutions to serve real needs. In many cases, large companies use the strategy of engaging with local communities to help them define their global goals.

A good example of this engagement is the story of Reinaldo Pamponet,[16] an Ashoka Fellow known for his social initiatives with his former company Eletrocoperativa. His new initiative is called ItsNoon, and it has attracted the interest and support of some of the largest Brazilian companies who can use it to engage with local communities of young people who they would normally not have access to. This new initiative is spreading fast throughout the world.

> ItsNoon, is a company created by Reynaldo Pamponet in Brazil in January 2010. Using a win–win schema, the company intends to link two fundamental assets in society – knowledge and money – which also means linking companies with young people at the bottom of the social pyramid.

Companies need the knowledge of the market that these youth have; therefore they must build bridges with these communities through new projects. At the same time, youngsters benefit from applying their knowledge to these new projects, not only because of the income they provide, but also because it leads to higher self-esteem. Together, companies and the youth, have the possibility to co-create new products and services that target real societal needs and desires.

ItsNoon is a virtual platform that creates a space where creators can show their creations and be valued by their peers and other people, while also being incentivized to think about challenging questions relevant for today's society.

The system works as follows:

A company or organization will sponsor a call based on a topic of interest to them. Corporate sponsors include Vivo, Bradesco, Itau, Telefónica Foundation, and Ashoka, other sponsors include governmental bodies, NGOs and other global organizations.

ItsNoon formulates a question and posts the call on its website (www.itsnoon.net). Questions focus on different areas relevant for today's society. Examples include: What would you do to preserve the environment? How do you feel about working with new technologies? What work can you do using your cell phone? What does music mean for you?

Network members respond by producing creative multimedia works such as music, videos, photos or poems. Some calls have received responses from more than 1000 creators.

A dialogue is conducted within the network and afterwards creations are jointly selected by ItsNoon, the sponsor and the rest of the network.

The number of selected creators varies with each call, normally it will be less than 300 with each of them earning an around R$300 (more or less US$180), a sum which varies depending on the call.

In 2011 a new complementary currency was created, the Girassol, which is also distributed in addition to Reales. Girassols can be awarded for having creations selected in calls, but also can be received by other members of the network and currently can be used to buy equipment. The Girassols allow ItsNoon to increase the number of its selected creations.

ItsNoon provides the client with a full analysis harvesting of what was learned during the call.

The company works following the principles of *sevirologia* (http://ItsNoon.net/sevirologia-2/): "believing that we all have knowledge inside of and thus we can use it to perform actions we never thought we could do, sevirologia has two aspects that work together: self-stimulus and learning as a group."

The company has a current network of more than 6000 creators, of which at least 70 percent have contributed with at least one submission, and more than ten sponsors including some of the largest companies in Brazil, organizations in South Africa and the Netherlands, the three places where the company operates.

During the first year, ItsNoon managed to inspire more than 10,000 creations submitted over 17 calls. Over the next five years, the idea is to have a network of more than 1 million creators. Sixty percent of the fees paid by the clients go to the network and the remainder is used to cover operating expenses.

Source:
http://www.ashoka.org/fellow/reinaldo-pamponet
http://ItsNoon.net/sevirologia-2/
(Accessed December 13, 2011.)

2   Diversity management revisited

The instruments described in the previous section have many different origins; some were developed by a particular company and then spread globally, others originate in the work of scholars, and many come from the creative drive of individuals who want to improve things in their companies. There is also variety in the ways these policies are managed inside the company; some, such as the flexibility schemes, are managed by the Human Resources or the CR departments, while other initiatives are managed directly by a particular business unit or by the innovation division.

Managing identities is increasingly perceived as an asset for every department in the organization, and for many companies it represents a move forward in their diversity strategies that they developed in the 1970s as a result of affirmative action laws. The diversity policies implemented by most international corporations during the last decades of the twentieth century have resulted in an important step forward towards the inclusion of people in organizations, regardless of their background or origin. While these policies have achieved indisputable gains for individuals as well as for the companies, their instruments were designed in a large part during the 1980s and 1990s based on the needs and realities of the twentieth century.

However, recent literature shows that the mismatch we have today of diversity management policies with the external and internal environments in which companies operate, has generated a *proliferation of negative perceptions over the value of diversity programs over the last decade.* So, this is a good moment to review these strategies and analyze them in light of new and emerging paradigms. How can these policies grow and be modified to help companies to adapt to the complexity of identities in the diverse world of the twenty-first century?

Corporate diversity management: 30 years on

Diversity management for the changing environment of the 1980s

According to Mor Barak, the term "Diversity Management" originated in America and referred to: the voluntary organizational actions designed to create greater inclusion of employees from various backgrounds into the formal and informal organizational structures through deliberate policies and programs (Mor Barak 2005, p. 208).

A clear development in the content of diversity strategies appeared in a number of articles during the late 1980s and 1990s, specifying how these policies tackled the advent of demographic and social changes in the work place. Scholars such as Taylor Cox, Stacy Black, and R. Roosevelt Thomas provided a vision and an agenda for the workplace diversity movement that emphasized the competitive advantage for organizations that manage diversity well. In particular, Cox and Blake highlighted six strategic benefits for companies that manage diversity, including: reduction of staff turnover; increase in productivity; gaining an edge in attracting talent; increase in successful markets targeting underexploited subpopulations; increased potential for creative problem-solving and innovation; and improved ability to adapt to other inevitable sources of change. These new perspectives revolutionized the nature and direction of research in demographics, and also changed practices relating to equal employment opportunity (Stockdale and Cao 2005, pp. 299–300).

These scholars documented and clarified a change in the corporate world that began at the end of the 1970s as an effort to adapt to major changes in the environments where organizations operated.

Anti-discrimination legislation. Among the changes that corporations faced at the end of the twentieth century was anti-discrimination legislation, of which equal opportunity laws were probably the most important.

The equal opportunity concept began with the United Nations in the 1948 Universal Declaration of Human rights, and continued with the equal opportunity movement in the United States and Eastern Europe during the 1960s, and blossomed in the 1980s and 1990s with constitutional revisions and a multitude of laws protecting the rights of individuals of diverse backgrounds (Mor Barak 2005, p. 17).

Some countries, such as the United States, Canada, and many European Union members, have broad-based anti-discrimination legislation covering a wide array of characteristics such as gender, race, ethnicity or country of origin, religious beliefs, physical disability, and sexual orientation. Managers in late 1970s and early 1980s reacted by quickly putting into place anti-discrimination policies to avoid costly consequences.

The main European Union anti-discrimination regulations are:

- EU Treaty Article 13, which takes action to combat discrimination.
- The 2000/43/CE Directive on equal treatment between persons, irrespective of racial or ethnic origin.
- The 2000/78/CE, directive on the establishment of a general framework for equal employment. (Both incorporated into Spanish Law through the Law 62/2003 of December 2003.)
- The 2003/88/CE, regulating working times.
- And 2002/73/CE, focusing on equality between men and women.

In addition to anti-discrimination laws, during the 1980s and 1990s positive action programs were put in place in different countries, all aiming to change business rules and provide advantages to groups that have been traditionally discriminated against. Affirmative Action programs go beyond assuring equal rights by attempting to correct past wrongs, providing measures for interventions to actively reverse past discrimination against specific groups and offer temporary solutions. The so-called quota laws for women on corporate boards are one of the best known examples of these positive action policies.

The Quota Law of Norway, January 2002

From November 2003, boards of directors were required to have a minimum of 40 percent from each sex. (At the time women made up 6.8 percent of boards.)

Public Limited Companies (ASA companies) had until December 2005 to fulfil the quota voluntarily. By December 2005 17.8 percent of directorship positions were held by women.

In January 2006, the law came into force and ASA companies had two years to comply, otherwise the company would be dissolved.

By January 2008 no company was dissolved as a result of noncompliance with the law.

The Equality Law of Spain, March 2007

Companies with more than 250 employees are required to develop gender equality plans as well as specific measures to counteract work/life imbalances.

Article 75: "Companies which are obliged to present unabridged financial statements of income will endeavor to include a sufficient number of women on their boards of directors in order to reach a balanced presence of women and men within eight years of the entry into effect of this law."

Positive actions tend to be very controversial. The quota for corporate boards has had important results in Norway and Spain, among them: a clear increase in the number of women in directing positions; a greater diversity in the selection process at the board level; a general move towards younger boards; the appearance of role models for future generations; and a general acceptance in the business sector of having women on boards. However, the quota laws have also suffered important drawbacks, such as: the stigmatization of the women who gain these positions who are being questioned of their capacities; the fact that a very few number of women hold multiple board positions; a tokenism effect, by which many boards have only marginal numbers of women; and probably the most important drawback is the fact that most women nominated to board positions tend to be independent and the number of executive positions is getting lower. That means that women still cannot find their way on the career ladder to the top positions.

Changes in the Labor Market. Second to the changes in legislation, another fundamental change in corporations during the last decades of the twentieth century has been the diversity composition of the workforce. Due to increased mobility but also to a general rise in education, the workforce in most companies is extremely diverse. We can appreciate this fact with the aid of some figures:

- 10 percent of the world's total population is Caucasian.
- 12 percent of the world's total population has a disability.
- 52 percent of the world's total population is female.

One of the effects of the changes in the labor market is the distribution of economic power, which, D'Souza shows, reflects a shift in companies traditional clients, as we can see in the following box:

Purchasing power of some groups in the UK

"LGTB Pound" – 6 percent of the population, £70 billion.
"Grey Pound" (over 50 years old) – 80 percent of national wealth, 45 percent of total consumption, £175 billion.
"Brown Pound" (ethnic minorities) – £32 billon in consumption.
"Disabled Pound" – £80 billion in purchasing capacity.

The changes we mentioned in legislation and workforce were the consequences of major changes in the technologies that democratized communication and information on a global scale, and as a consequence produced major changes in the financial global sectors. Due to all of these changes, the financial lives of products were also shortened. Before, a major technical product could last ten years; today probably no more than two, and as a result, the need for constant innovation has become the key for corporate survival. And, last but not least, there has been a fundamental change in social values, shifting in favor of a responsible company with a movement towards the inclusion of the excluded.

Faced with such a rapid changes and an ever-more-complicated background, management theories came to conclude that it was not possible to continue believing that there was a single way of managing an organization, nor a single best way of managing people. Each situation was different and the employees were increasingly different, and thus as a result, companies began to change their focus to become more responsive and flexible organizations capable of adapting to continuous changes (de Anca and Vazquez 2007, p. 121).

The traditional paradigm was based on a system of values that reflected the workforce and major clients of the time, basically Anglo-Saxon males. In that system, uniformity was the most appreciated value, and people different from the mainstream needed to either change in order to fit in, or accept exclusion. In the changing paradigm, management theories began to emphasize new values, among others: the conscious participation of individuals in the organization; looking at organizations as interactive systems; and organizations becoming based on permanent collective learning. These ideas were spread by the works of scholars such as Peter Senge (Senge, 1990) and Thomas Davenport (Davenport, 1999), and supported by new discoveries in science and information technology regarding living systems.

The changes in the environment and the reactions from companies resulted in the fact that by 2001, 75 percent of the Fortune 100 companies had invested in diversity initiatives of some kind (Agars and Kottke 2005, p. 56).

Diversity management as a corporate strategy

The diversity management strategy was designed to welcome into the corporation groups that for historical reasons had felt excluded. These groups tend to be classified into two levels. The first level has six primary dimensions: gender, age, ethnicity, physical abilities, race, and sexual orientation. The second level is made up of qualities that can be changed, such as: education, geographical location, social status, income, marital status, parental status, religious beliefs, work experience and so on (Loden and Rosener 1991, p. 20).

The classification of these groups, following mostly the primary dimensions, is a reflection of the US experience that categorizes diversity according to its mixed racial and ethnic population. This is the logical consequence of the fact that diversity management practices began in the United States, alongside the new civil rights laws of the 1970s. However, these narrow diversity definitions are based on categories drawn from the unique experience of the US and were not necessarily transferable or applicable to other cultures. The spread of diversity policies outside of the United States has been one of the primordial difficulties for global companies.

Diversity initiatives have some similarities across companies and sectors, typically covering five areas: management leadership; educational training; performance and accountability; work and life balance; and career development and planning. The most common approaches affect recruitment practices, and are embodied by awareness seminars provided to all employees. Many of tactical activities include ideas and strategies such as gaining top management support, developing mentoring opportunities, changing recruitment and selection practices, attending to career development, and providing ongoing training to address multicultural competence.

The instruments for diversity management have many features in common with the instruments used to introduce change in organizations; therefore, during the last three decades, scholars and consultants have developed models to enhance diversity strategies in organizations that have many similarities with models to introduce change, among which the following should be highlighted:

- In 1993, Powell designed a model for organizations to respond to equal opportunity issues. In this model organizations react differently to equal opportunities, and these reactions are classified into four main types: proactive, reactive, benign or neglectful. In his view, the most desirable attitude is proactive (Powell, 1993).
- Roosevelt Thomas (1991, 1996) uses a model that defines three basic responses organizations have towards the changing face of the workforce: affirmative action, valuing differences or managing diversity. To take the full advantage of diversity, organizations should change their cultures and systems to sustain coordinated efforts of a diverse workforce, and thus become an organization that manages diversity.
- Taylor Cox published his model in 2001 as an evolution from an earlier one. He advocates organizations becoming multicultural organizations as opposed to more primitive forms that do not manage plurality well – monolithic vs. pluralistic. In order to become a multicultural organization, managers need to take action in five areas: leadership, research and measurement, education, alignment of management systems, and follow-up. Cox's model also incorporates important processes such as: the need to assess organizational diversity competence (research and measurement); develop internal expertise and systems to enhance the learning process (education); and ensure the alignment of the system within the organization with management visions (alignment of management systems and accountability of the process follow-up).
- A more recent model, enacted by Agars and Kottke integrates the ideas of other scholars into a full integration theory. "The fully integrated theory is similar to the concepts of Cox's multicultural organization or Thomas' managing diversity organization, since all these organizations have developed policies and practices and culture to support diversity; where their model differs is how to explicate the process by which organizational change occurs." According to their model, organizations progress through three stages: 1) issue identification, during which they make managing diversity a priority; 2) implementation, during which existing practices are accepted and new policies implemented that support a diverse workforce; and 3) maintenance, during which formal and informal processes are established (Agars and Kottke 2005, p. 67).

Most of these models have been tested by companies and monitored by scholars and consultants. They have helped organizations advance in the implementation of diversity policies into a larger framework of company changes. Organizational change efforts are comprehensive, multi-level, planned, flexible, addressing specific policies, practices, norms, attitudes, values and behaviors of entire organizations or sizable units within organizations. Intervention may focus on structural, cultural or behavioral processes, or all three together.

Strengths and limitations of the current corporate diversity strategy

In their review of the empirical evidence from diversity management models and their effect in the company, Agars and Kottke recognize that while during the last decades there has been considerable work in the academic development of models for managing diversity, as well as research on diversity and its potential benefits, it is not easy to analyze their results because so few organizations have evaluated their diversity initiatives (Agars and Kottke 2005, p. 67).

The majority of the research that has been conducted at the organizational level comprises case studies that have monitored the implementation of diversity programs. Beyond these case studies some research has focused on comparing the workforce of organizations with their financial performance. Research conducted following both hypotheses – whether diversity leads to positive outcomes or to negative outputs – has been equally inconclusive. This is probably due the fact that diversity groups, as categorized by society (women, race, etc.), are considered to be homogenous, and thus company performance results are based on the "perception" of members of that group behaving similarly, regardless of differences in competence or personality. A famous example is the early study (Wright et al. 1995) that examined the stock prices of firms that had been awarded the department of Labor's Exemplary Voluntary Efforts (EVE) Award for affirmative action programs. This study showed that stock prices increased for firms that had been awarded the awards and decreased for firms that had the outcome of discrimination suits made public. However, when Bierman attempted a replication and extension of the same study in 2001, he found negative stock returns for EVE award winners (Agars and Kottke 2005, p. 70).

The difficulty of proving results also lies in the fact that these policies tend to be long-term strategies; the benefits of diversity management take time to emerge and are difficult to articulate to organizational leaders, leading to further difficulties with securing serious commitments because there is often a focus on short-term outcomes.

While stating than generally diversity policies implemented over the last 30 years have resulted in clear benefits for individuals, organizations and society in general, Stockdale and Cao classify the benefits of diversity management into three levels: the Individual; group and interpersonal development; and organizational (Stockdale and Cao 2005, p. 311).

These and other experts tend to agree in some of the clear positive outcomes of diversity policies, among them:

- **Individual level:**
  - Career tracking awareness
  - Individual strategies for women to overcome the glass ceiling
  - Individual access to advancement and job promotions
  - Improved economic benefits
  - More decision-making power for minority groups
  - Mentoring opportunities
  - Improved salary opportunities in minority groups
  - Gains in mental and physical health
- **Group level:**
  - Diversity awareness and counter-stereotype training
  - Expanding discussion on the forms of prejudice and oppression in diversity training
  - Developing multicultural competencies
  - Improving social networks through mentoring
  - Developing affinity groups
- **Organizational level:**
  - Business growth
  - Increase in productivity
  - Cost savings
  - Positive image of the company
  - Advances in talent recruitment
  - Increased employee loyalty
  - Strong connection between social and economic performance

However, diversity management has also had important limitations and serious obstacles: persistent discrimination covert or overt; perception of a threat to job security; perception of unfairness among traditional groups; economic pressures to demonstrate profitability; and lack of leadership to champion and sustain long term efforts, just to name a few.

Moreover, Barak claims that the three main characteristics of diversity management (voluntary policies, the use of a broad definition for diversity, and the focus on providing tangible benefits to the company) also constitute its main limitations. The fact that the company implements these policies voluntarily, leads to a situation where in times of crisis there is a clear withdrawal from these efforts. Mor Barak argues that defining diversity in its broadest sense may result in a limitation of resources for those minorities that deserve more attention, since efforts are spread too thin, thus diluting the message of past injustices. Finally, the perceived business emphasis may imply that if companies no longer perceive diversity management as profitable, it would disappear (Mor Barak 2005, p. 222).

The real question is whether diversity policies are put in place because of social justice and the requirements of the law, or if they are necessary for the business success of the company; and, then, to what extent both can be tackled using the same policies. Diversity management has thus a dual focus: the first is enhancing social justice by creating an organizational culture without privileges; and the second is increasing productivity and profitability through organizational transformation.

Also, as we saw in Chapter 2, there is a fundamental debate in terms of privileging individuals vs. privileging groups as the main recipients of policies. This debate is positioned sometimes in terms of liberal policies vs. multicultural practices and reflects in management in terms of the debate of meritocracy and colorblind policies vs. minority groups and affirmative action. These ideas are subject to complex arguments, as mentioned by Thomas, Mack, and Montagliani,

> The meritocracy myth, colorblind ideal, and melting pot metaphor have created a social climate that discourages diversity and privileges homogeneity and the defined norm of the dominant group. These systems of beliefs help to make the existence and maintenance of diversity myths socially acceptable. That is, diversity efforts can be opposed in socially acceptable ways by positioning diversity efforts as an unfair, inequitable, and inconsistent with these societal ideals. Yet these ideals themselves must be challenged. Organizations are microcosms of society. Individuals who work within organizations bring their attitudes, beliefs and stereotypes into the workplace ... Organizations can simultaneously pursue a workplace that is both cohesive in its values and that is diverse in order to enhance creativity, innovation, productivity and subsequently organizational effectiveness. Leadership support for diversity as a learning opportunity rather than a detriment is foremost in establishing an organizational context that can recruit and

retain diversity in order to reap its organizational rewards (Thomas, Mack and Montagliani, p. 51)

On the other hand, people opposed to diversity policies believe that the fact that diversity management tends to focus on minority groups, helps to produce a backlash from some members of the company that perceive individual unfairness. Also, some individuals belong to minority categories but do not have a strong affinity towards them, and for them diversity policies will provoke pressures to enter into these definitions in order to achieve corporate benefits.

The steps that organizations and their leaders must take to create and sustain diversity and inclusion are demanding and challenging, and in order to be effective, they require a substantial degree of planning, resources and commitment (Holvino, Ferdman, and Merrill-Sands, p. 275); therefore, many experts believe that in the actual period of crisis would be difficult to maintain the commitment.

3   Managing identities: An emerging paradigm for corporate development

As with everything in humanity, things are probably not right or wrong but only moving and changing along with the changes in history and human needs. Just as the human brain still has a reptile part, and around that base new developments have grown, wrapping up the older tissues, policies follow suit and wrap new ideas around older pillars. The policies of the 1950s were useful for companies at that time in which the goal was efficiency. Some practices from that era are still useful, while others have evolved. Diversity management helped organizations to open monolithic practices and allow for some more flexibility among their members, and some of these early practices will prove to remain useful in the future while others may change. The question now is: in these changing times, what are the new models of how companies need to evolve without eliminating diversity practices, but rather including them into larger frameworks?

In the newer definitions of diversity policies we can appreciate the new tendencies that are emerging. From a narrow definition of excluded groups in the 1970s, we have been moving towards a much broader definition of diversity during the last few years, implying a better understanding of the multiplicity of affiliations that make up Identity.

We can better understand this change in definition through the explanations of R. Hays-Thomas: One approach emphasizes the position of groups who have traditionally been victims of discrimination. It acknowledges power differentials among groups. The newer approach downplays power differentials and treats all bases of difference as more or less equivalent in terms of systemic analysis (Hays-Thomas 2005, pp. 11–12). For the author, the newer approach considers many dimensions of difference among people in organizations, thus conceptualizing diversity in terms of environmental complexity and change and shows that the challenges posed by diversity management are just one aspect of life in an increasingly complex organizational world. Complexity of thought and flexibility of behavior are required for success in contemporary organizations. An important consequence of this perspective is that diversity management is seen as a form of organizational development and change as well as a set of processes for increasing effectiveness and harmony in a workforce that varies along important dimensions (Hay-Thomas 2005, pp. 11–12).

If we analyze management theories in terms of diversity we can better understand the changes in company practice that are meant to adapt to new environmental stimuli, as shown in Figure E.1.

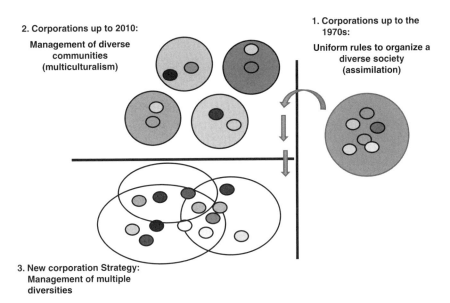

Figure E.1 Corporate diversity strategy: from assimilation to managing groups to the management of multiple identities

Up to the 1970s, the uniformity of procedures and rules was the best model to face the challenges of the time, in which efficiency was the goal most demanded by corporations. The best way to ensure efficiency was to put in place a set of procedures for everyone to follow, regardless of their differences. This management model forced the assimilation of many people that did not fit into the main value system. The system was efficient at the expense of creativity and the exclusion of many.

During the 1980s and 1990s, the environment changed, and, in addition to efficiency, companies required innovation and knowledge of diversity in order to penetrate new markets and to adapt to the purchasing power of new groups in society. Managing diversity in the various groups within the company was the best approach. Companies broke the patterns of uniformity and assimilation and liberated many people that did not fit into their uniform culture; in addition, new flexible policies allowed the further inclusion of formerly excluded groups.

However, in the first decade of the twenty-first century, the diversity policy has shown its limitations. Many people do not feel at ease clustered according to their communities of origin and what they want is to be able to act in their communities of aspiration; they want to be able to live in the multiplicity of their different identities.

To be able to manage at the same time both individuals and their actions within their multiple communitarian identities, is the key for the next decade. Managing multiple identities is a *better adapted model to the fluid and changing reality that characterizes our global society today.*

In the new emerging paradigm, one pre-requisite before being able to manage identities is clear: individuals need to be playing on an equal field to be able to give their full potential. Employees who feel they can be themselves and be appreciated for their qualities will feel more identified with the company, and then they will be able to act in a smaller community, inside the company itself, representing their potential aspirations.

For the last few years, together with my colleague Conchita Galdon at the Center for Diversity in Global Management of IE Business School, we have been analyzing the accumulated expertise and knowledge of research initiatives and program management in different regions throughout the world. We have been developing a model to capture what has worked well in past diversity policies and develop a *new model* that has the potential to be utilized to better tackle the management of multiple identities.

This new paradigm recognizes the variety of identities that compose each individual. As has been explained previously, the many identities held by men and women can be grouped into identities of origin and identities of aspiration. During each given moment in time, identities of origin are those that are already incorporated within the person (being a man, disabled, Vietnamese, and so on), whereas identities of aspiration are, as the name perfectly indicates, aspirational (being part of the marketing department, belonging to the runners' club, being perceived as a member of the country of destination with all the rights it entails). The model we propose is based on the elimination of barriers to integration, barriers to "belonging." It seeks to remove the barriers that prevent individuals from joining their identities of destination, without removing or underestimating the elements of the identity of origin that the individual might want to protect.

The model is based on observing a shift that has already happened in many companies that are implementing certain instruments and policies. Rather than trying to integrate minority groups, integrate individuals, eliminating whatever barriers an individual might face, companies have understood that individuals still face barriers because they belong to certain groups. They aspire to be perceived as members of their communities of aspiration and not be treated as part of the minority groups. To solve this paradoxical issue, some companies have invested in developing ways to achieve equal opportunities for all, beginning with their human resources departments; and if that policy is effective, other units can then fully harvest the potential of diversity.

Individuals may still have barriers in order to be on equal terms with others; some of these are barriers that have resulted from their belonging to certain groups of origin. These barriers that individuals carries within themselves are what we, at the Center for Diversity in Global Management of IE Business School, call individual barriers. For example, a lack of specific skills derives from a specific education that perhaps does not favor ambition and competition (this is often said of women and certain cultures men as well). This doesn't mean that all women show lack of ambition; it means that some women happen to be educated to be less ambitious just because they are female. When this occurs, these women reach the market with an individual trait that might be a barrier to their professional development. Other barriers can be the lack of access to support from leadership by being excluded from the main networks of power (also mentioned often in the case of women and certain minority groups). And the list of barriers can go on and on.

For example, in a context in which assertiveness might be considered to be directly related to professional success, training focused on developing assertiveness can be very beneficial for many women, but also for many men, particularly to those from cultures in which assertiveness is not perceived as a good value. If the course is labeled as a "women's initiative" or "specific culture development program," the initiative may produce a significant backlash from those belonging to the groups that happened to be assertive by nature; and many who perhaps are white and male, and who can also benefit from this training, might find it difficult to participate. The company should therefore list a series of instruments to help eliminating barriers without focusing on any specific minority groups. In this manner effectiveness will be achieved quickly. A course on assertiveness offered to every employee, or by a recommendation from a mentor or supervisor, might be made up mostly of women or people of certain cultures, but none will be there due to their identity of origin. In this way, other members of the community that the company might not have initially identified as needing the course can benefit from it.

On the other hand, there are other barriers people face that represent collective perceptions that others might have against somebody because they belong to a certain group; this is the case of prejudices against LGBT members, or against a race or religion. These barriers exist in the community outside the individual who faces them (and also outside his or her group of affiliation). They are what we call collective barriers. In this case companies are finding that the best approach is to tackle them specifically using awareness programs to make people self-aware of their own prejudices and work on them to make room for new possibilities.

By applying specific instruments to eliminate individual and collective barriers, it is possible to design quality-based indicators and procedures that go beyond traditional demographic indicators, to better measure the true effectiveness of these management policies. These indicators will quantify the impact of the implemented actions within the organization by the level of employee identification with the company. The research of Nobel Prize laureate George Akerlof (Akerlof and Kranton, 2005), shows that a greater degree of identification with the company by workers, increases their level of motivation and the perceived utility obtained by the worker from his or her professional performance.

In parallel to the development of policies to target specific individual and collective barriers, different units in the overall organization can learn how to better understand multiple identities and use the knowledge to create and innovate new processes, products or ideas, and engage effectively with the new emerging communities in a different co-creation process that is moving with the flow of the times. Akerlof himself states that identification occurs primarily through the groups that workers are in contact with (department or section), which reinforces the idea that an approach of collective creativity that incorporates the lower orders of a company structure will be essential to achieve inclusion.

Diversity is still the right word to express the world we live in. However, today we are concerned with the management of the multiple and mobile identities in all of us on a level playing field in which, among equals, we all can be different and bring our differences to work on a common goal.

Author's Note

1. Aristotle *Politique* I, 2, 1252 a 24 a cited in Pierre Hadot, p. 16.

Introduction

1. Second principle of Kybalion, anonymous based on Hermes Trimegisto, to be found in http://www.kybalion.org/kybalion.asp?chapter=II.
2. Ibn Khaldun: Abū Zayd 'Abdu r-Rahman bin Muhammad bin Khaldūn Al-Hadrami, May 27, 1332 AD/732 AH – March 19, 1406 AD/808 AH.

Chapter 1   Identity and the Self

1. French expression equivalent to Tool Kit, or Instruction booklet.
2. *Analects* translations in this section are taken from http://www.classicallibrary.org/confucius/analects/14.htm
3. In Athens in the fourth century BC and for three centuries after, four schools were active, the *Academia* (founded by Plato), the *Lyceum* (founded by Aristotle) The Garden (founded by Epicurus) and the *Stoa* (founded by Zenon).
4. The Enneagram, from Sufi old traditions was first formulated in the works of George Gurdjieff (1872–1949). Oscar Ichazo (Bolivian – 1971 Institutes Arica in the USA) and Claudio Naranjo (Chile November 1932 – Psychiatrist – Harvard, Berkeley – 1970) developed the system in its actual form; other current developers include: Don Riso (New Orleans, 1987 – Enneagram Jesuit tradition via Arica institute: Personality Types Co-founder of the Enneagram Institute), Russ Hudson (Co-founder of the Enneagram Institute in 1991, Enneagram professional training programs) www.enneagraminstitute.com..
5. Mark Anielski: *An Assessment of Sweden's No Interest Bank* http://anielski.com/wp-content/documents/The%20JAK%20Bank%20Report.pdf (accessed December 14, 2011), and Mark Burton Dissertation.
6. Giorgio Simonetti, *Jak Bank, per un modello finanziario sostenibile libero dal concetto di usura*,Dreossi Editore, Zoppola Aprile 2009.

7. Miguel Ganzo's report: *Introduction to JAK: ideology, structure and savings and loans system* http://jak.aventus.nu/download/JAK_Int/Introduction_to_JAK_-_JSE_2009.pdf (accessed December 14, 2011).
8. Miguel Ganzo's report and Alienski's report.

Chapter 2   Identity and Community

1. http://www.feirapreta.com.br/.
2. Approximately US$ 400,000 at the time (US$ 1 = R$ 1.7).
3. The word *arrastão* is taken from a common fishing term, and can be literally translated as a big dragnet. It refers to a collective robbery performed by groups of impoverished teenagers in public spaces such as street fairs, beaches and tunnels. This phenomenon was commonly observed between the 1990s and the early 2000s in some large Brazilian cities.
4. The words *preto* and *preta* are, in Brazilian Portuguese, informally used to refer to a black person (the formal words are *negro* and *negra*). Its meaning can range from a disrespectful to an affable manner to call a black person, varying in accordance to the content and the tone used in the sentence.
5. http://www.sebrae.com.br/.
6. Artemisia, http://www.artemisia-international.org/about.php.
7. http://www2.goldmansachs.com/citizenship/10000women/index.html.
8. See details at http://www.feirapreta.com.br/.
9. www.pretapretinha.com.br.
10. http://www.belezanatural.com.br/.
11. This case is a summary of a case study developed at IE Business School "Beleza Natural: The Coca-Cola of the hair? Offering self-esteem to the base of the pyramid" by Edgard Barki of the FGV, Newton Campos and Celia de Anca ref. GE1-121-I. It can be found at IE Business School. www.ie.edu.
12. US$ 1 was equivalent to R$ 1.6 in April 2011.
13. http://www.sebrae.com.br/.
14. http://www.endeavor.org/.
15. The research was conducted by IE professors from the Center for Diversity in Global Management and professors from the ONA Foundation Morocco between 2005 and 2008, using six structured focus groups of a total of 90 Moroccan and Spanish managers in

Morocco and Spain, following the methodology developed by the ONA and IE Foundations. The results of the focus group were validated in a think tank of 20 international experts that led to the design of a survey that was answered by 60 Spanish businessmen working in Morocco. Findings can be seen in *Cultural Diversity in International Business, The Spanish–Moroccan Business Context* http://centerfordiversity.ie.edu/sites/default/files/Cultural%20 Diversity%20in%20International%20Business-%20The%20 Spanish-Moroccan%20Business%20Context.pdf (accessed December 14, 2011).

16. Ali, Benmakhlouf, in *Cultural Diversity in International Business, The Spanish Moroccan Business Context*, Think tank found at http:// centerfordiversity.ie.edu/.

Chapter 3   Identity and gender: Between the self and the social

1. http://www.kybalion.org/kybalion.asp.
2. In English, since pronouns are neutral, the play between the feminine and masculine cannot be appreciated.

> Once in a dark of night
> Inflamed with love and wanting
> I arose (O coming of delight!)
> And went, as no one knows,
> When all my house lay long in deep repose ...

"The Dark Night Of The Soul," Saint John of the Cross, Translated by A.Z. Foreman http://poemsintranslation.blogspot.com/2009/09/saint-john-of-cross-dark-night-of-soul.html (accessed December 14, 2011).

3. Qabalah is the word normally used to describe Jewish mysticism, in particular referring to a school of thought concerned with the esoteric aspect of Judaism systematized during the 11th to the 13th century in its first development and a second development from Spain, in the 16th and in the Ottoman empire during the 18th century. During the 20th century its teachings have influenced modern western psychology as in the words of Parfitt:

> for many years the Qabalah appeared to be lost in obscurity, particularly in its practical applications, yet today, with so many people searching for spiritual roots, and looking for meaning and purpose in their lives, it is undergoing a remarkable comeback. Its influence

has not only been in the spiritual realms, however, for it has also exerted a profound and lasting effect on the ground of modern western psychology. Although he kept it secret, we know that Freud was interested in the Qabbalah, and in his letters Jung made many knowledgeable references to the Tree of Life. (Parfitt 1991, pp. 1–2).

The Qabalah seeks to define the nature of the universe and the human being, as well as the nature and purpose of existence, The Qabbalah is the revelation of our inner nature that comes with study and use. The spiritual map known as the Tree of Life, is a guide for the spiritual development, it deals with the whole person, in his body emotional and intellect characteristics, as well as reveals paths that the self can follow in his/her conscious spiritual development.

4. www.Catalyst.org.
5. In 2005, a study elaborated by Circulo de Progreso with the academic advice of professors from the IE Business School, attempted to provide a rigorous vision of the processes and conditionings that could answer the basic question: why are there so few women at higher decision-making positions in Spain? The study attempted a personal approach to the individuals, valuing options and decisions that have defined the professional careers of women in Spain (Círculo de Progreso 2005).

   150 women were interviewed in eight different professional paths: public administration, academia, arts, executive, business, politics, liberal professions and public institutions. The 8 types were structured around different professional levels defined by a specific professional maturity index that was developed for the purpose of this study. The results were somewhat surprising: the traditional hindering factors, such as equal opportunities in the access to higher education or job positions, were not perceived as an obstacle. The main hindrance limiting professional advancement was considered generally to be a matter of decisions rather than options. For many of the participants, the answer to the question as to why there are so few women at the top was for many due to personal factors, rather than social or job sector factors. The study led to the conclusion that women in Spain consider their personal value system as a catalyser or inhibitor for their careers (de Anca and Aragon 2007).

6. Locke, http://www.constitution.org/jl/2ndtr07.txt.
7. *Encyclopedie ou dictionnaire raisonne des sciences, des arts, et des metiers.* Reimpresion en fascimil de la primera edicion. Stuttgart-Bad Cannetatt, F.Froman Verlag, 1966 p. 483, vol 3) en Alicia puleo (comp) La ilustración olvidad. Barcelona: Antropos, 1993, en murillo p. 44
8. This case is a shorter version of a case study developed at IE Business School "Dana; *In the* Footsteps of Khadijah al-Kubra: Women Banking

at Abu Dhabi Islamic Bank," written by Fatimah M. Iliasu and Celia de Anca, that can be found at IE Business School. www.ie.edu.

9. Manuela Marín, "Women as Economic Agents in Al-Andalus: Our Common Legacy," a presentation from the conference "Arab Women in the XXI century: a business opportunity" which took place at the IE Business School, Madrid, June 30 to July 1, 2003. See also *Mujeres en Al Andalus* Marin, Madrid C.S.I.C, 2000, pp. 253–394.

10. Damisch, Kumar et al, "Leveling the Playing Field: Upgrading the wealth Management Experience for Women." Boston Consulting Group, July 2010. http://www.bcg.com/documents/file56704.pdf (accessed December 14, 2011).

11. *From my Experience, the Division of Man's Life Stages.* Saaed Bin Ahmed Al Lootah, UAE 2009. www.lootah.com.

12. www.centralbank.ae.

13. http://www.zawya.com/.

14. www.forteconsultancy.com/.

Chapter 4   Identity and the market

1. Abu Zayd 'Abd al Rahman B. Muhamad b. Muhammad Bin Khaldun, popularly known as Ibn Khaldun (1332–1406).

2. Abu-l Walid Muhammad bin Ahmad bin Rushd, also known as Averooes (1126–1198). For more information: Cruz Hernandez, M. 1998 *Abu-l Walid Muhammad B Ahmad B Muhammad Ibn Rushd, Vida, Pensamiento, Influencia.*

3. Exchange Value vs. Use Value: The metaphor of St Augustine comparing the value of a horse with the value of a slave is often quoted as one of the first attempts to understand the utility factor in the exchange process.

> These are the gradations according to the order of nature; but according to the utility each man finds in a thing, there are various standards of value, so that it comes to pass that we prefer some things that have no sensation to some sentient beings. And so strong is this preference, that, had we the power, we would abolish the latter from nature altogether, whether in ignorance of the place they hold in nature, or, though we know it, sacrificing them to our own convenience. Who, e.g., would not rather have bread in his house than mice, gold than fleas? But there is little to wonder at in this, seeing that even when valued by men themselves (whose nature is certainly of the highest dignity), more is often given for a horse than for a

slave, for a jewel than for a maid. Thus the reason of one contemplating nature prompts very different judgments from those dictated by the necessity of the needy, or the desire of the voluptuous; for the former considers what value a thing in itself has in the scale of creation, while necessity considers how it meets its need; reason looks for what the mental light will judge to be true, while pleasure looks for what pleasantly titillates the bodily sense. The City of God, St. Augustine of Hippo. http://www.newadvent.org/fathers/120111.htm

The metaphor of St Augustine was taken further by St Thomas Aquinas in the thirteenth century, with his thoughts on the value of economic goods, and his idea of utility.

> *Reply to Objection 3* As Augustine says (De Civ. Dei xi, 16) the price of things salable does not depend on their degree of nature, since at times a horse fetches a higher price than a slave; but it depends on their usefulness to man. Hence it is not necessary for the seller or buyer to be cognizant of the hidden qualities of the thing sold, but only of such as render the thing adapted to man's use, for instance, that the horse be strong, run well and so forth. Such qualities the seller and buyer can easily discover. *Summa Theologica*, Treati II cap 77 art 2

The conclusion of the *Summa Theologica* is that the value of economic goods is that which comes into human use and is measured by a monetary price, for which purpose money was invented. As Rothbard indicates, the value of things as stated by Aquinas, was clearly found in the Market. His works were widely used throughout economic history to build the theory of just price, and later thinkers, including Marx, viewed the cost of production through the idea of just price, and thus understood price as result of cost and not as a result of utility.

> Unfortunately, in discussing the just price, St. Thomas stored up great trouble for the future by being vague about what precisely the just price is supposed to be ... Aquinas felt obliged to incorporate the Aristotelian analysis of exchange into his theory, with all the ambiguities and obscurities that that entailed. St. Thomas was clearly an Aristotelian in adopting the latter's trenchant view that the determinant of exchange value was the need, or utility, of consumers, as expressed in their demand for products. And so, this proto-Austrian aspect of value based on demand and utility was reinstated in economic thought. On the other hand, Aristotle's erroneous view of exchange as "equating" values was rediscovered, along with the

indecipherable shoemaker–builder ratio. Aristotle's famous discussion of reciprocity in Exchange in book V of his Nichomachean Ethics talks of a builder exchanging a house for the shoes produced by a shoemaker. He writes "The number of shoes exchanged for a house must therefore correspond to the ratio of builder to shoemaker." Some have tried to see in this passage a forerunner of the labor theory of value, implying that the ratio referred to by Aristotle was the labor hours put into work. (Rothbart, 1995, p. 16)

Unfortunately, in the course of the *Commentary to the (Nichomachean) Ethics*, Thomas followed St. Albert in seeming to add to utility, as a determinant of exchange value, labor plus expenses. This gave hostage to the later idea that St. Thomas had either added to Aristotle's utility theory of value a cost of production theory (labor plus expenses), or even replaced utility by a cost theory (Rothbard 1995, p. 52).

Later, scholars declared that the just price was based on the cost of production and not on the idea that it was based on the common price of the market, as the majority of scholars had assumed, and the same assumption was followed by the Austrian School of Economics centuries afterwards.

For centuries, Christian scholars discussed the justice of a determined price, and thus who was entitled to set a just price: whether a just price must be set by market forces based on utility for the buyers; if it should be set by the producers based on their cost; or if just price should be set by the government in an attempt to strike a balance between the two sides, the utility of the buyer and the cost of the producer; centuries later, these ideas mainstreamed into modern economics.

Regardless of the meaning of a just price, what is important is the concept of utility. Aristotle's idea of utility was followed by a Christian tradition based on the importance of proportion between the possession of one thing and the possession of another, with each person assigning value according to their perception. The absolute value of things is not something tradable in economic terms.

Value is the quality a thing can never possess in privacy, but acquires automatically the moment it appears in public. This marketable value, as Locke very clearly pointed out, has nothing to do with "the intrinsic natural worth of anything" (Arendt 1978, p. 164).

The question is not so much whether value is objective or subjective, but whether it can be absolute or indicates only the relationship between things. For medieval thinkers, the value of a thing was either determined by its worth or by the objective needs of men, and the just price was normally the result of the common estimate.

The confusion in classical economics, according to the thinking of Hannah Arendt, comes about because the older term of worth, which we still find in Locke, was replaced by Marx with the scientific term of "use value." Marx could not find an absolute value so "in its stead he put the function things have in the consuming life process of men, which knows neither objective and intrinsic worth nor subjective and socially determined value" (Arendt 1978, p. 166). Arendt points out that no one finds it easy to accept the simple fact that no absolute value exist in the exchange market, which is the proper sphere for values.

In the words of Marx:

> The utility of a thing makes it a use value. But this utility is not a thing of air. Being limited by the physical properties of the commodity, it has no existence apart from that commodity. A commodity, such as iron, corn, or a diamond, is therefore, so far as it is a material thing, a use value, something useful. This property of a commodity is independent of the amount of labor required to appropriate its useful qualities. When treating of use value, we always assume to be dealing with definite quantities, such as dozens of watches, yards of linen, or tons of iron. The use values of commodities furnish the material for a special study, that of the commercial knowledge of commodities. Use values become a reality only by use or consumption: they also constitute the substance of all wealth, whatever may be the social form of that wealth. In the form of society we are about to consider, they are, in addition, the material depositories of exchange value.
>
> ... As use values, commodities are, above all, of different qualities, but as exchange values they are merely different quantities, and consequently do not contain an atom of use value. If then we leave out of consideration the use value of commodities, they have only one common property left, that of being products of labour. ... A use value, or useful article, therefore, has value only because human labour in the abstract has been embodied or materialised in it. How, then, is the magnitude of this value to be measured? Plainly, by the quantity of the value-creating substance, the labour, contained in the article. The quantity of labour, however, is measured by its duration, and labour time in its turn finds its standard in weeks, days, and hours. Capital, Chapter 1, Section 1: the two factors of a commodity use-value and exchange value (http://www.marxists.org/archive/marx/works/1867-c1/ch01.htm#S1)

Marx presupposes that the sin of capitalist society is changing the use value for the exchange value. His idea of value is determined by labor, and thus exchange value must also be a function of production cost.

Although a bit tedious the above discussion of the use value vs exchange value is important to understand current misunderstandings in recent debates on the usability of objects, as described in the next section, (defined by the utility we obtain from them) which has nothing to do with the debate of use vs exchange value as some confused incorrectly.

4. www.ebay.com/.
5. http://www.etsy.com/.
6. (http://thecinema.blogia.com/2004/120101-guantanamera-1995-tomas-gutierrez-alea-y-juan-carlos-tabio-.php).
7. Conversations with History: Institute of International Studies, UC Berkeley http://globetrotter.berkeley.edu/people/Castells/castells-con5.html (accessed December 14, 2011).
8. http://www.artofhosting.org/events/.
9. http://uk.zopa.com/ZopaWeb/.
10. www.crunchbase.com/company/hub-culture.
11. A good explanation is the story of Banco Palmas in Brazil, as told by one of the most renowned exponents of the complementary currencies movement, Bernard Lietaer http://www.lietaer.com/2010/05/bancodipalma/.
12. http://www.youtube.com/watch?v=pWe7wTVbLUU.
13. http://the-hub.net/.

Chapter 6   Moving Civilizations

1. Mirabeau (Victor Riquetti, marquis de); Quesnay (François); *L'Ami des hommes, ou Traité de la population.* Avignon, s.n., 1756–1758–1760. 6 parties en 6 volumes in 12.
2. UNESCO was the organization created to unite all human cultures, defined in line with the conception of culture following the German tradition, which we can still see in their mission statement:

   UNESCO works to create the conditions for dialogue among civilizations, cultures and peoples, based upon respect for commonly shared values. It is through this dialogue that the world can achieve global visions of sustainable development encompassing observance of human rights, mutual respect and the alleviation of poverty, all of which are at the heart of UNESCO'S mission and activities (http://www.unesco.org/new/en/unesco/).

3. This reflects in genetic studies that categorize human beings in different branches (Cavalli-Sforza 1993, 1994, p. 135):

- The African family, with more genetic variety among individuals.
- The rest of the world that divides into two big groups:
- South East Asia, Pacific Islands New Guinea and Australia and
- North and Arctic Asians, American Indians, European Caucasian and non-European Caucasian.

4. Ibn Khaldun: Abū Zayd 'Abdu r-Rahman bin Muhammad bin Khaldūn Al-Hadrami, May 27, 1332 AD/732 AH–March 19, 1406 AD/808 AH.
5. The information of this section is mainly taken by from Quigley and from *El Atlas de las civilizaciones*.
6. Ibrahim Abouleish, *A sustainable Community in the Egyptian Desert*, Floris Books, Edinburgh 2005.
7. Enien, R. A. et al. (2000): "A New Research Paradigm for Sustainability Research in Egypt" *Experimental Agriculture*, 2 265–271; and Ibrahim, F. N. and Ibrahim, B. (2003): *Egypt: An Economic Geography*, London: I.B. Tauris.
8. Rudolf Steiner; *Basic Issues of the Social Question*, Chapter Two, "Finding Real Solutions to the Social Problems of the Times." http://wn.rsarchive.org/Books/GA023/English/SCR2001/GA023_c02.html (accessed December 14, 2011).
9. Ibrahim Abouleish p. 158.
10. Ibrahim Abouleish p. 206.
11. SEKEM sustainable report p. 36.
12. SEKEM sustainable report p. 39.
13. Ibrahim Abouleish, *A Sustainable Community* p. 47.
14. "Emission reduction through organic farming in Egypt's desert. Waste management, compost production and carbon sequestration."
15. UNFCCC/CCNUCC. 2007. Approved baseline and monitoring methodology AM0039. "Methane emissions reduction from organic waste water and bioorganic solid waste using co-composting" AM0039 / Version 02, Sectoral Scope 13, EB 35.
16. http://www.youtube.com/watch?v=g-dORzILk4Q&feature=fvwrel.
17. Mohammed Arkoun died in September 2010. Born in Algeria, he was a philosophy professor at the Sorbonne.
18. For further information on the concept of honor in the Mediterranean the works of Carmel Cassar are of interest (Cassar 2005).
19. A term coined by the historian James Henry Breasted to define the regions of Mesopotamia and the Levant in the Middle East.
20. For more information on Iranian Mysticism, the works of Henri Corbin are probably the best analysis.

21. The word "brother" is used in a larger sense as a greeting protocol with Christian communities, which are spread out among Arabs, but also has an ethnic meaning of pointing to a common ancestor. In this case, the characters exchanging the letter recognize their common Arabic origin, even though they are actually in different families and tribes.

22. Djins were spirits of nature, living inside stones, trees, water sources, etc. There was no barrier between djins and gods, both of which in fact were considered to be different degrees of integration between nature and tribal power. These beliefs laid the groundwork for the great unity of Arabs that occurred after Mohammed's prophecy.

23. ENPI information center; http://www.enpi-info.eu/index.php?lang_id=450, Euro-Med portal http://www.enpi-info.eu/indexmed.php?lang_id=450.

Epilogue

1. http://www.pwc.com/us/en/about-us/pwc-professional-development.jhtml.
2. https://kpmentoring.org/about.php.
3. For more information: http://www.expansion.com/especiales/empleo/premioseye/estudio_presentacion.html.
4. https://www.wellsfargo.com/about/diversity/past_present_future/diversepresent.
5. http://www-03.ibm.com/employment/us/diversity_partnerships.shtml.
6. http://nikerunning.nike.com/nikeos/p/nikeplus/en_US/.
7. Botsman and Rogers, p. 201.
8. http://www-03.ibm.com/employment/us/life_ibm.shtml.
9. http://www.jpmorgan.com/pages/jpmorgan/about.
10. http://www.ford.ca/app/fo/en/our_company/careers/our_culture.do.
11. http://www.businessknowhow.com/manage/flex-work.htm.
12. http://www.cvalora.com/empresa-flexible.html.
13. http://www.artofhosting.org/home/.
14. http://www.openspaceworld.org/, see also, http://www.artofhosting.org/home/.
15. http://www.nhne.org/news/NewsArticlesArchive/tabid/400/articleType/ArticleView/articleId/6617/language/en-US/Wal-Mart-Unveils-Plan-To-Make-Supply-Chain-Greener.aspx.
16. http://www.ashoka.org/fellow/reinaldo-pamponet.

REFERENCES

Addiss, S. and Lombardo, S. *Tao Te Ching: Lao-Tzu* (Indianapolis: Hackett Publishing Company, 1993).

Agacinski, S. *Metaphysique des sexes masculin/ féminin aux sources du christianism* (Paris: Editions Seuil, 2005).

Agars, M. D. and Kottke, J. L. "Models and Practice of Diversity Management: A Historical Review and Presentation of a New Integration Theory" In M. Stockdale and F. Crosby, eds. *The Psychology and Management of Workplace Diversity* (Malden, MA: Blackwell, 2004, 2005) pp. 55–77.

Akerlof, G. and Kranton, R. E. "Economics and Identity" *Quarterly Journal of Economics* 115 (3) 715–53 (2000).

Akerlof, G. and Kranton, R. E. "Identity and the Economics of Organizations" *Journal of Economic Perspectives* 19 (1) 9–32 (2005).

Akerlof G. and Kranton R. E. *Identity Economics* (Princeton University Press, 2010).

Alba, S. *Las reglas del caos, apuntes para una antropología del mercado* (Barcelona: Anagrama, 1995).

Anderson, B. *Imagined Communities* (London: Verso, 1983, 2006).

Appiah, K. A. *The Ethics of Identity* (Princeton University Press, 2005).

Arendt, H. *The Human Condition* (University of Chicago Press, 1958, 1998).

Arendt, H. *The Life of the Mind* (New York: Harcourt, 1978).

Arkoun, Mohammed "Actualité d'une culture méditerranéenne" *Les Cahiers du TAPRI*, 49 (Tampere: Tampere Peace Research Institute, 1990).

Arkoun, Mohammed "Langues, societes et religion dans le Magreb independent" In M. A. Roque, ed. *Les cultures du Maghreb* (Paris: L'Harmattan, 1996).

Arkoun, Mohammed "Religious Reason, Scientific Reason, Philosophical Reason in Islamic Contexts" In *The Frontiers of the Mind in the 21st Century* (Washington, DC: Library of Congress, 1999).

Arkoun, Mohammed "Repenser l'espace méditerranéen: au-delà des dialogues interreligieux et interculturels dissertatifs" *Quaderns de la Mediterrània*, 14 45–51 (2010).

Barth, F. "Los grupos étnicos y sus fronteras" In *La organización social de las diferencias culturales*. Introducción. (Mexico: D.F. FEC, 1976) pp. 9–49.

Bauman, Z. *Community: Seeking Safety in an Insecure World* (Cambridge: Polity Press, 2001).

Beck, D. E. and Cowan, C.C. *Spiral Dynamics* (Malden, MA: Blackwell, 1996, 2006).

Blanco, O. "La querelle feministe en el siglo XVII ponencia del seminario Feminismo e Ilustración" Madrid Universidad Complutense, 1991.

Botsman, R. and Rogers R. *What is Mine is Yours: The Rise of Collaborative Consumption* (New York: Harper Collins, 2010).

Bouchara, M. "Una sociedad civil en el Maghreb" In M. A. Roque, ed., *Identidades y conflicto de valores, diversidad y mutación social en el Mediterráneo* (Barcelona: Icaría, 1997).

Braudel, F. *El mediterraneo* (Barcelona: Espasa Calpe, 1989). (Based on the two original titles; *La Mediterranée; L' espace et l' histoire* and *La Mediterranée: les hommes et l'héritage*, Paris: Flammarion, 1985, 1986.)

Braudel, F. *Civilization and Capitalism, 15th–18th Century*, Vol. I: *The Structure of Everyday Life* (University of California Press, 1992).

Brown, T. "Innovation Through Design Thinking" (2006) http://mitworld.mit.edu/video/357/ (Accessed December 13, 2011).

Brubaker, R. and Cooper, F. "Beyond 'identity' " *Theory and Society* 29(1) 1–47 (2000).

Butler, J. "Of Personal Identity" In J. Perry, ed. *Personal Identity* (Berkeley: University of California Press, 2008) pp. 99–107.

Carbonell, E. and Sala, R. *Planeta Humano* (Barcelona: Ediciones Península, 2000).

Cassar, C. *L' honneur et la honte en Méditerranée* (Aix-en-Provence: Edisud, 2005).

Castells, M. *The Rise of the Network Society. The Information Age: Economy, Society and Culture* Vol. I (Cambridge, MA; Oxford, UK: Blackwell, 1996, 2nd edition, 2000).

Castells, Manuel *The Power of Identity: The Information Age: Economy, Society and Culture* Vol. II (Cambridge, MA, Oxford, UK: Blackwell,1997, 2nd edition, 2004).

Castells, Manuel *End of Millennium: The Information Age: Economy, Society and Culture* Vol. III (Cambridge, MA, Oxford, UK: Blackwell, 1998, 2nd edition, 2000).

Cavalli-Sforza, Luca and Cavalli-Sforza, Francesco *¿Quiénes Somos? Historia de la diversidad humana.* (Original: *Chi siamo: la storia della diversita Umana.* Milan: Arnoldo Mondadori, Editore SPA 1993; traducción castellana, Barcelona: Editorial Crítica, 1994).

Círculo de Progreso *Mujer y Empleo. Opciones y Decisiones* (Madrid: CP, 2005).

Coase, R. H "The Nature of the Firm" *Economica*, 4(16) 386–405 (1937).

Corbin, H. *Avicenne et le récit visionnaire* (Paris: Verdier, 1999).

Co-working Wiki (2011). http://wiki.coworking.info/w/page/16583831/ FrontPage (Accessed December 14, 2011).

Cox, T. *Creating the Multicultural Organization: A Strategy for Capturing the Power of Diversity.* (San Francisco: Jossey-Bass, 2001).

Cruz, Hernandez, *M. Abu-l-Walid Muhammad B Ahmad B Muhammad Ibn Rushd: Vida, Pensamiento, Influencia* (Cordoba: Caja Sur Pub, 1997).

Davenport, T. *Human Capital. What It Is and Why People Invest In It* (San Francisco: Jossey-Bass, 1999).

de Anca, C. "Women on Corporate Boards of Directors in Spanish Listed Companies" In *Women on Corporate Boards of Directors: International Research and Practice*, Susan Vinnicombe, Val Singh, Ronald J. Burke, Diana Bilimoria and Morten Huse, eds. (Cheltenham: Edward Elgar, 2008).

de Anca, C. and Aragon, Salvador *La mujer directiva en España: Catalizadores e inhibidores en las decisiones de trayectoria profesional* (En Academia, Revista Latino Americana de Administración; Publicación del consejo Latinoamericano de escuelas de admistración no. 38, 2007).

de Anca, C. and Vazquez, A., *Managing Diversity in the Global Organization* (Basingstoke: Palgrave Macmillan, 2007).

de Beauvoir, S. *The Second Sex* (New York: Knopf, 1953).

Descola, P. "¿Que es Una civilización?" In *El Atlas de las civilizaciones* pp. 22–24.

D'Souza, S. and Clarke, P. *Made in Britain: Inspirational Role Models from British Black and Minority Ethnic Communities* (Harlow: Pearson, 2005).

Durkheim, E. *De la division du travail social* (Paris: Les presses universitaires de France, 8e édition, 1967).

El Atlas de las civilizaciones (Valencia: Fundación Mondiplo, 2010).

Fericgla, J. *Los chamanismos a revisión* (Barcelona: Kairos, 2000, 2006).

Fisher, H. *The First Sex*, (Toronto: Ballantine Publishing, 1999).

Foucart, S. "Mesopotamia, los albores de la Historia" In *El Atlas de las civilizaciones*, pp. 32–36.

Friedman, T. *The Lexus and the Olive Tree* (New York: Anchor Books, 1999, 2000).

Fumaroli, M. "¿que es una civilización ?" In *El Atlas de las civilizaciones*, pp. 17–19.

Goleman, D. *Emotional Intelligence* (New York: Bantam Books, 1995).

Hadot, P. *Qu'est-ce que la philosophie antique?* (Paris: Gallimard, 1995).

Hall, E. T. *The Silent Language* (New York: Doubleday, 1990).

Hawken, P. *Blessed Unrest* (London: Penguin, 2007).

Hays-Thomas, R. "Why Now? The Contemporary Focus on Managing Diversity" In M. Stockdale and F. Crosby eds., *The Psychology and Management of Workplace Diversity* (Malden, MA: Blackwell, 2004, 2005) pp. 3–30.

Hewlett, S. A. "Executive Women and the Myth of Having It All" *Harvard Business Review*, 80(4) 66–73, 125 (2002).

Hogg, M. A. "Social Identity Theory" In *Contemporary Social Psychological Theories,* ed., P. Burke (Stanford University Press, 2006) pp. 111–137.

Holvino, E., Ferdman, B. and Merrill-Sands, D. "Creating and Sustaining Diversity and Inclusion in Organizations: Strategies and Approaches" In M. Stockdale and F. Crosby, eds. *The Psychology and Management of Workplace Diversity* (Malden, MA: Blackwell Publishing, 2004, 2005) pp. 245–275.

Hume, D. "Of Personal Identity" In J. Perry, ed. *Personal Identity* (Berkeley: University of California Press, 2008) pp. 161–173.

Huntington, S. *The Clash of Civilizations and the Remaking of World Order* (New York: Simon & Schuster, 1996; paperback edition 2003).

Ibn Al Árabi *La Joya del Viaje a la Presencia de los Santos.* Murcia: Editorial Regional de Murcia, 1990.

Ibn Khaldun *Al-Muqaddimah, Introducción a la Historia Universal,* (Mexico: Fondo de cultura económica, 1997).

Ibn Khaldun *The Muqqaddimah, An Introduction To History.* Translated by Franz Rosenthal, edited and abridged by N. J. Dawood (Princeton: Bollingen Series, 1989).

Jenkins, R. *Social Identity* (New York: Routledge, 1996, 2004, 2008).

Jung, C. "Approaching the Unconscious" In *Man and His Symbols* (London: Macmillan, 1964, 1978) pp. 1–95.

Jung, C. *Arquetipos e insconsciente colectivo* (Barcelona: Paidos, 1970).

Jung, C. *Symbols of Transformation* (Princeton University Press, 1956) as quoted in the Spanish edition C. Jung *Simbolos de transformación* (Barcelona: Paidos, 1982).

Klein, N. *No Logo* (New York: Picador, 2000, 2002).

Kybalion http://www.kybalion.org/kybalion.asp (Accessed December 14, 2011).

Lacoste, Y. "El Mediterráneo una Cuenca con Identidad Propia" In *El Atlas de las civilizaciones* pp. 100–102 (2010).

Lajoie, D. H. and Shapiro S. I. "Definitions of Transpersonal Psychology: The First Twenty-Three Years" *Journal of Transpersonal Psychology* 24(1) 79–95 (1992).

Lippa, R. A. *Gender, Nature, and Nurture*, (2nd edition, London: Lawrence Erlbaum Associates, Publishers, 2005).

Locke, J. "Of identity and Diversity" In J. Perry, ed. *Personal Identity* (Berkeley: University of California Press, 2008) pp. 33–53.

Locke, J. "Of Political or Civil Society" Chapter VII of *The Second Treatise of Civil Government, 1690* http://www.constitution.org/jl/2ndtr07.txt (Accessed December 14, 2011).

Loden, M. and Rosener, J. *Workforce in America: Managing Employee Diversity as Vital Resource* (Homewood, IL: Business One Irwin, 1991).

Maffesoli, M. *Le temps des tribus. Collection sociologies au quotidien* (Paris: Le Livre de Poche, 1988).

Maslow, A. H. *Toward a Psychology of Being* (New York: John Wiley, 1958, 1968, 1999).

Miller, J. "Daoism and Ecology" *Earth Ethics* 10(1) 26–27 (1998).

Mor Barak, M. E. *Managing Diversity, Toward a Globally Inclusive Workplace.* (London: Sage, 2005).

Murillo, S. *El mito de la vida privada, De la entrega al tiempo propio* (Madrid: Siglo XXI, 2006).

Parfitt, W. *The Elements of the Qabalah* (Shaftesbury: Element, 1991).

Pitt-Rivers, J. "Las culturas del mediterráneo" In Maria Angels Roque, ed., *Nueva Antropologia de las cociedades Mediterráneas* (Barcelona: Icaria, 2000).

Powell, G. N. "Promoting Equal Opportunity and Valuing Cultural Diversity" In G. N. Powell, ed, *Women and Men in Management* (Thousand Oaks, CA: Sage, 1993) pp. 225–52.

Quigley, C. *The Evolution of Civilizations* (Indianapolis: Liberty Fund, 1961).

Ramos, P. *Feminismo y música* (Madrid: Narcea SA, 2003).

Rederikse, M. E., Lu, A., Aylward, E., Barta, P., Pearlson, G. "Sex Differences in the Inferior Parietal Lobule" *Cerebral Cortex* 9 (8) 896–901 (1999).

Reinventingmoney.com (2011). http://www.reinventingmoney.com/documents/wir.html (Accessed December 14, 2011).

Robinson, P., ed. *Social Groups and Identities: Developing the Legacy of Henri Tajfel* (Oxford: Butterworth-Heinemann, 1996).

Roque, M. A. *Antropologie du quotidienne en Mediterranée* (Aix-en-Provence, Edisud, 2005).

Rothbard, M. N. *Economic Thought Before Adam Smith* (Cheltenham: Edward Elgar, 1995).

Sabbatini, R. M. E. "Are There Differences between the Brains of Males and Females?" http://www.cerebromente.org.br/n11/mente/eisntein/cerebro-homens.html (Accessed December 14, 2011).

Said, E. *Orientalism* (New York: Vintage Books, 1979).

Schlaepfer T. E., Harris G. J., Tien A. Y., Peng L., Lee S. and Pearlson G. D. "Structural Differences in the Cerebral Cortex of Healthy Female and Male Subjects: A Magnetic Resonance Imaging Study" *Psychiatry Research* 61(3) 129–35 (1995).

Schumpeter (2010) "The Business Of Sharing" http://www.economist.com/node/17249322?story_id=17249322&fsrc=rss (Accessed December 14, 2011).

Seligman, M. E. P. and Csikszentmihalyi, M. "Positive Psychology: An Introduction" *American Psychologist* 55(1) 5–14. (2000).

Senge, P. M. *The Fifth Discipline: The Art and Practice of the Learning Organization* (New York: Random House Business, 1990).

Snow White and the Seven Dwarfs. Illustrated by Dinah. (London: Raphael Tuck and Sons, [c. 1936]) pp. 1–14.

Stevenson, L. and Haberman, D. L. *Ten Theories of Human Nature* (Oxford: Oxford University Press 1974, 1987, 1998, 2004).

Stockdale, M. S. and Cao, F. "Looking Back and Heading Forward: Major Themes in the Psychology and Management of Workplace Diversity" In M. Stockdale and F. Crosby, eds. *The Psychology and Management of Workplace Diversity* (Malden, MA: Blackwell, 2004, 2005) pp. 298–316.

Thatcher, Margaret Interview for *Women's Own*, September 23 1987 http://www.margaretthatcher.org/document/106689 (Accessed December 14, 2011).

Thomas, K., Mack, D. and Montagliani, A. "The Arguments Against Diversity: Are They Valid?" In M. Stockdale and F. Crosby eds. *The Psychology and Management of Workplace Diversity* (Malden, MA: Blackwell Publishing, 2004, 2005) pp. 31–51.

Thomas, R. R. Jr. From Affirmative Action to Affirmative Diversity. *Harvard Business Review* 2, 107–17 (1990).

Thomas, R. R. Jr. *Beyond Race and Gender: Unleashing the Power of Your Total Workforce by Managing Diversity* (New York: AMACOM, 1991).

Thomas, R. R. Jr. *Redefining Diversity,* (New York: AMACOM, 1996).

Toynbee, A. *A Study of History* (Oxford: Oxford University Press, 1957).

Tropennaars, F. *Riding the Wave of Culture* (Chicago, Irwin, 1994).

Trotman, C. J. "Introduction" In C. J. Trotman, ed. *Multiculturalism: Roots and Realities* (Indiana University Press, 2002) p. ix.

Tylor, E. B. *Primitive Culture: Researches into Development of Mythology, Philosophy, Religion Language Art and Custom* 7th edition (New York: Brentano's, 1924 [orig. 1871]).

von Franz, M. L. "The Process of Individuation" In Jung, C. *Man and his Symbols* (London: Mcmillan 1964, 1978) pp. 157–255.

Weber, M. *Peasants into Frenchman: The Modernization of Rural France; 1870–1914* (Stanford University Press, 1976).

Weber, M. *Essays in Sociology* 1st edition (London: Routledge, 1991).

Weber, M. *The Protestant Ethic and the Spirit of Capitalism* London: Routledge Classics, London, 2001).

Wilson, E. O. *Sociobiology* (Cambridge, MA: Harvard University Press, 1992).

Wilson, R. *Economics, Ethics and Religion: Jewish, Christian and Muslim Economic Thought* (London: Macmillan, 1997).

Woolf, V. *A Room Of One's Own* (London: Penguin, 2004; first published 1928).

Zelding, T. *An Intimate History of Humanity* (New York: Harper Perennial, 1994).

INDEX

Page numbers in italics refer to information represented in maps, table and figures.

Middle Eastern names are presented in direct form i.e. not inverted in the form surname, forename. Names beinning with "Mc" or "St." can be found with entries 'Mac' or "Saint" respectively.